CONFLICT AND POLITICAL CHANGE
IN VENEZUELA

BY DANIEL H. LEVINE

Conflict and Political Change in Venezuela

PRINCETON UNIVERSITY PRESS

LC: 75-39790
ISBN: 0-691-07547-6

This book has been composed in Linotype Caledonia

Printed in the United States of America
by Princeton University Press

To Phyllis, Peter, and Paul

CONTENTS

TABLES

FIGURES

ACKNOWLEDGMENTS

WRITING acknowledgments is a risky business. The peril of forgetfulness, leaving valued friends unmentioned, is mixed with the danger of inadvertently betraying confidences and confidential sources. But debts incurred should be acknowledged. Research overseas, especially for the first time, is an enterprise full of pitfalls and disappointments, and only the constant goodwill and counsel of many saved this inexperienced scholar from crisis and disillusionment.

The research on which this book is based was conducted in Venezuela from October 1967 to June 1969. Support was provided by several sources: first, a Doherty Fellowship from the Henry L. and Grace Doherty Charitable Foundation, Inc.; and later, a Latin American Teaching Fellowship. In addition, a small grant was awarded by the Creole Foundation to cover extra costs of typing and duplication of materials in Venezuela. I am indebted to these institutions and to their personnel for making this work possible. I am also indebted to the Council on Comparative and European Studies of Yale University for an award to help defray the costs of typing an earlier version of this book which was presented as a Ph.D. dissertation to Yale University.

Many individual debts are owed. Dr. Willard Leeds of the University of Wisconsin, then of the Office of Planning of the Ministry of Education, EDUPLAN, and Dr. José A. Silva Michelena of CENDES, helped set me on my way. The continued interest and helpfulness of Dr. Lorenzo Monroy, then of the Universidad de Oriente and now of the Ministry of Education, were invaluable at many stages. For the study of Catholic-secular relations, I am particularly indebted to Professor Adelso González, of the MEP, and to

ACKNOWLEDGMENTS

Dr. José Luis Aguilar, of the Catholic University, for opening many doors and sharing their time and understanding with me. The officers of the Federación Venezolana de Maestros, the Colegio de Profesores de Venezuela, the Asociación Venezolana de Educación Católica, and the Federación de Asociaciones de Padres y Representantes de la Educación Católica also generously shared their knowledge with me. The late Padre Manuel Aguirre, S.J., helped clarify many aspects of the recent history of the Church in Venezuela.

For the study of student politics, acknowledgments become more difficult since many of the persons interviewed remain active participants in the political struggle, legal and illegal. Therefore, rather than thank any particular person, let me extend a blanket acknowledgment to the university authorities, deans, professors, and students, and to regional and national leaders of all political parties who so generously contributed information to me.

A researcher who goes to another country and simply collects his data without getting "involved" practices a not so subtle form of academic and cultural colonialism, leaving his hosts and himself the poorer. In Venezuela, I was fortunate to have the opportunity to teach political sociology in the Escuela de Ciencias Sociales of the Universidad Catolica Andres Bello. For this opportunity, I am indebted to Dr. José Luis Aguilar, Vice-Rector, Dr. Arístides Calvani, founder of the school, Dra. Maritza Izaguirre, then director of studies, and to the students. I was also associated with the Instituto de Estudios Políticos in the Faculty of Law of the Universidad Central de Venezuela. I am indebted to Dr. Gustavo Planchart Manrique, then dean, for suggesting the affiliation, and to Dr. Manuel García-Pelayo and Dr. Juan Carlos Rey, of the Institute, for making the experience such a pleasant and rewarding one.

General intellectual debts are owed, above all, to two men. Kalman H. Silvert is, in a way, responsible for the whole thing, by virtue of having convinced me long ago of the combined fascination of political science and Latin America. His friendship and encouragement can never be completely acknowledged. The friendship, intellectual guidance, and example of Robert A. Dahl have been invaluable every step of the way. Without his comments, criticisms, and unflagging interest, this book would have had a much harder time emerging from the initial steps of proposal, field work, and dissertation to its present form.

Parts of the manuscript have been read and criticized by Thomas Anton, Ronald Inglehart, Kenneth Langton, Richard Morse, Kalman H. Silvert, Eric Veblen, and John Waterbury. The entire manuscript has benefited from careful readings by Frank Bonilla, Robert A. Dahl, Juan Linz, Juan Carlos Rey, Alfred Stepan, and Eric R. Wolf. It goes without saying that their criticisms and suggestions have improved the book enormously. Of course, the final responsibility for analysis and factual errors is mine alone.

Perhaps my greatest debt is to my wife Phyllis, whose constancy and encouragement helped me through difficult periods in my work. Her great warmth and energy helped widen our circle of friends in Venezuela, making our initial residence more of a pleasure than a chore, and our subsequent visits a genuine reunion with friends.

D.H.L.

Ann Arbor, Michigan
November 1971

CONFLICT AND POLITICAL CHANGE
IN VENEZUELA

CHAPTER 1

The Problem

VENEZUELA presents a continuing paradox to the political scientist. With only three years of civilian rule in the first half of this century, it has built since 1958 one of the few effective, competitive, democratic political orders in Latin America. Ridden with conflict, civil violence, and systematic guerrilla warfare since the early 1960's, it has nevertheless managed three peaceful transfers of power in recent years (1958, 1963, and 1968). These were the first consecutive transfers of power through mass popular elections in the nation's modern history, and the 1968 elections marked the first time power had ever been handed over to an opposition party—with a plurality of barely 30,000 votes out of almost 4 million ballots cast. It has one of the longest and bloodiest histories of military dictatorship in Latin America, and yet has spawned a powerful, highly organized, and far-reaching system of mass political parties—a system with few parallels in the entire region.

Some analyses of Venezuelan politics have taken a narrow focus, considering planning on a national[1] or regional[2] level, the evolution of political parties,[3] politics in the urban slums,[4] or the development of key leadership generations.[5]

[1] See, for example, J. Friedmann, *Venezuela from Doctrine to Dialogue* (Syracuse: Syracuse University Press, 1965), or F. Levy, *Economic Planning in Venezuela* (New York: Frederick A. Praeger, 1968).

[2] J. Friedmann, *Regional Development Policy: A Case Study of Venezuela* (Cambridge: M.I.T. Press, 1966).

[3] J. Martz, *Acción Democrática: Evolution of a Modern Political Party in Venezuela* (Princeton: Princeton University Press, 1965).

[4] T. Ray, *The Politics of the Barrios of Venezuela* (Berkeley: University of California Press, 1969).

[5] J. Martz, "Venezuela's 'Generation of '28': The Genesis of Polit-

3

THE PROBLEM

Others have taken a global view, arguing that the polity is marked by a profound "cultural heterogeneity,"[6] which reinforces deep social and political cleavages, hinders the formulation and implementation of rational social policy, and saps the strength and vitality of the system.

This book grew out of a general concern with problems of conflict, conflict resolution, and the development of institutions for routine conciliation of disputes. Although the work was initially inspired by the idea of cultural heterogeneity as a key to the understanding of political conflict, that approach was abandoned as inadequate to explain the Venezuelan experience. Instead, I try to answer two broad questions: (1) why has the Venezuelan political system changed the way it has; and (2) given deep and often cumulative cleavages (both organizational and ideological in origin), how has the society learned to manage conflict, building an effective political system in a relatively free, pluralistic, and democratic social order?

My concern, therefore, is with how conflicts are managed, and not with the "dysfunctionality" of conflict, or with the degree to which it inhibits rational policy formation.[7] The

ical Democracy," *Journal of Inter American Studies*, 6, No. 1 (January 1964), 17-33, or a fuller analysis, María de Lourdes Acedo de Sucre and Carmen Margarita Nones Mendoza, *La Generación Venezolana de 1928: Estudio de una élite política* (Caracas: Ediciones Ariel, 1967).

[6] This work, conducted jointly by the M.I.T. Center for International Studies and the Center for Development Studies of the Universidad Central de Venezuela (CENDES) has so far produced three books and many articles and papers. The three major books are F. Bonilla and J. Silva Michelena, eds., *The Politics of Change in Venezuela: Volume I, A Strategy for Research on Social Policy* (Cambridge: M.I.T. Press, 1967), F. Bonilla, *The Politics of Change in Venezuela: Volume II, The Failure of Elites* (Cambridge: M.I.T. Press, 1970), and J. Silva Michelena, *The Politics of Change in Venezuela: Volume III, The Illusion of Democracy in Dependent Nations* (Cambridge: M.I.T. Press, 1971). These volumes are hereafter referred to as the CENDES studies.

[7] The system is ridden with conflict, yet the system functions fairly effectively. How? One contributor to the comparative study

4

book examines a crucial transition in the life of a political system: the development of representative democratic regimes in a country lacking strong democratic roots or traditions. These facts are approached in several ways. In terms of the political system as a whole, I analyze the evolution of modern mass political organizations, the changing structure and content of social and political conflict, and the gradual development of common norms governing political behavior. My central concern is the development of political legitimacy in Venezuela—legitimacy in the sense of shared norms as to criteria of power (ballots or bullets, to use a crude example), proper methods of political action, and proper arenas for political action. The learning of norms is central to recent Venezuelan experience—norms governing behavior in conflict situations, norms governing the use of organizations, and norms concerning resources and arenas appropriate to political action. It is important to note that these interests do not specify or require any general substantive consensus in the society. Rather, I will describe and explain the process by which commonly accepted "rules of the game" were developed, shared among key elites, and imposed (by force if necessary) on recalcitrant oppositions, no matter what their ideological coloring.

My conclusions about the political system as a whole are based primarily on several case studies in political conflict. In books of this kind, case studies provide valuable perspectives on the actual behavior associated with general system change. Overall commitments to "democracy," "development," "conciliation," and the like, are all too often

---

of these questions has been Arend Lijphart. See his *The Politics of Accommodation: Pluralism and Democracy in the Netherlands* (Berkeley: University of California Press, 1968), and his articles, "Typologies of Democratic Systems," *Comparative Political Studies*, 1:1 (April 1968), 3-44, and "Consociational Democracy," *World Politics*, 21:2 (January 1969), 207-223. See also Val Lorwin, "Segmented Pluralism: Ideological Cleavages and Political Cohesion in the Smaller European Democracies," *Comparative Politics*, 3:2 (January 1971), 141-176.

merely fine phrases, rhetoric which collapses under the strain of actual conflict. Case studies let us see the development of new norms and patterns of action in conflict situations and provide valuable historical perspective on changes in the structure of issues, the use of social and political organizations, and the attitudes to conflict and opposition characteristic of contending groups.[8]

The use of case studies, selected on a theoretical basis, allows us to look at behavior in institutionally defined situations. In this way, it is possible to see what form ideal public norms take in concrete social settings. In such contexts, constraints on action are present which may not exist in the world of public formulas. Indeed, as we shall see, people may compartmentalize their worlds so that effective patterns of action continue in paths seemingly incongruous with publicly expressed values and attitudes.[9] Particular institutional definitions of roles and role expectations may create pressures which move action away from ideal goals.[10] Given my concern with questions of motivation and perception, I relied heavily on interviewing. In all, 105 interviews were carried out with 89 respondents. Subjects were chosen in five major areas: (1) leaders of the Church and Catholic associations; (2) leaders in secular education (the parties, teachers' associations, and the Ministry of Education); (3) university professors and authorities; (4) student leaders and party youth leaders; (5) high officials of the PCV and ex-high officials of the MIR. The interviews were unstructured, lasting from one to three hours, and designed to find out about behavior in conflict situations, perceptions of the

[8] Of course, principles of political analysis can neither be deduced nor induced from any finite number of cases, but general principles can be used to explain the cases, thereby adding to the existing body of comparative knowledge.

[9] See Chapter 9 below. For a full discussion, see Daniel H. Levine, "Issues in the Study of Culture in Latin America" (forthcoming).

[10] For a useful discussion of this point, see J. Steward, *Theory of Culture Change* (Urbana: University of Illinois Press, 1963), especially pp. 46ff.

opposition, and norms concerning the resources, methods, and goals appropriate to political conflict.[11]

There are two primary case studies. First, the evolution of Catholic-secular relations is studied in the context of conflicts over educational reform. Of particular interest here are changes in the structure of issues; the impact of past severe conflict in leading all sides to seek accommodation and avoid future conflicts; changes in the organizational base of the Catholic sector; and the changing perceptions on both sides of conflict and opposition as social processes (e.g., are they normal, legitimate, or aberrant?). My basic concern is to explain the conditions under which a traditional sector of the society (Catholic groups and institutions) moved from violent, all-out opposition to the political system to a position of accommodation and acceptance of new norms of organization and action. The overall consequences of the accommodation of Catholic and lay sectors are also of interest, especially insofar as the bargain struck between these sectors was made at the expense of others— in this case, the parties of the extreme Left, who grew increasingly alienated from the system.

The second case study examines the role of students in politics, with special reference to the integration of students into national patterns of conflict and opposition. In the burgeoning literature on students and politics,[12] relatively

[11] The interviews were, of course, intended to explain a process of behavior, and not to provide the basis for generalization to a universe represented by the respondents. For a sensitive and helpful discussion of the problems of interviewing of this kind, see L. A. Dexter, *Elite and Specialized Interviewing* (Evanston: Northwestern University Press, 1970). I was fortunate in that my stay in Venezuela coincided with the release from jail (and return from exile) of many Communist leaders. Only ex-MIR leaders were interviewed because the current MIR leadership was still involved in the guerrilla movement, and hence, underground. I was able, however, to talk at length with the MIR student leaders at several universities.

[12] See, among others, D. Emmerson, ed., *Students and Politics in Developing Nations* (New York: Frederick A. Praeger, 1968) and S. M. Lipset, ed., *Student Politics* (New York: Basic Books, 1968).

little attention has been paid to students as political actors—their resources, organizations, and relations with other social forces.[13] Primary emphasis here is given to the role assigned to students by the different political parties, and to the structural ties binding students and student organizations into national patterns of conflict and opposition. The key norms in question are those concerning the use of organizations—the proper relationship between conflicts at different levels, or concretely, students and national political parties.

At this point, it may be worthwhile to outline the content of the new norms and patterns of behavior which came to dominate Venezuelan politics after 1958. Basically, Venezuelan politics can be described as a party system. The basic vehicles of political action are parties, the fundamental legitimate political resource is mass consent and votes, and power is transferred through elections. A crucial norm in Venezuelan politics is organizational concentration: the parties are monopolists of political action. The concentration of forms of action reflects a conscious desire to avoid situations where conflict gets out of hand, to maintain (through party organization) a high degree of control over the consequences of action. Opposition and conflict are tolerated, and indeed, built into the system, but opposition is constrained to work within a set of common procedures and forms. Politics is supposed to work through elections, the congress, elected officials, and the like—through explicitly political mechanisms. Forms of action which are difficult to control (such as mass street demonstrations) are discouraged and often suppressed.

The emphasis on concentrating political action in a few common organizational vehicles reveals a conscious decision to avoid what Huntington has called a praetorian society:

13 A useful exception for Latin America is K. H. Silvert. "The University Student," J. J. Johnson, ed., *Continuity and Change in Latin America* (Stanford: Stanford University Press, 1964), pp. 206-226.

8

In a praetorian system social forces confront each other nakedly; no political institution, no corps of professional political leaders are recognized or accepted as the legitimate intermediaries to moderate group conflict. Equally important, no agreement exists among the groups as to the legitimate and authoritative methods for resolving conflicts.[14]

As we shall see, political elites in many sectors are concerned with the dangers of praetorianism for Venezuela. Hence, a common line of analysis in the case studies is the relation of political parties to sectoral organizations and changes in the salience of any particular group as opposed to the parties per se in political organization and conflict. The role of political parties in mediating and moderating conflict is given special emphasis, and seen as a relatively independent set of variables, creating autonomous pressures and constraints.[15]

Articulating a concern for the way in which Venezuela's political institutions manage conflict has a particular, specific meaning. Although this chapter is not intended to present or justify any detailed conceptual or theoretical framework, it may be useful to describe one fundamental concept now. As used here, the scope of conflict means the degree to which any conflict joins actors in various functional spheres and arenas.[16] The more spheres or arenas joined on a single line of conflict, the greater the scope. The scope of conflict has "objective" and "subjective" dimensions. The

[14] S. Huntington, *Political Order in Changing Societies* (New Haven: Yale University Press, 1968), p. 196.

[15] Janowitz calls this the institutional view in political sociology. See his useful discussion in M. Janowitz, *Political Conflict: Essays in Political Sociology* (Chicago: Quadrangle Books, 1970), Chapter 1.

[16] By functional sphere I mean economic, social, cultural, political, etc. activities. If, for example, a person's politics are wholly determined by his job or religion, or if he perceives his position in all his social roles (as worker, religious communicant, etc.) as determined by one line of conflict, then we can say that conflict cuts across, or unifies action in a number of functional spheres and that the situation is polarized.

objective scope refers to the degree to which the organizations involved in a conflict cut across a variety of social spheres, linking any member's actions in one arena to his actions in all others. In this way, conflicts in different arenas are joined through common organizational affiliations of the participants. For example, the actions of students in university politics follow the lines of national politics because the students' behavior is governed by the political party to which they belong—both in their general role as citizens and their more specialized role as students. The subjective scope of conflict refers to the way in which the issues, as perceived, structure the commitments of the actors to the conflict.

Let me define the concept of scope with a negative example. Isolation of conflict implies that relations in one arena do not determine relations in all others. The evolution of industrial conflict in this century in the United States and Great Britain offers a good example of the institutional isolation of conflict:

> In terms of its issues, industrial conflict increasingly becomes *industrial* conflict without reference to general social and political problems. Secondly, this narrowing down of the issues of industrial conflict means that the individual worker is concerned with them only in his role as worker. In other roles, he is moved by other things; as consumer or citizen, he is no longer worker.[17]

If conflicts are not isolated, and ever-greater numbers of arenas are fused on unified lines of conflict, then we have polarization. The continuum from isolation to polarization is central to this investigation, for conflict management hinges on the ability to isolate a given dispute and resolve it in limited terms. Not every conflict need involve more general questions of political structure and legitimacy. Ability to isolate conflict, however, requires prior agreement

[17] R. Dahrendorf, *Class and Class Conflict in Industrial Society* (London: Routledge and Kegan Paul, 1959), p. 274.

10

on questions of political legitimacy, as defined above. A major premise of this book is that as long as legitimacy questions remain unresolved, conflicts will be pervasive and difficult to isolate. When legitimacy questions are at stake, and the form and proper procedures of political institutions are in question, conflict runs rapidly up the hierarchy of arenas until institutions themselves are involved. Legitimacy conflicts, in short, take priority.[18]

UNANSWERED QUESTIONS

This book is strongly influenced by theories of pluralism. The perspective offered on pluralism, however, is different from the one which has dominated most recent research and writing, and it may be well to set out these differences at the outset. My goal is not principally to decipher "who has the power," or "who governs." It lies, rather, one step back, in identifying the conditions of different patterns of conflict and conciliation. I am not so much concerned with who wins, as with why the players act as they do—why and how criteria of legitimate power, methods of action, and basic attitudes to conflict and opposition change. Who has the power remains, of course, a central concern of political analysis. But the answer to that question—whatever it may be—is insufficient in itself to explain the scope of conflict in a society, and less so to explain goals pursued, levels of intensity and violence, and the choice of different arenas for conflict.

All these are as important to political understanding as mapping the distribution of power. The study of conflict, focused sharply on the evolution of common procedural norms, offers important insights on the emergence and survival of competitive political systems. These are perspec-

---

[18] This does not, of course, imply that legitimacy conflicts are in any sense "irrational" or "unreal." On the contrary, very real and concrete interests, both symbolic and material, may be at stake. For a fuller discussion of legitimacy conflicts, see Chapter 8 below.

tives drawn from group interaction and its characteristics, not from the analysis of relative strength and power alone. This book is not a general descriptive survey of Venezuelan politics, nor does it pretend to be. The case studies were selected to illustrate dimensions of conflict that have theoretical relevance. They hang together theoretically, if at all. Thus, not all important groups are studied; not all salient issues or problems receive detailed attention. The conclusions and generalizations advanced are based on the case studies, related research of my own, and a critical reading of the existing literature on Venezuela.

Initially, my design emphasized a close analysis of microsituations of conflict, with great attention to the personal qualities of participants. A rigid and violent conflict was taken as a sign of rigid and violence oriented personalities, closed to contact and communication with others. This approach proved unsatisfactory, consistently leading to pure tautologies or useless propositions. Many blind alleys were explored in the first stages of research. As work progressed, it became clear that the patterns of conflict and conciliation so visible in Venezuelan politics could not be explained in terms of individual psychological characteristics, but rather through analysis of the priorities and organizational structures of groups, which together defined the scope of conflict and provided a concrete basis for interaction. Continuing to focus on personal characteristics implies an unjustified identification of the characteristics of individuals with the traits of social and political systems. Keeping in mind the distinction of these two levels of analysis, it becomes clear that a person can act in a conflict so as to increase its overall rigidity and violence, while remaining personally a friendly and open individual. Personality traits are, of course, not irrelevant—they are simply not necessary or sufficient to explain the conflicts.

A closer and more reflective look at the data further emphasized the impossibility of analyzing any conflict apart from broader trends in the political system, and from the participants' own perceptions of these trends. These considerations dictated closer attention to the ties binding actors in any given conflict to issues and conflicts in other arenas. Analysis and explanation thus moved from the case studies as such, back to the structure and formulation of issues and to the organizations tying different arenas and levels of action together—the modern, mass political parties that pervade every aspect of Venezuelan political life.

A candid recognition of these changes in perspective led me to abandon earlier plans for an orienting theoretical chapter—an analytical framework of the now conventional kind. The final scheme of analysis, and the propositions and generalizations advanced, are less a format than a product of the analysis itself. I have therefore placed all theoretical syntheses, generalizations, and comparative analyses, in the concluding chapters. In this way, the range of generalization intended, the degree to which any of the propositions advanced is meant to have limited or more general applicability, will be clearer than if theoretical conclusions were presented as a tight analytical framework.

CHAPTER 2

The Setting

MODERN political life began for Venezuela in 1936. The forces unleashed, the organizations created, and the positions assumed in that year set the pattern for subsequent political change and conflict. The relative youth of most social and political organizations means that the past is present in many aspects of contemporary life—the issues that define its conflicts, the organizations that guide them, and the institutions that contain and channel them are all of recent vintage.

The contemporaneity of the past in Venezuela thus obliges us to analyze the origins and evolution of the structural setting which defines the situation for political actors. Chapters 2 and 3 try to draw from recent history a series of themes that help us understand contemporary political change. The major dimensions which emerge from the analysis are four: (1) the growth of political organizations and their penetration into all spheres of social life; (2) the changing bases of political power and hence the declining power of groups not specifically political, such as students; (3) the emergence and consolidation of a party system based on a series of mutual guarantees among power factors in the society; and (4) the defeat of opposition to the party system.

Social change is subversive. The firmest dictatorships often unwittingly lay the foundations for subsequent expansion and liberalization of political life. Venezuela is a good example. From 1908 to 1935, Venezuela suffered through the bloody dictatorship of Juan Vicente Gómez. His autocratic regime unified the country administratively and politically, effectively eliminating all traces of the nineteenth-century heritage of regional conflict and civil war. The oil revenues that began to flow in the 1920's reinforced the Gómez regime and helped create a national army and national bureaucracy—in short, an effective state machine for the first time in Venezuelan history. The sheer growth and potential power of the central government is reflected in the expansion of overall state income and expenditure in the Gómez period. Actual income substantially exceeded expected income in most years (Table 2.1), particularly as petroleum

TABLE 2.1

Overall State Income in Selected Years*

(in thousands of *bolívares*)

Year	Budgeted	Collected
1905-06	55,000	49,335
1910-11	48,000	69,862
1915-16	39,550	65,674
1920-21	59,612	81,561
1925-26	69,148	172,098
1930-31	202,599	210,259
1935-36	164,594	189,125
1936-37	215,861	274,003

* The data are drawn from "Ingresos, Egresos, y Reservas del Tesoro Nacional, Años Económicos 1900-01–1965 (en miles de bolívares)," in the *Anuario Estadístico de Venezuela, 1965* (Caracas: Taller Gráfico, 1967), pp. 285-286.

revenue became important. Expenditures of the national government also rose dramatically. (Table 2.2.)

Average annual state expenditures thus rose from 44,454,000 *bolívares* in the first decade of this century to 249,752,900 *bolívares* in the period from 1930 to 1939.[1] The

[1] Calculated from data in *Anuario Estadístico de Venezuela, 1965* (Caracas: Taller Gráfico, 1967). The value of government services and incomes as shown by these data was little affected by inflation. Their real value rose roughly as shown. The *bolívar* appreciated in value in the 1930's.

15

TABLE 2.2

Overall State Expenditures in Selected Years*
(in thousands of *bolívares*)

Year	Authorized	Spent
1905-06	55,000	50,345
1910-11	48,000	61,640
1915-16	39,550	57,930
1920-21	58,539	102,656
1925-26	66,280	163,118
1930-31	201,800	260,291
1935-36	164,594	233,186
1936-37	215,861	285,317

* The data are drawn from "Ingresos, Egresos, y Reservas del Tesoro Nacional, Años Económicos 1900-01–1965 (en miles de bolívares)," in the *Anuario Estadístico de Venezuela, 1965* (Taller Gráfico, 1967), pp. 285-286.

bulk of this new income came from oil royalties. Although the petroleum industry has never employed more than a small percentage of the economically active population, its impact was gradually reflected in the social structure in a variety of ways. Throughout the nineteenth century, Venezuela had been primarily an agricultural economy, exporting coffee, cacao, sugar, tobacco, hides, etc. As oil exports began to dominate the economy, however, agricultural exports of all kinds actually declined, both as a share of total exports, and in absolute terms as well.[2]

The decline in volume of all agricultural exports reflects the tremendous impact of petroleum on the rural social structure. The drop in agricultural production was accompanied by a progressive depopulation of the countryside. While population grew only slowly during the Gómez period (especially as compared to later rates of growth), some areas grew more rapidly than others. Industrial and

[2] See Tables 7 and 8, pp. 54 and 55 in Acedo de Sucre and Nones Mendoza, *op.cit.*

16

urban areas grew much faster than essentially agricultural areas.[3]

Although specific estimates of the rural-urban mix of the population are not available for the pre-1936 period, the decline in agricultural production and the more rapid growth of industrializing and urban areas reveal a consistent trend to urban growth. After 1936, the relative decline of the rural population is striking. While 65.28 percent of the population was classified as rural in 1936, this dropped to 46.19 percent by 1950 and to only 32.56 percent by 1961. Current projections foresee only 17.2 percent of the population as rural by 1981.[4] The difference in rates of growth is even more dramatic: while the urban population grew by 99.86 percent from 1941 to 1950, and 95.02 percent from 1950 to 1961, rural population grew by only 0.38 percent from 1941 to 1950 and 5.36 percent from 1950 to 1961.[5]

These different rates of population growth are a useful indicator of the tremendous geographical mobility that has marked recent Venezuelan history. The proportion of people living outside their native state grew from 3.9 percent in 1920 to 14.2 percent in 1941 and 20.4 percent in 1961.[6] Migration has been widespread, pulling people out of all regions and all levels of the social structure.[7] Moreover, among those social groups which are now heavily urban

[3] See A. Uslar Pietri, *Sumario de Economía Venezolana* (Caracas: Fundación Eugenio Mendoza, 1960), pp. 63-72 for data on internal migration over time.

[4] Persons living in centers of less than 1,000 population are classified as rural in Venezuela. Data are drawn from "Cuadro 7. Población Total por Areas, Censos de 1961, 1950, 1941, y 1936," *Noveno Censo General de Población* (26 de febrero de 1961), *Resúmen General de la República, Parte A* (Caracas, 1966), p. 11. The projection to 1981 is from the *Compendio Estadístico de Venezuela* (Caracas, 1968), p. 44.

[5] Data are from "Cuadro 7. Población Total." The population classified as urban includes those living in towns of over 2,500 persons. The category of "intermediate" is used for towns between 1,000 and 2,500.

[6] J. Silva Michelena, *op.cit.*, p. 79.

[7] *Ibid.*, pp. 90-91, Table 4.3.

17

(50 to 90 percent in urban areas), the incidence of migration is even higher. In this regard, J. Silva Michelena points out that rates of residential mobility are particularly high among peasants. Between 33 and 43 percent of rural workers sampled in 1963 had already lived in three or four different places. This statistic points to a backlog of movement directed to the cities[8]—many people are still on the way. The relative depopulation of rural Venezuela is also reflected in long-term changes in the occupational structure. The proportion of the labor force employed in agriculture dropped from 71.6 percent in 1920 to only 33.5 percent by 1961, while employment in services (public and private) rose from 7.6 percent in 1920 to 24.8 percent by 1961. Employment in industry more than doubled in the same period.[9]

All of these changes (population, residence, occupation) have political significance as they reveal that the experience of change and movement has been widespread in Venezuela for a long time, even during the politically static Gómez period, when the lid of repression was clamped down firmly. The broadly based nature of social and economic change helped release people from old social ties all across the regional and class spectrum. As we shall see, the parties that began to form after 1936 fit into this situation in two important ways: (1) the weakness of old ties made many persons available for new forms of social organization and commitment; and (2) the successful parties were all broadly based, with a wide range of appeals, reflecting the variety of groups on the move in Venezuela. Single-class parties (attempts to build parties based solely on industrial workers, for example) have had little success in Venezuela.

It is important to note that while economic pressures helped pull people into new jobs and residences, the social bonds and loyalties which might have held them in the old areas, or at least provided social continuity to the transition,

[8] *Ibid.*, p. 91.　　　　[9] *Ibid.*, p. 55, Table 3.1.

did not exist. In political terms, a crucial aspect of the Gómez regime was the elimination of regional military power, hence wiping out the social basis for the regional divisions and civil wars which had characterized the nineteenth century in Venezuela.[10] Once the central government was able to purchase planes and machine guns and maintain a well-equipped standing army,[11] the days of the regional *caudillo* were over. There was too much power at the center. Gómez also managed to wipe out all traces of the traditional political parties—Liberals and Conservatives—which had dominated nineteenth-century political alignments. It was very difficult for any kind of organization to exist in Venezuela during the rule of Gómez, and the unprecedented length of his regime completely destroyed the traditional parties. Indeed, a famous motto of the Gómez regime was *Gómez único* (Gómez alone, nothing but Gómez). *Gómez único* was more than a slogan; it was a social reality as well.[12]

The possibilities of opposition to Gómez were extremely limited. Power was highly centralized, and no expression of organized political life was tolerated. The only group able to generate consistent opposition of a potentially popular kind was the university students. The origins of modern politics in Venezuela lie in this group. Under Gómez, Venezuela had only two universities, the Central University (UCV), in Caracas, and the University of the Andes (ULA), in Mérida. Significant political actions were effectively limited to the students in Caracas. Even this limited base of opposition was restricted by Gómez as he closed

---

[10] See R. L. Gilmore, *Caudillism and Militarism in Venezuela, 1810-1910* (Athens, Ohio: Ohio University Press, 1964).

[11] Gilmore argues forcefully that Gómez was the last *caudillo* since he was the first to recruit and equip a regular professional army, and thus institutionalize military forces that had previously been raised on an ad hoc personal basis by regional and local elites. See Gilmore, *op.cit.*, pp. 60ff.

[12] See A. Arellano Moreno, *Mirador de la Historia Política de Venezuela* (Caracas: Ediciones Edime, 1967), pp. 19-21.

the UCV from 1912 to 1922, after a series of antigovernment political actions by students. The strikes in 1912 marked the first important student opposition to the rule of Gómez, and led to the dissolution of the General Association of Students. There were brief revivals of student action in 1914 and 1918, culminating in student participation in a trolley car strike, one of the first instances in twentieth-century Venezuela of student cooperation with nonstudents in political action. A later attempt to reconstitute student organizations failed in 1918, and it was only in 1921 that the Federación de Estudiantes de Venezuela (FEV) could be organized. With the reopening of the UCV in 1922, the basis of future oppositions began to emerge. The FEV itself was dissolved in the mid-twenties, and reorganized in late 1927, in time to lead the opposition to Gómez in the famous events of Student Week in February 1928. The events of this week have been extensively studied and commented upon; hence I will limit myself here to a brief outline of the most important aspects.[13]

Student Week was originally planned as a series of events to raise funds for the construction and outfitting of a Student Residence. The intentions of the students were, at least to begin with, entirely nonpolitical. In the course of the week, however, the students designated to speak at various events all gave speeches easily interpreted as antigovernment—as calls for liberty.[14]

[13] The best work on the subject is *La Generación.* . . . Other useful sources are J. Martz, *op.cit.,* Chapter 1; J. Gabaldón Márquez, *Memoria y Cuento de la Generación de 1928* (Caracas, 1958); R. Betancourt, *Venezuela: Política y Petróleo* (Caracas: Editorial Senderos, 1967), Chapter 1; and J. B. Fuenmayor, *Veinte Años de Política, 1928-1948* (Caracas, 1968).

[14] A particularly striking incident came in the reading of a poem dedicated to the Student Queen, Beatrice I, by the poet Pío Tamayo. After telling her of his own lover, the poet went on:

> Trembling in shadows I loved her in fear.
> In my veins ran fears for her life.
> And one day they stole her from me,

The government reacted swiftly, with many arrests. But the contrast to earlier events soon became clear as great numbers of students, in solidarity, presented themselves to the police and demanded to be arrested, 214 in all finally being sent to the "Castle" of Puerto Cabello. This new attitude introduced an entirely new approach—someone willingly submitting to arrest in protest—and it was soon joined by another—mass popular protest—as a wave of spontaneous demonstrations swept Caracas and other cities, pressuring Gómez into releasing the students after only 11 days in jail.

Contact with many political prisoners in the jails, and the obvious popular support their actions aroused, encouraged student leaders to go further, seeking the complete overthrow of the dictatorship. Students participated with young military officers in an abortive coup in April 1928. Once again, many were arrested, some remaining in jail until Gómez's death in late 1935.[15] But even this dose of defeat and repression was insufficient to liquidate student opposition. In October 1928, the FEV sent a letter to Gómez, calling for the release of those arrested in February and April. Thirty-two of the signers of the letter were immediately arrested, and in the days that followed, many more voluntarily submitted to arrest. Most were sent to forced labor on the highways, where the combination of malaria and brutal treatment guaranteed that few would survive.

Those who evaded arrest participated from exile in sev-

And one day they took her away. . .
. . . and the name of this lover is much
like your own:
She was called Liberty.

Quoted, in R. A. Freytes, *Vida de un Adelantado* (*Intento Biográfico Sobre José Pío Tamayo*), Caracas: Editoral Universitaria, 1948), p. 30. (Translations from the Spanish are by the author.)

[15] For an account of the April 1928 revolt by a nonstudent participant, see F. Betancourt Sosa, *Pueblo en Rebeldía* (Caracas: Ediciones Garrido, 1959).

eral armed attempts to overthrow the regime during 1928 and 1929. All were easily defeated, and the nation relapsed into the peace of dictatorships. But the events of 1928 had significance far beyond their immediate success or failure. Students, in exile and underground within Venezuela, now turned to the formation of mass political parties. This turn to party organization is of the utmost importance, for it indicates that the uprisings of 1928, although sparked and led by students, were in fact the last autonomous student political movements Venezuela was ever to see. Students realized that to defeat Gómez, it was not enough to kill him and hope for the best. To change Venezuela, the system had to be changed, and this required a reorientation in thinking about politics and the redirection of all efforts into the formation of mass organizations. The idea of mass parties was itself something new for the nation. Political parties in Venezuela had traditionally been parties of notables, armed factions rather than permanent and continuous organizations. The mass of the population was involved only minimally in their conflicts.

The most important aspects of the Gómez era were, then: (1) the consolidation of an effective national army and state machine; (2) the eradication of the traditional political parties and the absence of any organized political groups; (3) the erosion of traditional social structure (above all in the rural areas), and the setting in motion of large masses of people all across the social spectrum; (4) the concentration of opposition in student groups able to operate autonomously in politics; and (5) the emergence from these student groups of a new orientation to political action, directed to mass organization as the appropriate vehicle for political change.

While Gómez lived, his political system remained firm, and the organization and expression of new potential power sources based on mass organization were effectively suppressed. With his death, on December 17, 1935, however, things began to move very quickly, and the entire political landscape changed beyond recognition in a few short months.

As we have seen, on the death of Gómez, Venezuela had no political parties,[16] and popular organization of any kind was extremely rare. The nation lacked a tradition of political struggle outside of the universities. Not surprisingly, then, the first group to react publicly to Gómez's death was the FEV, which had reorganized secretly in early December 1935. The FEV launched a public manifesto calling for the liberation of political prisoners, the return of exiles, and the restoration of civil and political liberties.[17]

However, once the exiles did, in fact, begin to filter back, and set about organizing political parties, trade unions, and associations of all kinds, political action soon got beyond the potential resources of the FEV alone. The FEV, of course, retained great prestige, but the most notable aspect of the political changes following Gómez's death is precisely the growth of organizations with a broad social base—unions, civic leagues, political parties, etc. Although these groups were generally founded and led by returning exiles of the 1928 generation, the organizations themselves were general in scope and not limited to students. Students as a power group per se soon faded from the scene. They provided the catalyst for party organization, but never again would they wield autonomous power. In 1936, power began to pass to those who could organize the masses.

Following a wave of popular riots against the Gómez family and close collaborators, the former Minister of War, General Eleazar López Contreras, was able to consolidate his position in the presidency. He faced intense pressures for liberalization. Agitation continued throughout the month of January 1936, as the exiles returned and set to

[16] An attempt was made to form a Communist Party of Venezuela in May 1931. This was, of course, carried out in great secrecy but to no avail since the party functioned only with the greatest difficulty, with their meetings being repeatedly broken up by the police.
[17] See Eduardo Montes [pseud.], "La Historia Pública de la Federación de Estudiantes," El Nacional, February 17, 1966.

work. Among the earliest groups to form were Organización Venezolana (ORVE), led by Rómulo Betancourt, the Partido Republicano Progresista, made up mainly of Communists, but promoting a broad alliance of the democratic Left, and the Unión Nacional Republicana, a group of Center-Left business and professional people. At the same time, in the oil fields of Zulia state, one of the original founders of the Communist Party, Juan Bautista Fuenmayor, began to reorganize the PCV, also participating in a broad regional alliance of the Left, the Bloque Nacional Democrático.[18]

The other major group operating politically was the student federation. To comply with a provision of law that prohibited student groups from engaging in political actions, the FEV was reorganized as FEV-OP (FEV-Political Organization). This group was identical to the FEV, and existed solely for calling meetings, issuing manifestos, and the like. Its leader was Jóvito Villalba, a major figure in the 1928 events. It is important to note the different organizational orientations of those who had the experience of exile and contact with modern political organizations and currents of thought, like Rómulo Betancourt, who immediately began to organize parties, and those, like Villalba, with limited experience (Villalba was in jail from 1928 to 1936), who started in 1936 where they had left off eight years earlier—in the student movement.

The key test of strength between the regime and the new opposition came in the convocation of the Congress (made up of Gómez appointees) to confirm López Contreras in office and review and amend the Constitution.[19] The new groups formed an "April Bloc" to press for social and politi-

[18] For an account of the reorganization of the Communist Party underground and its relations with the Bloque Nacional Democrático in Zulia, as well as a valuable description of the first union organizing and calls for strikes among oil workers, see Fuenmayor, *op.cit.*, pp. 121-188.

[19] A good description of the events leading up to the congress is found in Martz, *Acción. . .*, pp. 26-28.

cal reforms in the Congress. But when the Congress finally met, it merely confirmed the election of López Contreras and granted no reforms at all. The revised Constitution was actually *regressive* since it reduced the legal basis of suffrage to literate males, over 21, thus eliminating the great majority of the population,[20] and added a clause banning Communists and Communist groups from all political activities.

The growing strength and confidence of conservative forces was manifest in the passage of the "Lara Law" (named after the sponsoring senator), a repressive measure which tightened the screws on democratic groups. In protest, the opposition demanded the dissolution of Congress, new general elections, withdrawal of the Lara Law, and the confiscation of all remaining assets of the Gómez family. A twenty-four hour general strike was called in Caracas. The strike was so effective that it was extended to other cities, and lasted five days in all, from June 9 to June 13. In a way, the strike marked the beginning of the end for the Left since it proved too great a strain on the new organizations' capacities, and, moreover, helped unify the Right behind López Contreras since the fear of similar strikes brought conservative elements together.[21]

The end became clear when elements of the Left sought legalization for a new, unified party, the Partido Nacional Democrático (PDN). Their application was rejected in November 1936, on the grounds that both the component groups and the proposed members were Communists, and hence barred by the Constitution from political action. This blow was followed by brutal repression of an oil workers'

---

[20] Suffrage had previously included all males over 21 for elections to municipal councils and state legislatures. The councilmen and state legislators then elected the national congressmen who chose the president. The voter was thus twice removed from the presidential election. The 1936 Constitution limited voting to literate males over 21.

[21] For an account of the Lara Law and the June strike, see Betancourt, *Venezuela. . .*, pp. 103-107, and Martz, *Acción. . .*, pp. 31-33.

strike and official dissolution of the Congress of Venezuelan Workers which had been formed on a national scale in December 1936.

The final stage in repression came after the January 1937 elections. Even under conditions of restricted suffrage and indirect election (members of Congress were elected by municipal councils), elements of the PDN managed to elect several deputies and senators. Almost immediately, leading figures of the Left were arrested, component groups of the PDN (ORVE, PRP, and others) were dissolved, and the election of their representatives invalidated. On March 13, 1937, the process was rounded out with a decree exiling most of the leaders of these parties. Only a few, like Rómulo Betancourt or Juan Bautista Fuenmayor, managed to evade the police and these few set to work organizing the PDN and the Communist Party of Venezuela (PCV) on an underground basis.

Although the new organizations had clearly met a crushing defeat, the important fact is that simple decrees were no longer enough to eliminate political opposition. It went underground. Both the PDN and the PCV (reorganized in August 1937 as a separate party) continued to operate throughout the López Contreras regime. The significance of the events of 1936 and 1937 may be summarized as follows: (1) the formation of mass political organizations for the first time in Venezuelan history; (2) through these groups, the introduction of new political resources into Venezuelan life (organized popular pressure); and (3) the beginnings, under party auspices, of secondary associations of all kinds, most importantly industrial and rural trade unions.

CHAPTER 3

The Party System: Conflict, Conciliation, and Exclusion

THROUGHOUT the López Contreras period, the Communists and the PDN operated underground, concentrating on the formation of leadership cadres and the elaboration of programs for future action. There was no real change in the effective structure or distribution of power during the period López Contreras was in office, and the organizational base slowly being created by the clandestine groups found no expression in political power.

Toward the end of his regime, however, López Contreras grew more lenient, and the PDN was allowed to participate de facto in the presidential elections held in April 1941. Its candidate was Rómulo Gallegos, the novelist and educator. Although Gallegos' candidacy was largely symbolic, in this case the symbol was important: it provided the first public platform in modern times for opposition to the tradition of *continuismo* (an outgoing president continuing his power by placing his own men in office).

The new president, General Medina Angarita, had been Minister of War under López Contreras, and was handpicked for the succession. Yet it was Medina Angarita, universally regarded at the time as a puppet of López Contreras, who initiated the process of political liberalization and freedom of organization in Venezuela. These reforms probably stemmed from Medina's need to establish an entirely separate base and distinctive image from that of López Contreras, and, moreover, to the impact of World War II and the relation to the allied powers. Whatever the reasons, the reality of liberalization was clear and the PDN, sensing

27

this change of climate, applied for legalization shortly after Medina took office. Authorization was quickly granted and the party, its name changed to the present Acción Democrática, was formally constituted on September 13, 1941. Immediately, the party began a vigorous organizational drive destined to cover the country from end to end with centers composed of party members. According to Rómulo Betancourt, from the very beginning "The leadership of AD established for itself the watchword of: 'Not a single district, not a single municipality without its party organization.' "[1]

Every major political party to follow AD has heeded this advice. Today, if one travels in the most remote and isolated areas of Venezuela, almost every collection of houses big and permanent enough to be called a town has several party headquarters. Acción Democrática pioneered the building of a new kind of political party with a permanent organizational base—full-time parties, which operated all year round, at election time and between elections, at the national level, and in every locality. Each party built its organization both vertically and horizontally: vertically the parties reach all levels, from neighborhood through region to nation; horizontally, the party is affiliated with and sponsors functional groups like student wings, labor sections, women's fronts, and the like.

For a long time, AD was the only party with a national organization of this scope and depth. This gave it an incalculable advantage, above all in the early years of party activity. In a situation resembling an organizational vacuum, AD was the only force to fill the gap. A prominent Christian Democrat later acknowledged the unique character of the early years of AD, noting that "Acción Democrática was the meeting place of anti-Gómez Venezuela. The mental state of our country facilitated the growth of AD."[2]

[1] Betancourt, *Venezuela. . .*, pp. 163-164.
[2] R. J. Cardenas, *El Combate Político: Sólo Para Líderes Nuevos* (Caracas: Editorial Doña Bárbara, 1966), pp. 20-21.

During the Medina period, the other important forces operating politically were the Communists and a party founded by the government. The Communists were split into several factions, but basically operated through Unión Popular, a poli-class organization of the popular front type, reminiscent of the PRP of 1936, and through an underground organization of the PCV proper.[3] The government party was first organized as the Partidarios de la Política del Gobierno (roughly translated this means Partisans of Government Policies), later changed to the Venezuelan Democratic Party (PDV), an organization which brought together many leading intellectuals, along with Communist sympathizers whose participation in the PDV reflected Communist support for Medina.[4]

The growth of party organization brought with it the penetration of many sectors of national life along party lines. For example, organizers went out to aid in the formation of labor unions, and the entire Medina period witnessed a quiet, dirty struggle for control of the labor movement. By 1945, AD had clearly taken the upper hand. A similar drive was conducted for the organization of peasant unions.[5]

In this way, a whole new set of political roles emerged in Venezuela, fundamentally reshaping the political landscape. Roles such as union organizer or party official gradually occupied the center of the political stage, channeling the energies previously dispersed, or only sporadically represented by student movements. Student movements per se lost importance. In this context, it is instructive to look brief-

[3] The formal legalization of the PCV as such came late in Medina's period in office.

[4] Communist support for Medina was largely due to Venezuela's key role as a supplier of oil in the anti-Nazi struggle.

[5] On peasant organization, see J. D. Powell, *The Role of the Federación Campesina in the Venezuelan Agrarian Reform Process,* Land Tenure Center Research Paper, No. 26, University of Wisconsin, December 1967. Powell provides useful figures on the growth of peasant unions from 1936 on.

ly at the changing political role of students, and their evolving relation to political parties. The FEV increasingly became a battleground for rival political forces, losing its autonomy and unity. These internal divisions grew stronger after the political liberalizations of the early 1940's, when AD and the Communists could compete openly among students. The rival parties formed their own youth groups. The Communists and their allies joined in the Venezuelan Confederation of Youth (CJV) while AD worked through the Association of Venezuelan Youth (AJV). These organizations gradually took over the role of the FEV and drew off its membership. Later these organizations (the CJV and the AJV) were replaced by formal party youth wings.

As for the FEV, it simply languished—no one is sure just when it died, as no one really cared at the time. It had lost its membership and was merely a battleground for opposing party factions, each seeking the prestige of "controlling" the name of the FEV. A student leader of the period describes the process: "The FEV simply languished and died unnoticed. By that time it had become an army of generals. In those days we tried to speak of a 'fevist' spirit, but the political groups simply ridiculed this as romanticism, lack of realism . . . they insisted that one had to be political."[6]

The most significant development for the student movement came earlier in 1936. In that year, the FEV divided, with a group of Catholic students leaving to form a rival organization, the National Student Union (UNE). The emergence of the UNE marks the first political expression in Venezuela of Catholic social doctrine, and its formation presented to the nation a brilliant new political generation, led by Rafael Caldera. Members of the UNE were greatly influenced by the development of social doctrine in the Venezuelan Church, as embodied in a series of study circles organized within the UNE from 1937 on.

[6] Interview D-25, October 28, 1968.

30

The UNE soon became a nationally organized rival to the FEV. As its founding generation left the universities, they formed several political parties with a Catholic orientation: Acción Electoral in 1941, Acción Nacional in 1942, and finally COPEI (Comité de Organización Política Electoral Independiente) in 1946. In forming as a social-Christian party, COPEI absorbed the UNE and later formed its own youth wing, the Revolutionary Copeyano Youth (JRC).

Thus, by 1947, there was no unified, autonomous student organization left in Venezuela. Instead party youth wings appeared, the most important being the Youth of AD, the Communist Youth, and the Revolutionary Copeyano Youth, in that order.

It is worth noting that although organizations of all kinds emerged in Venezuela in the post-Gómez thaw, these were generally leftist in orientation, and traditionally prestigious sectors of society were left out of (or did not join) the organizational race. Traditional social and economic elites found shelter of a sort in the Sociedades Cívicas Bolivarianas, groups supporting the policies and programs of López Contreras. However, these were essentially creations of the government, and not representative associations in any strict sense of the word. The Church, a pillar of traditional values, was largely without organization. Outside of the UNE and a tiny Catholic Action movement, there were no major Catholic secondary associations. The Church, indeed, was barely present in many parts of Venezuela. In 1945, there were only 664 priests in the entire country, an average of over 15,000 persons per priest.[7]

The Venezuelan Church had traditionally been weak, never enjoying the wealth, prestige, or power of the Church in Colombia or Peru. This weakness dates from the late nineteenth century, when the dictator Guzmán Blanco exiled

[7] I. Alonso, M. Luzardo, G. Garrido, and J. Oriol, *La Iglesia en Venezuela y Ecuador* (Bogotá: FERES, 1962), Table, p. 54, and Table 4, p. 155.

the Archbishop of Caracas, expelled the Jesuits, closed the seminaries for the training of priests, and instituted a civil registry and civil marriage.[8] The slow rebuilding of the Church began in the early years of the twentieth century.[9] Over half the dioceses and all the vicarates in the Church were founded after 1900.[10] This renovation centered on the reestablishment of Catholic education. Catholic *liceos* were opened in Caracas (the first in 1916) and soon acquired tremendous social influence, especially among elite groups. By 1945, Catholic *liceos*, which then formed the bulk of private secondary education, accounted for almost half the total enrollment in secondary education.[11] But even though education was a sensitive area for the Church, it was unable to establish and maintain any national organization in this field until 1945. This despite the fact that the Venezuelan Federation of Teachers, a militantly anticlerical group, was organized in 1936.

On the eve of the Revolution of October 18, 1945, then, in which Acción Democrática (a party with an anticlerical image, and strongly committed to educational reform) took power, the Church had a major stake in education.

In general, the Church was profoundly alienated from the newer trends in Venezuelan politics, and yet organizationally incapable of responding to them. When crises arose

[8] For a full discussion of these nineteenth-century conflicts, see J. L. Mecham, *Church and State in Latin America* (Chapel Hill: University of North Carolina Press, 1966), Chapter 4, and M. Watters, *A History of the Church in Venezuela, 1810-1930* (Chapel Hill: University of North Carolina Press, 1933).

[9] A good account of the history of the Church in Venezuela is J. Rodríguez Iturbe, *Iglesia y Estado en Venezuela (1824-1964)* (Caracas: Imprenta Universitaria, 1968). This is a comprehensive politico-juridical account of Church-state relations.

[10] American University, *U.S. Army Handbook for Venezuela* (Washington: U.S. Government Printing Office, 1964), p. 197.

[11] Enrollment in private *liceos* accounted for 49 percent of the total *liceo* enrollment in 1943-44, and 46 percent in 1944-45. Chapter 4 will present data on the dramatic decline of this percentage during the AD government of 1945-48. A breakdown of private education into Catholic and secular is not available for these years.

32

which affected the Church, it had to intervene directly, in open political defense of its rights and privileges. While the lack of an associated organizational network forced the Church to intervene directly in politics, it also made the results of that action more difficult to control. Lack of organization naturally inhibits control over the actions of supporters. As we shall see, it has only been with the consolidation of COPEI, as a Catholic-inspired, yet non-confessional political party, that the Church has been able to withdraw from direct political action while at the same time growing in influence and prestige within the political system.[12]

THE CONSOLIDATION OF THE PARTY SYSTEM

As we have seen, the potential bases of participation expanded greatly in the Medina period. Nevertheless, the political system remained restrictive of actual participation, denying ultimate legitimacy to the new power factors being forged by the political parties—votes and mass popular consent. The expansion of participation in a system which denies results to organized participation implies that the loyalties generated by the new-found opportunities to participate will go to the parties and the leaders of the opposition, not to the system or its institutions.[13]

This concentration of loyalties in the new party organizations[14] reinforced a structural tendency to define

[12] Vallier notes that this is a common feature of those Latin American countries with strong Christian Democratic parties. See I. Vallier, "Religious Elites: Differentiations and Developments in Roman Catholicism," S. M. Lipset and A. Solari, eds., *Elites in Latin America* (New York: Oxford University Press, 1967), pp. 190-232, especially p. 209.

[13] J. Silva Michelena, *op.cit.*, pp. 5-6, emphasizes this point with admirable clarity.

[14] The development of organization-focused loyalties in a new party system is explored for the United States in R. Hofstadter's *The Idea of a Party System: The Rise of Legitimate Opposition in the United States, 1780-1840* (Berkeley: University of California Press, 1970),

social cleavages primarily in terms of party affiliation—party ties cutting across functional spheres to unify workers, students, peasants, professionals, etc., along party lines. In some cases, we might expect that party organization would merely encapsulate traditional structures. Change would then be superficial, and the underlying structure of power and loyalties would continue to be dominated by traditional patterns. However, if the picture I have drawn of the pre-1936 social structure in Venezuela is accurate, then the weakness of traditional bonds paves the way for a more powerful penetration by the new organizations. Although the new structures might represent a cross-section of interests—farmers, workers, shopkeepers, students, etc.—the organization itself builds up great reserves of organization-focused loyalties and internal discipline. Party identification in this sense (particularly among activists) is a key feature of Venezuelan political life. Loyalty to the party as an organization often overrides particular sectoral and pragmatic interests.[15]

The Medina regime remained one that fundamentally shut off access to power to AD and its growing, vigorous organization. This helps explain the fact that when AD received an unexpected invitation to join a military conspiracy against the Medina government, the reaction was one of cautious acceptance. Only a very small number of officers were committed to the coup (perhaps 150 out of an officer corps of several thousand), and feeling insecure in their numbers and ability to control the country, the conspirators sought an alliance with Acción Democrática. Outside of the army and the bureaucracy, AD was, in effect, the only or-

especially Chapter 6, which discusses the rise of professional politicians and party loyalty as exemplified in the career of Van Buren.

[15] In the case studies that follow, great importance is attributed to the role of party discipline in permitting parties to play a mediating role in political conflict. For a fuller discussion of the genesis of these organization-focused loyalties, see Chapter 8 below.

ganization of truly national scope in Venezuela.[16] The coup was launched on October 18, 1945, and after several days of fighting, the Medina government was replaced by a civil-military junta, composed of four members of AD (Rómulo Betancourt, Raúl Leoni, Gonzalo Barrios, and Luis B. Prieto),[17] two military officers (Major Carlos Delgado Chalbaud and Captain Mario Vargas), and one independent civilian (Dr. Edmundo Fernández). The three-year period of government which followed the coup, commonly known in Venezuela as the *trienio*, witnessed the firm rooting of the party system in Venezuelan political life.

At this point, let me clarify what I mean by the term "party system." As used here, the phrase implies at least four dimensions:

1. the fundamental instruments of political mobilization and action are political parties;

2. as a result of "1," the fundamental, legitimate resource of politics becomes that characteristic of modern political parties—the vote and the mobilization of consent;

3. as parties come to dominate the political scene, certain methods of political action become prevalent—mass meetings, extensive propaganda, and reliance on elections, for example;[18] and

[16] Joseph Doyle, "Venezuela 1958: The Transition from Dictatorship to Democracy" (Ph.D. dissertation, Department of History, George Washington University, February 1967), p. 32.

[17] Of the four AD members, Betancourt was president from 1959 to 1963, Leoni was president from 1964 to 1969, and Barrios and Prieto were the chief contenders for the AD nomination in 1968. Barrios won the nomination and Prieto formed his own party, the MEP (People's Electoral Movement), taking with him the more socialist wing of the party.

[18] One good question which might be raised is what difference it would make if the parties were nonelectoral. Clearly the character of the system would change. This, however, was never a real alternative since the basic ideological choices made in the formation of the parties were always keyed toward elections as the source of legitimate power. AD always insisted, to its credit, on using power not to consolidate itself in a single-party dictatorship, but rather to ensure free elections.

4. as parties dominate politics, they become the principal agencies for the organization and channeling of political conflict. Conflicts are expressed primarily through political parties, and this organizational concentration opens the possibility of agreement between parties on the legitimate bounds of conflicts—that is, a procedural consensus on the means of limiting the scope of any given conflict becomes a possibility.

The potential present in the last-named dimension, that is for a procedural consensus on the limitation of conflict, is the determining factor in the stabilization of a party system. If such agreements cannot be reached, then it is likely that conflicts will simply get beyond the capacity of settlement which the parties possess and, moreover, will be defined in terms that imply the illegitimacy of the new system. As we shall see shortly, it was precisely a lack of this procedural consensus—the absence of agreement on legitimate criteria of power and methods of action in politics—that contributed in large measure to undermining the strength and vitality of the regime that began with such high hopes on October 18, 1945.

Party organization in the *trienio* was in general free,[19] and the stimulus to organization was increased through a fundamental reform of the election laws which eliminated all qualifications for suffrage outside of age and citizenship. The age barrier itself was lowered from 21 to 18. In addition, direct popular election of president, deputies, senators, and local councilmen was instituted. The *trienio* witnessed the formation of COPEI (in January 1946). COPEI soon became the center of opposition to AD. In addition, Unión Republicana Democrática (URD) was formed in December 1945, and soon became the personal vehicle of Jóvito Villalba, the former student leader. This party basically rep-

[19] There were some limitations on this freedom. For example, just after the coup, police destroyed and closed down the offices of the PDV (Medina's party). For a critical account, see Fuenmayor, *op.cit.*, p. 335.

resented the non-Communist left wing of the forces that had backed Medina. In 1947, the various factions of Communists came together in a Unity Congress, to form a single Communist Party of Venezuela.[20]

In general, avenues for the expression of interests were expanded and the costs of organization reduced. This was reflected in the rapid expansion of trade union organization. In 1946 alone, more than 500 new unions were formed.[21] The Confederation of Venezuelan Workers (CTV) was formed in November 1947, and by the time of the overthrow of President Gallegos in November 1948, claimed over 300,000 members, a sixfold increase over the figure for 1945.[22] The same organizational explosion occurred in the countryside, where, with the encouragement of the parties, the Venezuelan Peasant Federation greatly increased both in numbers of component unions and in total membership.[23] The expansion of peasant organization accompanied extensive agrarian reform that fundamentally altered the rural power structure, transferring the authority formerly wielded by agents of the central government (the *jefes civiles*) and by the local landowning class to the union official *cum* party organizer.[24] Thus the social bases of political power changed profoundly in rural Venezuela. Agents of the central government of course continued to wield great power, but the range of social interests represented through their actions, and the forces acting upon them, changed dramatically.

The rapid expansion of political participation during the *trienio* was, in some ways, too much of a good thing, as the country was subjected to an almost interminable election campaign for three full years. Elections were held for a National Constituent Assembly on October 27, 1946, to

[20] A small group stayed out of the unification process, forming the Partido Revolucionario del Proletariado, known as "Black Communists." This group worked with the regime almost until the end, reuniting with the "Red Communists" in a single PCV after 1958.
[21] Figures are from Betancourt, *Venezuela. . .*, p. 336.
[22] Martz, *Acción. . .*, p. 260.   [23] J. D. Powell, *op.cit.*
[24] *Ibid.*, p. 13.

select delegates to a convention which was to draw up a new Constitution. Elections were held again on December 14, 1947, to select a president and the congress. And elections were held once again on May 9, 1948, for positions on municipal councils throughout the nation. The strain of continuous election campaigns increased the apprehensions of opposition elements, and helped keep tensions at fever pitch at all times. There was hardly any time for cooling off.[25]

Political conflict in the *trienio* was in general quite bitter. The major opposition to the government stemmed from COPEI. It was indeed in this period that the term *adeco*, now a household word for members of AD, was coined. The term itself reflects the depth of political divisions, as it implies "*AD-CO* mmunist"—that AD was only Communism in disguise.[26] A prominent political figure associated with COPEI recently recalled his first political meeting in these terms:

> I remember very well the second meeting I conducted— I was stoned out of the first one. In that meeting I defined the problem in these terms . . . "Rómulo Betancourt is a Communist and AD means Communism. We must fight Communism and save Venezuela from Communism. The family demands it, the Fatherland demands it, Liberty demands it."[27]

Strong partisan feelings were further inflamed by religious conflicts which arose in 1946 out of the educational policies of the AD regime. AD came to power with a firm commitment to expanding public education, reinforced by a deep-rooted anticlericalism. Many of the founders and leaders of AD were also key figures in the Venezuelan Federation of Teachers, and leaders in public education. The sheer expan-

[25] It is perhaps significant that since 1958 elections have been consolidated: everything is decided at five-year intervals.
[26] Interview A-16, February 14, 1961.
[27] *Ibid.*

sion of the state educational system was enough to put the Church on guard. But the threat perceived by the Church was altered in quality and vastly amplified after the publication of a decree regulating the examination system in public and private schools. In effect, the decree put the private schools at a disadvantage. As the largest single component of private education, the Church saw the measure as an attack on the entire Catholic educational system, and through it, on the Church itself, in a drive to impose a lay, atheist, and socialist regime on Venezuela. Opposition to the decree was widespread and the antigovernment demonstrations that took place are important since they marked the first expression of large-scale public opposition to AD's rule.

It is important to note that this opposition was basically religious in inspiration. It was neither initiated nor controlled by COPEI, although the Christian Democrats did act as spokesman for these interests both in the Constituent Assembly and in the congress that followed.[28] As we shall see, COPEI as a political party was simply swept up in the wave of religious opposition to AD. Its identity as a political party was insufficiently developed to let it fill the role of mediator between the Catholic sector and the new regime.

From the publication of the decree until the fall of AD in November 1948, relations between the Church and the government were hostile and tense. From the Church's point of view, the conflict clearly centered on the very legitimacy of the AD regime, and the party system it epitomized and espoused. The threat perceived by the Church, and its fundamental rejection of the legitimacy of the new system, are nicely expressed in the fact that the fall of AD was greeted by the Jesuit magazine, *SIC*, with an editorial entitled "God Has Saved Us":

[28] Chapters 4 and 5 will show how the religious nature of this opposition precluded any possible role for COPEI as a mediator or moderating force in the conflict.

The most solid hopes appeared broken before the cold, hard reality which day after day the saddened Venezuelan community experienced. But faith did not die. And parallel to the prudent, measured and persevering activity of those who by mission and duty had to confront the chaos which devoured us, there was another attitude, quieter and more hidden, but of undeniable value: it was the attitude of those who suffered, sacrificed, and prayed incessantly, and hoped, firm in their faith that the God of our fathers would "intervene with His provident hand" and save us.

And God saved us. This is the phrase we have heard over and over in these days from mature and even hardened men: "How great is God!"[29]

While AD encountered often savage opposition, it must be noted that it offered little incentive of its own to cooperation and compromise with other parties. During the *trienio*, the *adeco* attitude to other parties was one of undisguised scorn and hostility. Acción Democrática has always been strongly anti-Communist, and as for URD and COPEI, the other opposition parties, Martz points out that: "the relations of the AD with both the URD and COPEI were charged with animosity and the thought of even minimal accommodation was alien to the *adeco* mentality."[30]

Quite apart from party-based hatreds, AD also managed to arouse the dislike and mistrust of many sectors ranging from the Church, landowners, and foreign investors, to former members of the Gómez, López Contreras, and Medina regimes, angered by the well-publicized trials of former officials for embezzlement.

The new criteria of power and legitimacy espoused by AD—votes and popular consent—were simply not accepted by many elements of the opposition. The Church rejected

[29] SIC (*Revista de Orientación*), No. 110 (December 1948), 485.
[30] Martz, *Acción. . .*, pp. 321-322.

the idea that the majority (of voters) could go against the "obvious" wishes and interests of the Catholic majority. The military in particular rejected the new system. If AD argued that its government was legitimate because it was based on victories in elections, the military attitude was that governments always won elections, and that nothing had, in essence, been changed. On the other hand, the army felt threatened by AD's attempts to remove deliberative and policymaking functions from its sphere of competence.[31]

AD finally fell in a bloodless coup on November 24, 1948, and was replaced by a triumvirate of military officers. The fall of AD is in large part attributable to the fact that its continued rule threatened too many interests, symbolic and material. In a sense, the party system initially implanted in the *trienio* fell under the weight of its own immaturities and excesses of zeal. Organization had spread and new forces had been mobilized and unleashed in political life without sufficient experience in democratic coexistence and without the construction of common norms for the limitation and management of conflicts. AD failed to establish a set of mutual guarantees with major sectors of the society, from foreign investors to the Church and the military. In the absence of such guarantees, these institutions felt their most cherished values threatened—even their immediate survival. As we shall see, on its return to power in 1959, AD was careful to avoid the fatal errors of the *trienio*.

The long and bloody dictatorship that controlled Venezuela from 1948 to 1958 is of specific interest here only insofar as the situation faced by the military rulers reflected the

[31] The Decree of December 7, 1948, which justified the coup, argued that AD had tried to distort the institutional essence of the armed forces: "Considering that the said Party attempted to separate the National Armed Forces from their essential nature, in order to convert them into an instrument for its designs," quoted in P. Taylor, *The Venezuelan Golpe de Estado of 1958: The Fall of Marcos Pérez Jiménez* (Washington: Institute for the Comparative Study of Political Systems, 1968), p. 46.

long-term structural impact of the *trienio* reforms on national politics. For the military regime faced the systematic opposition of political parties, trade unions, students, and other groups. This opposition differed from previous anti-dictatorial movements since it was composed of political parties and their branches—among labor, students, etc.

Perhaps the most important result of the lengthy resistance to military rule was the cooperation that resistance forced on the parties. The common experience of persecution and the common effort to overthrow Pérez Jiménez softened many of the antagonisms so bitterly felt during the *trienio*.[32] This softening of divisions led to clear decisions among the top leadership of AD, COPEI, and URD to seek a permanent reduction of the sectarian and partisan tone of political conflict, thereby enhancing the chances for the maintenance of a stable, democratic system in the postdictatorship era.

It is important to remember, however, that these arrangements were made largely at the level of top party leadership. For AD this posed a sharp problem. For of all the major parties, AD was the most bitterly persecuted. Its underground organization was shattered and rebuilt many times. The net result was a growing dissociation between top leadership in exile and those who carried on the day to day struggle underground.

While AD's exile leaders agreed on the need for cooperation with URD and COPEI, the major allies of AD's underground cadres were the Communists. When the exile leadership returned to take over the party, and began to press for concessions to old enemies as the necessary price of stability and survival, they met growing opposition from the underground generation of leaders. As we shall see, these men rejected the new alliances, and the concessions made, and later came to form the nucleus of revolutionary opposition

---

[32] Martz, *Acción. . .*, pp. 322-331, discusses the experience of the resistance and its impact on inter-party relations. Doyle, *op.cit.*, Chapters 3 and 4, gives a detailed account of inter-party cooperation in the overthrow of Pérez Jiménez.

to the post-1958 political arrangements, expressing their opposition in guerrilla warfare.[33]

The new unitary spirit, known as the Spirit of the 23rd of January (the date of Pérez Jiménez's fall) took concrete form in a pact between COPEI, URD, and AD—the Pact of Punto Fijo. In this agreement, signed on October 31, 1958, the three parties pledged to respect the outcome of the forthcoming elections and to work for a common minimum program. The pact laid the bases for a coalition government of the three parties which initiated the constitutional period of Rómulo Betancourt's presidency. On taking office, Betancourt himself described the pact, and the changes it implied for national politics:

Inter-party discord was kept to a minimum, and in this way the leaders revealed that they had learned the hard lesson the despotism gave to all Venezuelans. Underground, in prison, in exile, or living in precarious liberty at home, we understood that it was through the breach opened in the front of civility and culture that the conspiracy of November 24, 1948—of unmistakable regressiveness and supported by some with ingenuous good faith—was able to pass, a conspiracy which overthrew the legitimate government of Rómulo Gallegos.[34]

The attempt at a new style of relations among the parties reflected a general lowering of tensions and a drawing together of AD and many of the sectors that had offered such bitter opposition in the *trienio*. The case of the Church is particularly clear and important. From the very beginning of the Provisional Government, the Church sought to establish and maintain improved relations with the non-Commu-

[33] A good account of these divisions in AD is J. D. Cockcroft, *Venezuela's Fidelistas—Two Generations* (Washington: National Student Association, 1963).
[34] R. Betancourt, *Tres Años de Gobierno Democrático* (Caracas: Imprenta Nacional, 1962), I, 13. This work, in three volumes, is a collection of Betancourt's speeches and messages in his first three years in office. It is a valuable source for the period.

nist Left. Meanwhile, the new government, under the control of forces formerly seen as inimical to the Church, substantially increased the subsidy traditionally paid by the government to the Church, for salaries, repair and construction of churches, travel costs, etc. From 1957 to 1958 (the last year of the dictatorship) to 1958-1959, this subsidy almost tripled, and thereafter leveled off at an amount more than double the figures paid out during the 1950's. (See Table 3.1.)

A cordiality unimaginable in the late 1940's was general. This stemmed initially from the Church's key role in gen-

TABLE 3.1

Subsidies to the Church: 1951-68
(in *bolívares*)

Year	Subsidy
1951-52	3,688,200.00
1952-53	3,826,400.00
1953-54	2,803,348.50
1954-55	3,528,000.00
1955-56	3,794,800.00
1956-57	3,770,800.00
1957-58	3,815,400.00
1958-59	10,752,776.00
1959-60	7,304,014.00
1960-61	6,925,694.00
1961-62	4,935,091.03
1962-63	5,264,882.00
1963-64	5,264,882.00
1964-65	5,264,882.00
1965-66	6,582,534.00
1966-67	6,533,362.00
1967-68	6,577,072.00

SOURCE: *Presupuesto General de Ingresos y Gastos Públicos Para el Año Fiscal* (for the years 1951-52 to 1967-68). These are the years for which separate figures are available. Note that these are budgeted amounts. Thus, figures are sometimes repeated three years in a row. Actual disbursements were modified each year by a number of additional credits for specific items.

erating and sustaining opposition to Pérez Jiménez.[35] This basis for accommodation was reinforced by clear decisions taken within the Church to seek understanding and increased contacts with the forces in control of the government. One among many examples was the unprecedented participation of representatives of the Catholic schools in the deliberations of the militantly anticlerical Venezuelan Federation of Teachers and the Venezuelan College of Professors (a parallel group for secondary school teachers). Both these organizations were under AD control, and AD played a major role in urging its teachers to cooperate with the Church.

On a general level, as well, AD set out to mend fences with the Church. In his inaugural address, Betancourt promised a full reexamination of the legal bases of Church-State relations, with a view to a complete revision of the traditional system of ecclesiastical patronage, which subordinated the Church to the state.[36]

In the process of integrating the Church and the entire Catholic sector into the political system, encouraging a reconciliation of AD and the Church and a growing cooperation in common organizations, the participation of COPEI in the governmental coalition of 1959 to 1963 was of fundamental importance. For political motives—a desire to broaden the scope of the system and ensure the institutional stability of the new democratic regime—COPEI constantly stimulated this type of cooperation and common effort, often

[35] The Church wanted to avoid another dictator like Pérez Jiménez, and feared a take-over by the Left. In this context, AD, its old enemy, began to look better as an alternative. As we shall see, AD and its coalition government became in a sense the only alternative for the Church. See Chapter 5 below. Doyle, *op.cit.*, Chapter 2, gives a detailed account of the Church's role in the opposition to Pérez Jiménez.

[36] See Rodríguez Iturbe, *op.cit.*, and Betancourt's own inaugural address. These policies resulted in the signing of a modus vivendi between the Vatican and Venezuela in 1964. A concordat was impossible because Venezuela has civil divorce.

serving as go-between in consolidating better relations between the two sectors. A high-ranking *copeyano* legislator, with ample experience both in the *trienio* and in the post-1958 period, describes the role of COPEI in this way:

> If the Church found resistance within AD, it is clear that AD also found resistance within the Church, and it is here that we in COPEI played a basic role, in the government of Betancourt, as initiators and promoters of a greater understanding and cooperation between these two sectors.
>
> We have been like Saint Paul, with a Pauline message: "go and work among the people." The old thesis in the Catholic sector and even within COPEI was that Catholics should stay on their side and all others on their own side, isolated and apart. Our constant effort has been to increase work with other sectors, to increase common efforts and cooperation wherever possible.[37]

Increased mutual tolerance took form in many other fields. Within trade unions, for example, the principle of proportional representation for minorities dates from after the fall of Pérez Jiménez. Proportional representation allowed unions to function with several political groups competing internally, and eliminated the previous all-or-nothing system which had encouraged the multiplication of parallel unions, each inspired by a different political party.[38] The "Spirit of the 23rd of January" was also evident in student organizations, where the rule of proportional representation was established in 1960.

Betancourt's policy of attempting to conciliate old enemies, mending fences with groups which had offered bitter opposition in the past, is also visible in his relations with the military. The regionally based cliques which had dominated the military from Cipriano Castro and Gómez to Pérez

[37] Interview A-15, January 21, 1969.
[38] As we shall see, the trade union movement did eventually divide, unity falling victim to the growing tensions between the government and the Left.

Jiménez were purged and hemmed in within the army by a new corps of officers who were committed to and dependent on the regime. Betancourt also provided concrete benefits to the military, in terms of improved salaries, better housing, low-cost loans, and opportunities for professional training. In this regard, it is worth remembering that professional criteria for advancement in the armed forces had gone by the boards under Pérez Jiménez, and his capricious authoritarianism had eventually led to the imprisonment and torture of military officers.[39]

In this way, AD's leadership began correcting the errors which had led to their downfall twenty years earlier. Whereas in the *trienio* AD was perceived as a threat to the survival of the Church, foreign business, and the military, after 1958 AD deliberately sought to bury those fears. Its efforts in this regard were reinforced by the increasing alienation of the extreme Left. Perhaps more than any other factor, the development of a left-wing strategy of insurrection and guerrilla warfare helped consolidate the AD regime. Old enemies, like the Church and the military, came to see AD and its regime as the only viable alternative standing between them and total liquidation at the hands of a successful revolution. The example of Cuba, where the traditional military was completely destroyed after the revolution, was used to great effect by Betancourt.[40]

The alienation of the Left[41] arose from the convergence

[39] On Betancourt's relations with the military, see E. Lieuwin, *Generals vs. Presidents: Neomilitarism in Latin America* (New York: Frederick A. Praeger, 1964), pp. 86-91; Taylor, *op.cit.*, pp. 68-71; R. Alexander, *The Venezuelan Democratic Revolution* (New Brunswick: Rutgers University Press, 1964), pp. 105-117; and A. Sugon, *El Papel de los Militares* (Edinburgh: Centro de Estudios Latinoamericanos, 1963). Sugon's work is directly addressed to Venezuelan officers, and warns them that the military as an institution fares very poorly under military dictatorships, for then personal favoritism and caprice take over. He argues strongly that the best interests of the military lie in backing the constitutional regime.

[40] For a fuller discussion, see Chapter 9 below.

[41] The radical differences between the Left on the one hand and the Center and Right on the other in identifying problems and solu-

47

of at least three basic factors: (1) the decision of Betancourt to refuse the cooperation of the Communists in his government; (2) the generational-ideological split, already noted, between top-level exile leadership and the underground leaders (particularly acute in AD and URD); and (3) the tremendous impact of the Cuban Revolution, which convinced many in the Venezuelan Left that a similar revolution could be carried out at home. One leader of this younger generation summed up the situation in a recent interview. After describing the civil-military movement against Pérez Jiménez, he noted:

A year later came the Cuban phenomenon. This was decisive. In [his party] we began to see that the movement against Pérez Jiménez in 1958 should have taken the same orientation as that which Fidel Castro gave to his movement in 1959, and we concluded that our struggle in Venezuela had been very superficial. Although intended to produce basic changes, it ended with renewed domination by the old dominant classes and power groups. Along with this rethinking came a notable convergence of the youth movements of URD, AD, and the Communist Party. This was the nucleus of what lamentably was never to be, but which could have been a great new movement of the Left, aimed not only at an ideological position of great importance, but also at the replacement of the old leaders.[42]

A fundamental aspect of the reconciliation of AD with its old enemies was the agreement to concentrate political action in common organizational vehicles. This tacit bargain

---

tions for Venezuela are starkly revealed by J. Silva Michelena. In his "Desarollo Cultural y Heterogeneidad Cultural en Venezuela," *Revista Latinoamericana de Sociología*, 67:2 (July 1967), he presents survey data which show that while the "Unstable Center" and the "Center Right" were correlated .72, each was correlated with the Left only .47. The Left was not only isolated, but also much more divided internally than either the Center or Right.

[42] Interview E-6, March 18, 1969.

was designed to ensure greater control over the consequences of political actions. Appropriately, then, the first open clash between the Left and the government came in what was, in effect, a dispute over proper methods of political action. The government began by banning all unauthorized street demonstrations, and a clash soon came over police repression of a demonstration by unemployed workers in Caracas in January 1960, which left many injured. The Communists argued that "the streets belong to the people," and therefore could be used for demonstrations of any kind, at any time. Betancourt's reply marks a watershed for the subsequent course of political conflict in Venezuela. He argued that the disposition of the streets was a function of the forces of public order:

> The thesis that the streets belong to the people is false and demagogic. The people in abstract is an entelechy which professional demagogues use in seeking to upset the social order. *The people in abstract does not exist . . . the people are the political parties, the unions, the organized economic sectors, professional societies, university groups.* Whenever any of these groups seeks authorization for a peaceful demonstration, in a building or in the streets, there will be no difficulty in granting it. But any time uncontrolled groups go into the streets, on whatever pretext, they will be treated with neither softness nor lenience. For a country cannot live and work, acquire culture and forge riches, if it is always threatened by the surprise explosions of street violence, behind which the ancient enemies of democracy, totalitarians of all names and colors, seek to engineer its discredit.[43]

Betancourt's thesis is basically a call for the institutional channeling and delimitation of political conflict, and an argument for the rejection and exclusion of certain methods of political action from the new, revised spectrum of democratic politics.

[43] Betancourt, *Tres Años. . .*, I, 245 (italics added).

49

The entire period of Betancourt's presidency was played out in the midst of the most extreme social and political tensions. A convenient indicator of the level of tension is the fact that during his term in office constitutional guarantees were suspended five times in the entire nation, for a total of 778 of the 1,847 days Betancourt was in office. Suspension of guarantees usually affected the inviolability of the mails, limited free personal movement, severely restricted the right to hold meetings and publish "news affecting public security," and gave the government extensive powers of arrest and preventive detention. Although Betancourt and friends of AD have argued that these measures did not affect the lives of ordinary citizens, this is hardly the point. Suspension of guarantees is designed to restrict certain kinds of political action, and the parties of the Left clearly saw it as one more link in a chain of events hemming them in, cornering them, and limiting their ability to confront the government on equal terms.

The alienation of the Left became manifest in the organization of the Movement of the Revolutionary Left in April 1960. The MIR represented the expulsion from AD of its most radical wing. When the MIR left AD, it took with it almost the entire student wing of the parent party. This force, combined with the votes of Communist students and those of the extremely radicalized student wing of URD, ensured firm left-wing control of student organizations in the UCV and other major universities.

As violence between the government and the Left grew, the role of universities as centers of opposition became even more prominent. The tradition of university autonomy, which sanctioned an effective inviolability of the campus from police intrusion, allowed the universities to maintain full freedom for meetings, speeches, propaganda, etc. The availability of this forum, combined with the initial strength of the Left among students, naturally encouraged the PCV and MIR to entrench themselves within the universities. The critical nature of university strength for the Left was further increased by two measures. First, Communist and Mirist leaders were expelled from the trade union confederation, and formed a parallel organization, in March 1962.[44] Second, in November 1962, the government closed all student organizations in public secondary schools. These organizations had been centers of intense antigovernment organization and action. Elimination of student opposition at this level was reinforced by government action to root out leftist teachers in primary and secondary education.

Fundamental differences soon appeared between the government and the Left over the proper role of students as a politically active group in a democratic society. Betancourt insisted that although student opposition was justified in a dictatorship, once there was a democratic regime, with free access to institutions through freely organized political parties, no justifiable basis for student political action remained. Here again, Betancourt is arguing for a compartmentalization of politics, separating students from direct, overt political action: urging them to study and leave politics to the political parties. The Left, of course, rejected Betancourt's arguments, viewing the university as an important front, one among many, of struggle against the government. These differences reflected important disagreements as to what constitutes legitimate political resources and arenas of political action.

In this way, a series of restrictions and defeats combined to inflate the importance of the universities for the Left, while driving these parties further toward a full-fledged strategy of insurrection. As tensions rose throughout 1960, 1961, and 1962, the PCV and the MIR gradually became convinced of the possibility of a successful insurrection. Massive unemployment in these years, reaching 14.4 percent nationally (and probably higher in Caracas in 1962),[45] com-

[44] This reversal of earlier unitary trends went hand in hand with a drastic decline in left-wing influence among trade unionists.
[45] J. Silva Michelena, *The Politics of Change in Venezuela: Volume III*, 69.

bined with a general economic crisis and the presence of obvious divisions in the armed forces and the government[46] were interpreted by the Left as signs that the regime would be a pushover.[47]

The basic decisions committing the Left to insurrection were taken in the course of 1961. The strategy was reaffirmed for the Communists in the Plenum of the Central Committee which met in December 1962:

> . . . the Plenum concluded that in the concrete conditions of Venezuela, the struggle of democratic and patriotic forces for the taking of power and its maintenance necessarily implied the use of violence. This period evidently involves a difficult and lengthy struggle for the people of Venezuela, in which all forms of struggle must be used, but in which *armed* struggle will have fundamental value.
>
> Therefore the Plenum called on our Party and other popular forces to take on the task of preparing a popular army to unite all Venezuelan patriots, taking as our goal national liberation from foreign rule, replacing the present government and thus permitting the beginning of a process of transformation of the structures of the country.[48]

These decisions found their first major expression in two abortive uprisings by military officers sympathetic to the Left: at Carúpano on May 4, 1962, and the bloody rebellion

[46] URD had left the coalition in late 1960 in disagreement over Betancourt's policy toward Cuba, and the remaining partner, COPEI, seemed willing at the time to leave.

[47] Gumersindo Rodríguez, a founder of the MIR who left in protest against the insurrection policy wrote a series of eight articles with the general title of *El Fracaso de la Insurección* (The Failure of the Insurrection) published in *La República* from September 3 to September 10, 1962. These articles offer valuable insights into the tactical ideas of the MIR.

[48] Carlos López [pseud.], "El Partido Comunista de Venezuela y la Situación Actual en el País," *Principios*, segúnda época, No. 3 (March-April 1965); *Principios* was the organ of the central committee of the PCV (italics in original).

of Puerto Cabello, on June 2, 1962. The Carúpano revolt provoked the government to suspend the operations of the PCV and the MIR, and arrest many leaders and members of these parties. The appearance about this time of the first scattered guerrilla units indicated that for the Left, only three forums remained: the congress, the universities, and the mountains. After the arrest of the Communist and Mirist parliamentarians in the fall of 1963, only the universities and the mountains remained.

The guerrilla movement never got off the ground. The Left's call for abstention from the 1963 elections was a spectacular failure (92.21 percent of those registered voted for president, and 90.78 percent of those registered voted for congressional candidates).[49] Although the fighting continued with strong backing from the MIR and the PCV through mid-1965, prospects of success were clearly becoming remote.

Doubts soon began to appear within the Communist Party. In April 1965, the PCV launched the slogan of "A Government of Democratic Peace," initiating a tentative withdrawal from the armed struggle, and seeking renewed contacts with freely operating political parties. Communist withdrawal from the guerrilla actions was furthered by an internal split in late 1966 when those favoring armed struggle, led by Douglas Bravo, left the party, taking with them the bulk of its armed personnel. The split was soon followed by the virtual liquidation of the urban guerrilla apparatus and the severe battering of the rural fronts under Bravo's control.

Complete withdrawal from armed struggle was authorized for the Communists in the Eighth Plenum of the Central Committee, held in April 1967, which concluded that the guerrilla movement had become isolated and had turned into a blind alley. This Plenum further authorized the Party

---

[49] Figures from B. Bunimov-Parra, *Introducción a la Sociología Electoral Venezolana* (Caracas: Editorial Arte, 1968), p. 131.

to form organizations for participation in the forthcoming
elections of December 1968. The consensus among Communist leaders was that the guerrilla movement had been defeated not so much militarily as politically: never able to
generate mass support or get off home base in its operations
against the government. Pedro Ortega Díaz, a Communist
Deputy in the 1959-63 congress, has provided the key to the
Communist analysis of their defeat. His comments provide
the clearest possible example of the full significance of that
defeat for the strength and long-term viability of Venezuela's political institutions:

> We must never tire of repeating the distinction that must
> be made in fighting a government based on open military
> dictatorship and combatting a class dictatorship based on
> representative democracy, and respectful of certain forms.
> Our own case is all too expressive. The dominant classes
> were able to isolate the revolutionary vanguards in Vene-
> zuela, because we did not know how to adjust our strug-
> gle to the fact that there existed a form of domination
> based on representative democracy. . . . I repeat this be-
> cause it is always easier to continue in the same simplistic
> vein:
> "They are the same, both try to maintain Yankee rule."
> "Both serve the same boss."
> "Both use the army and police when their rule is threat-
> ened."
> And though all this be true, *nevertheless we must learn
> to fight the two forms of domination in different ways.*[50]

Recognition of the strength of political institutions led
the Communists to seek reintegration into national politics.
This decision took form in the appearance, in 1968, of the
Union for Progress (Unión Para Avanzar, *UPA*), a legal
facade for the Communist party. Under the name of UPA,

[50] P. Ortega Díaz, "La Ideología Pequeño-Burguesa en las Ideas de
Regis Debray," *Documentos Políticos*, No. 9, pp. 46-47 (italics added).

54

Communist candidates were run for deputies, senators, and municipal councillors throughout the nation. The reintegration of the Communists into parliamentary politics coincided with a prior trend in the universities toward a neutralization of this front by the Communists. The PCV began a reorientation of student activities away from an exclusive emphasis on harassing the government and toward the stimulation of a broad range of university centered actions and contacts. This reorientation was bitterly opposed by the MIR, which, remaining firm in the armed struggle, continued to insist that student organizations be oriented largely in terms of support for revolutionary war.

For our purposes, the decision to launch a revolutionary war is crucial as it represented a clear challenge to the party system: a complete rejection of its institutions as illegitimate and its methods as ineffective for identifying and solving national problems. The abandonment of revolutionary war, on the other hand, reflects a tacit acceptance of the party system, and a decision to work within the limits it sets. The Communist decision to de-activate the student front is significant in this regard: it represents acceptance of the Betancourt thesis on the need to compartmentalize conflict, avoiding rigid fusion of student organizations and actions with national political structures and problems. Seeking a place within the framework of constitutional democracy, the Communists have sought to define a role for their university membership which does not depend exclusively upon national political strategies and tactics.[51]

CONCLUSIONS

Any attempt to summarize the development of a political system, and to predict possible future trends, is always a

[51] This does not, of course, imply any weakening of the organizational ties binding students, as party members, to their parties. What does change is the use made of these ties, and the role parties give to students as political actors. See Chapter 7 below.

risky business. Nevertheless, certain aspects of post-1958 events are of particular importance.

A system of mutual guarantees has been evolved and accepted among major sectors of the society. Mutual confidence was promoted by the decision to form and maintain a coalition government in the 1959 to 1963 period, and was further reinforced by the common threat posed by leftist revolutionary warfare, which drew many old enemies together in common defense. The system of mutual guarantees has permitted the legitimation of conflict between these sectors, with increasing use of common methods and arenas of conflict.

Moreover, this process has been aided by the greater balance of the party system after 1958. The overwhelming hegemony of AD in the 1940's has disappeared, and the political system now seems increasingly balanced between AD and COPEI (each taking about 30 percent of the vote), with numerous smaller parties in between.[52] This growing balance is illustrated in Tables 3.2, 3.3, and 3.4, which show the distribution of first and second places in the four major presidential elections to date, and the percentage distribution of the vote in these elections. Taken together, these data reveal a significant increase both in the numerical balance of the parties, and in their geographical balance—all major parties are now national parties.[53]

[52] The post-1958 period has seen a great deal of atomization of parties, but this has normally been limited to interelection periods, with the splinter groups often liquidated when elections come around. There has also been a consistent nonparty vote, above all in Caracas. Nevertheless, in national terms, the major parties manage to control over three-quarters of the vote between them, and the system seems solid, even if independents can win seats on antiparty platforms.

[53] The figures for first and second place reflect the vote received by the candidate of the major party, not only by the party itself. Thus, although COPEI received the largest vote of any party in the Federal District in 1968, first place here is attributed to Miguel Angel Burelli Rivas, candidate of the URD-FDP-FND coalition. The percentages given are figures received on the party line alone. Voting is compulsory in Venezuela, and sanctions exist, and are applied, for failure to register and vote. Voting has consistently attracted over 90

TABLE 3.2

Presidential Elections, First Places in States
and Territories

Year	Party			
	AD	COPEI	URD	Other
1947	21	2	—	—
1958	16	2	5	—
1963	15	3	2	3[a]
1968	12	8	2[b]	1[c]

[a] In 1963, FND, with Uslar Pietri as candidate.
[b] In 1968, URD in coalition with two other parties ran a joint candidate.
[c] In 1968, the People's Electoral Movement (MEP) formed from a split in AD, with Luis B. Prieto as candidate.

TABLE 3.3

Presidential Elections, Second Places in States
and Territories

Year	Party			
	AD	COPEI	URD	Other
1947	2	21	—	—
1958	6	3	14[a]	—
1963	6	6	8	3[b]
1968	6	8	3[c]	6[d]

[a] URD backing the popular candidacy of Admiral Larrazábal, head of the provisional government that replaced Pérez Jiménez.
[b] FDP, running Larrazábal.
[c] URD, in coalition with two other parties.
[d] The MEP, backing Prieto.

TABLE 3.4

Presidential Elections, Vote Percentages
by Party[a]

Year	Party				
	AD	COPEI	URD	PCV	Other
1947	74.47	22.40	—	3.22	—
1958	49.18	15.70	30.66[b]	3.23[c]	—
1963	32.80	20.18	17.50	—[d]	27.79[e]
1968	27.49	28.65	21.87[f]	—[g]	17.33[h]

[a] Percentages do not always sum to 100; sometimes micro-parties
have won fractions of a percent of the total vote.
[b] URD, backing Larrazábal.
[c] PCV ran Larrazábal on its own line.
[d] PCV boycotted the 1963 elections.
[e] This figure includes 16.08 percent for FND (Uslar Pietri), 9.43
percent for FDP (Larrazábal), and 2.28 percent for Ramos Gímenez,
for AD-OP, product of a 1961 split in AD.
[f] URD in coalition split the vote with its partners as follows: 11.85
percent for URD, 6.47 percent for FDP, 3.55 percent for FND.
[g] As UPA, the Communists ran candidates only for congress, municipal councils, and state legislatures, taking 2.81 percent of the vote
at this level.
[h] MEP, backing Prieto; some other minor parties ran Prieto on their
own lines.

One way to analyze the strengths of the party system is
to consider the defeat of oppositions to its methods and institutions. A convenient way of summarizing these oppositions is to identify the major ideologies which have offered
solutions to Venezuela's problems of growth and change.
First, there is a military-technological ideology, epitomized
in the "New National Ideal" promoted by the Pérez Jiménez
regime. This ideology justified the suppression of democratic
politics and political conflict in the name of national material progress and efficiency. It called for dictatorship as a

percent of those registered. I do not have exact figures on the percentages of eligibles who register. Figures for the 1968 election were
not available at the time of writing.

necessary tool of progress. Second, there is a general reformist ideology, in which I would group parties otherwise as different as AD, COPEI, and URD. These parties are united by a common desire for social change through evolutionary reform; a common, self-conscious limitation of conflict; and a mutual commitment to constitutional forms and institutionalized political processes. And third, there is a revolutionary leftist ideology, which, rejecting the "sham" of bourgeois democracy, seeks its overthrow through armed struggle as a means of achieving rapid growth through revolution.

It is worth noting that both the military and the revolutionary Left argue for the suppression of political conflict as a necessary prerequisite for progress. Taking these three ideologies as competitors for the privilege of guiding Venezuela's future development, it is clear that the post-1958 period has seen the defeat of the military-technological alternative as well as the defeat of the revolutionary Left. The party system has managed the full incorporation of the Catholic sector and of others, which though still suspicious and jealous of their rights, seem to have decided to seek compromise and benefits from working within the system. One of the clearest and most significant implications of the growing balance of the party system is that now anyone (not only AD) can win according to the rules of the new system. The overall picture could be described as one of defeat of the extremes, both Left and Right, with the incorporation of previous oppositions to the party system itself facilitated by the movement of AD away from many of the more socialist elements of its programmatic traditions. The entire system has stabilized, in a conservative direction.[54]

[54] This has been most visible in the many divisions of AD. In 1960, the MIR split off, taking the most left-wing elements. In 1961, the ARS group split off, in an attempt by younger leaders to win control of the party machine. At the end of 1967, the MEP split off, invoking the socialist traditions of the party. The tendency has consistently

The significance of the consolidation of the party system lies in the provision of an open-ended framework for the expression and conciliation of conflict. The imposition of a party system—through the exertions of its supporters and the defeat of its opponents—also means the exclusion of certain resources and methods of political action. Thus political conflict in Venezuela is not eliminated, or reduced, or sublimated. Rather it is institutionally provided for, and increasingly channeled, delimited, and guided by commonly accepted procedural norms. The fact that the system is open-ended and not, for example, rigidly closed to Communist participation, is revealed in the government's decision to permit the Communists, once free of active commitment to the guerrilla movement, to participate in the 1968 elections under the facade of UPA. In this vein, it is worth noting that one of the first acts of the Christian Democrats, after taking office in 1969, was to legalize the Communist Party.

As general conclusions, let me offer the following observations:

1. The period from 1936 to 1948 saw the emergence of national organizations of power in the form of parties that penetrated all spheres of social life. These were the first nonofficial organizations of this scope ever to exist in Venezuela (the official ones being, of course, the state and army).

2. The emergence of these structures was not accompanied by the development of procedural norms of conflict behavior which could have limited the scope of political conflicts. The overwhelming hegemony of AD during the *trienio* contributed to the failure of this party to recognize its own lack of omnipotence, and the resulting need to seek mutual guarantees with other sectors of society.

---

been for the more socialist elements to split off, turning the party gradually into a party of the center, with a general commitment to reform and development. Chapter 9 below takes up this theme again in greater detail.

3. The experience of the dictatorship of Pérez Jiménez and the challenge of a leftist insurrection combined to push reformist parties into a series of mutual compromises which helped consolidate a viable, open-ended party system. This accomplishment implied the defeat of oppositions and the exclusion of their characteristic criteria of legitimate power, methods, resources, and solutions.

CHAPTER 4

Catholics and Seculars:
Toward Polarization

THE Revolution of October 18, 1945 unnerved many groups
in Venezuela, but few saw their interests so immediately
and gravely endangered as the Catholic Church did. The
threat perceived by the Church, which provided a motive
force for conflict throughout the *trienio*, lay in the educational policies of the new regime. This chapter will describe
and explain the conflict over educational reform that dominated Catholic-secular relations in this period.

The conflict was one of traditional defense. A weakly organized traditional institution (the Church), faced with
the new political forces and criteria of power embodied in
the revolutionary government, responded with all-out opposition. Catholic leadership saw the survival of the Church
and of religious values in general to be threatened by the
educational reforms proposed by the new regime. Questions
of political legitimacy clearly underlay the entire series of
conflicts in education. As an issue, education was merely
the tip of the iceberg, an effective catalyst in bringing more
basic fears and conflicts to the surface.

ORGANIZATIONAL WEAKNESS AND PERSPECTIVES
ON CONFLICT

Since its renovation at the turn of the century, the
Church had invested a large proportion of its energies and
personnel in building an educational system. As we have
seen, by 1945 the Catholic Church had a major stake in
education—many primary schools, almost half of the sec-

ondary schools, and more than half the normal schools. Nevertheless, the Church itself was weak as an organization. There was no effective network of Catholic secondary associations. There was no Christian Democratic Party, and few political figures were publicly identified with the defense of Catholic values and interests. Moreover, the Church had a class-bound image, its services and above all its schools being limited to the children of those able to pay.

The organizational weakness of the Church magnified the threat posed by a radical, secular mass movement. As Vallier has pointed out, traditional Churches in Latin America have rarely sought to organize their membership on a systematic basis.[1] Parish life has been limited in scope, and the Church as a religious community has barely existed in many areas. Rather, the position of the Church in the institutional order was guaranteed through political agreements and alliances with socioeconomic and political elites. To survive as an organization, the Church had only to cultivate these ties. Thus, for example, the dominant influence strategy of the Church involved horizontal contacts, with elites at corresponding levels, rather than vertical contacts, with a membership base within the Church.

Mass membership was rarely organized in a systematic way, because the loyalty of the masses to the Church and Catholic values was itself guaranteed through their continued participation in existing social and political arrangements which in themselves secured a place for the Church. In a society where existing institutions are strong, these relations naturally produce a strong position for the Church. However, what gives strength in one social order may be a source of weakness in another. For, as the social bases of existing institutions begin to erode, the Church is at a grave

---

[1] I. Vallier, *op.cit.*, p. 196. See also I. Vallier, "Towards a Theory of Religious Change: Extraction, Insulation, and Re-entry," H. Landsberger, ed., *The Church and Social Change in Latin America* (South Bend: University of Notre Dame Press, 1969), pp. 9-38, and I. Vallier, *Catholicism, Social Control, and Modernization in Latin America* (Englewood Cliffs: Prentice-Hall, Inc., 1970).

63

disadvantage. Lacking organization, and lacking an orientation to organization, the Church is suddenly faced with competitors for mass support—trade unions, political parties, and the like.

In Venezuela, the Church's poverty of organization implied that in the event of crisis, the Church would (1) feel deeply threatened and vulnerable, and (2) react directly, intervening in politics to fight its own battles. In some cases, direct action by poorly organized groups may limit conflict as the group is unable to mobilize, or even to find, its potential followers. There is another possibility, however, epitomized in Venezuela, where the lack of organization helps expand the scope and intensity of conflict. More extreme appeals are required to reach and activate a following not normally enrolled in organizations. Thus, when they join the conflict, they do so on the fringes.[2] Moreover, lack of organization also implies that once the Church calls for a Holy War, it has little control over the actions of its followers. And finally, lack of organization hinders the establishment of contacts through which a settlement might be reached. Of course, contacts per se do not guarantee conciliation. But without them, negotiations of any kind can be started only with great difficulty. And without the experience of organization, regular contact, and negotiation, a group can initiate and profit from negotiations only with great difficulty.

Catholic leadership did not understand the new bases of legitimate power and authority derived from the political reforms of the *trienio*. They continued to operate on the unspoken assumption that the Church, by definition, represented the interests and "will" of the majority. Throughout the *trienio*, one finds the "wishes of the Catholic majority" advanced in opposition to the "mandate of the majority of the voters." This opposition contributed greatly to the depth of conflict, for the Catholic sector, although certain of its

---

[2] A good discussion of this point is J. Coleman, *Community Conflict* (New York: Free Press, 1957).

majority status, could gain no effective majority power under the new political rules. Thus, the legitimacy of the revolution and its political system were called into question from the earliest clashes of Church and state over education. The new criteria of power sanctioned in the *trienio* put the weakly organized Church at a disadvantage. The system was perceived as biased, somehow distorting political processes so that the "true" weight of Catholic interests was not accurately represented. The Church and Catholic elites in general saw the new institutions as openly and deliberately anti-Catholic.

In such a conflict, there are few incentives to compromise. The Church sees its most cherished privileges and values threatened by a sudden, unexpected reversal of the rules of the game. The new holders of power see their developing institutions endangered by the defensive reaction of the traditional sectors. The deep threat perceived by all sides helps define the conflict in terms of legitimacy. Legitimacy conflicts put political forms and processes into question. It is hard to conciliate such conflicts within the framework of existing institutions: the institutions themselves are at the root of the conflict.

Moreover, there is little experience (on either side) in the give and take of bargaining. The organizations and institutions involved are too new. The idea of conflict and opposition as normal, legitimate social processes is also too new. And "newness" implies further that loyalties to institutions are weak. As we shall see, this means that political appeals for conciliation, appeals based, for example, on a concern for institutional stability, have little impact.

To complement our understanding of the pressures created by AD's sudden rise to power, let me offer a brief resumé of its program, both in general and specifically in education. Acción Democrática came to power as a reformist, socialist party. In the context of Venezuelan society, its programs were extremely radical and far-reaching: agrarian reform, full adult suffrage with no qualifications other than age, direct popular election of officials, trade union organization, expansion and reform of education, etc. A concern for educational reform was characteristic of AD, and many of its most prominent leaders were also founders and leaders of the most important lay institutions in education.[3]

AD's educational program is best understood in historical perspective. In 1936 the government invited a mission of Chilean educators to plan and implement the reform of secondary education. Through their efforts, the National Pedagogical Institute was founded. Its graduates soon constituted the core of the educational reform movement, dominated the teachers' organizations, and were heavily concentrated in AD.

What were the goals of this movement and its leadership? The philosophy they proposed is usually summarized under the name of *estado docente* (educator-state). In Venezuela, the label of *estado docente* implies at least the following:

1. Education is an essential public function and therefore the rights of the state are prior to those of any other institution. Hence, collaboration is admitted by the state, but always under public supervision and control.

2. Since the major nonofficial group involved in education is the Church, *estado docente* takes on an explicit anticlerical tone.[4]

3. *Estado docente* is strongly nationalist. Education is to be nationalized in two senses: (1) made more relevant to national experience (less dependent on foreign models, methods, and texts); and (2) taught by Venezuelan teachers, with certain subjects like national history and geography restricted to teaching by Venezuelan citizens by birth. The Church, heavily dependent on foreign teaching orders

[3] Such as the teachers' associations.

[4] Anticlericalism, centering on differences over education, is a common theme in Western development. See, for example, S. M. Lipset and S. Rokkan, eds., "Introduction," to their *Party Systems and Voter Alignments* (New York: Free Press, 1968). A fuller discussion of such conflicts is provided in Chapter 8 below.

(mainly Spanish) naturally saw a direct, concrete threat here.

4. Religious education is provided for only outside the normal class schedule, and only for those children whose parents specifically request it.

5. The training of teachers is to be exclusively a public function, above all for secondary education, centered in the National Pedagogical Institute.

The position of *estado docente* has been summarized by Luis B. Prieto:

> As a representative of the general interests of the collectivity, it is the function of the State to indicate the form in which these interests should be administered and directed, creating norms for the respect, defense and development of these interests. This attribution is based on the sovereignty of the State, which by definition is exclusive of any other power. . . . Private education is a form of collaboration within the teaching function of the State. It is a delegation of a public function, exercised within the norms set by the State. It cannot be explained in any other way. As a collaborator, it may not create its own norms, for collaboration is not a contract among equals.[5]

Up to 1945, the Church had waged a long and largely successful struggle against these ideas. The Catholic position is simple and it is worthwhile to outline it here. As a matter of doctrine, the Church has traditionally argued that the right to determine and orient a child's education rests primarily in the family and the Church. Hence, public action in education is by nature collaborative, secondary to the initiative of the family and the Church. These arguments are summed up in the phrase *libertad de enseñanza* (freedom of education) which calls for complete freedom in educational organization—no control or regulation by the state.

[5] Luis B. Prieto, *Problemas de la Educación Venezolana* (Caracas: Imprenta Nacional, 1947), pp. 5-6.

As to religious education, the Church favored giving religious instruction during regular class hours to all children except those whose parents requested exemption, with the teachers approved by the ecclesiastical hierarchy.

Historically, the Church won a tremendous victory in 1914 when the Supreme Court overturned the Code of Instruction of 1910, ruling that in providing for regulation of private education, the law violated constitutional guarantees of *libertad de enseñanza*. This decision left private education completely free of controls of any kind—outside of examinations, which continued to be set by the Ministry of Education. The result apparently was utter chaos, and the situation was altered in the Law of Education of 1924.

> Until 1958, the state in Venezuela, although giving relatively little money to education, has nonetheless been ideologically very dedicated to state control of all education. This has been the pattern at least since 1922. And state education here in fact means lay education and the inculcation of an anti-Catholic atmosphere. In 1936, with the importation of the Chilean educators in the reorganization of the Pedagogical Institute, this lay orientation became Marxist as well.[6]

The two doctrines, *estado docente* and *libertad de enseñanza* are compared in Table 4.1.

These issues and the fundamentally opposed philosophies they reflect guided the course of the bitter and often violent clashes of Church and state during the *trienio*. In a sense, these conflicts were inevitable, as the Revolution of October marked the emergence in Venezuela of a party offering a message of general social reconstruction, with the ideas and tools to carry it out. The Church, meanwhile, continued to believe itself invested with diffuse moral authority, and hence with the legitimate power to orient social life. When the familiar political props of the Church's position were

[6] Interview A-13, January 26, 1969.

TABLE 4.1

Issues Summarized in the Competing Slogans of
Estado Docente and *Libertad de Enseñanza*

ISSUE	Slogan	
	Estado Docente	*Libertad de Ensenañza*
1. Control and supervision	State control	No control
2. Function to educate is essentially proper to	State	Family-Church
3. Private education then, is	Collaboration	Basic right (state collaborates)
4. Religious instruction	On request, outside schedule	For all, inside schedule
5. Training of teachers is	State monopoly	No monopoly

swept away, insecurity grew apace. When the keystone of that orienting function—education—appeared threatened, the conflict exploded and it was never possible to limit it to technical grounds.[7]

EDUCATION IN THE *Trienio*

Before getting into the details of conflict, let us review the actual impact of AD's educational policies. First of all, there was a tremendous expansion of funds available, as the education budget of the central government more than tripled from 1945 to 1948. Indeed, one of the very first acts of the revolutionary government was the promulgation of additional money for education. The total budget of the Ministry of Education rose from 38 million *bolívares* in 1945

[7] The fact of revolution is important in itself as it gave the government the power to legislate by decree, thus avoiding the process of congressional debate and delay which often serves to modify controversial measures.

to over 119 millions in 1948.[8] This figure of 119 millions, moreover, does not include over 120 millions more spent by the states, by other ministries (such as Agriculture for rural schools, or Public Works in school construction), and in the construction of the new University City in Caracas.

From 1945 to 1948, the number of children in primary schools more than doubled. In secondary education, the number of official *liceos* jumped from 29 to 47, while the total number of *liceo* students more than doubled. Expansion of public education meant, in effect, a drastic decline in the relative position of private education. This was particularly true in secondary education, where the proportion of pupils in private *liceos* dropped from 49 percent at the end of the 1944 school year to a little over 20 percent by 1948-49. (See Table 4.2.)

AD's educational program was in large measure fulfilled, and the relative position of the Church cut down tremendously. This alone, however, would not have been sufficient to touch off open conflict. AD's goals were clear from the outset and the Church offered no direct opposition as long as no immediate threat was posed to its educational establishment and clientele. The direct threat which changed the quality of the confrontation was provided on May 30, 1946, by Decree 321: "On Grades, Promotions, and Examinations in Primary, Secondary, and Normal Education."

THE TERMS OF CONFLICT: A NARRATIVE

In Venezuelan education until 1946, promotion was determined exclusively by grades on examinations set by the

[8] The budget of the Ministry of Education rose as follows:

1945	38 millions
1946	65 millions
1947	97 millions
1948	119 millions

Figures come from "Presentación," by Rómulo Betancourt to Luis B. Prieto, *De Una Educación de Castas a Una Educación de Masas* (Havana: Editorial Lex, 1951), p. 7.

TABLE 4.2

Pupils in Secondary Education: 1943-49*

Year	Type of Education			
	Public		Private	
	No.	Percent	No.	Percent
1943-44	4,638	51	4,379	49
1944-45	6,337	54	5,361	46
1945-46	7,508	56	5,825	44
1946-47	11,024	68	5,110	32
1947-48	13,037	77.2	3,859	22.8
1948-49	17,019	76.3	5,280	23.7

* Data are elusive for these years, above all for private education. When the military took over, no Annual Report for Education was published until 1952, when a four-year volume, with many gaps, was brought out. These data are from the *Memoria y Cuenta del Ministerio de Educación*, for the respective years.

Ministry of Education for all primary, secondary, and normal schools, public and private. Decree 321 was intended to reform the examination system, by taking into account the yearly work of a student, and thereby eliminating the all-or-nothing character of the July examinations. To this end, the Decree established a complex set of rules governing the conditions of examination. The Decree is of Byzantine complexity, but since subsequent conflicts often hinged on specific provisions of the measure, it may be useful to review its contents here.

In primary education, for pupils in official schools, final grades were to be obtained by averaging 60 percent for grades over the year with 40 percent for the final exam. In private primary schools, the average was composed of 20 percent for grades over the year and 80 percent for the final examination. This provision, however, applied only in the fourth and sixth years. In the first, second, third, and fifth years, students with an average of 15 or more (out of

71

20) on bimonthly exams could be excused from the final. This exemption was applied to official schools in all grades.

For secondary and normal education, the Decree divided private institutions into two types: Type I, where at least 75 percent of the subjects were taught by instructors with the official title of "professor" in their specialty; and Type II, where less than 75 percent of the subjects were taught by instructors of this type. To be classified in Type I, then, a private institution had to have 75 percent of its teaching staff made up of graduates of the National Pedagogical Institute, the only institution authorized to grant the official title of "professor." In all public *liceos* and normal schools, grades were again to be an average of 60 percent for yearly work with 40 percent for the final examination. Students with a yearly average of 15 or more were exempt from final examinations. In private schools, however, final grades were composed of 20 percent for yearly work and 80 percent for the final examination. Moreover, in Type I private schools (75 percent professors with official title), all pupils in the second cycle of *liceos* (second half) or fourth year of normal school with a yearly average of 10 or more had to present final examinations. In private schools of Type II, all students with averages of 10 or more had to take the finals. An average of less than 10 is equivalent to failure and removes the right to present examinations. The Decree also established certain differences in the composition of examination boards between public and private schools, and between private schools of the two types. On the whole, for private schools more examiners were external to the school, and the student was required to pay a larger share of the fees given to the external examiners.

Despite the complexity of the Decree, its general thrust is quite clear: reform the examination system while imposing stricter control over private schools. The Decree sparked immediate, widespread opposition based on several key points: (1) students in Catholic schools opposed it as discriminatory, imposing more stringent criteria of promotion on them; (2) the Catholic sector in general opposed it as some of the conditions simply could not be fulfilled, and hence were viewed as merely punitive;[9] and (3) the distinctions drawn between official and private schools were explicitly grounded in the principles of *estado docente*, repugnant to Catholic doctrine. In the text of the Decree these distinctions were justified as follows: "The reasons and bases for establishing such distinctions rest on the philosophic conception we feel should be sustained in relation to the educative process in general, in which the only body responsible for its orientation must be the State which directs, channels, and supervises Education."[10]

The Church took the Decree, and its explicit philosophical bases, as the opening shot in a war of extermination against Catholic education. In the first Annual Report of AVEC, published in 1951 and reviewing the *trienio* events, an attempt was made to explain why the Catholic reaction had been so swift and strong:

In the first place, the very motivation of the Decree, of a clearly socialist orientation, was itself cause for alarm. It was affirmed that it was a function of the State to orient Education, organize it, and give it structure. By virtue of this principle, the State believed itself capable of introducing odious distinctions between official and private schools, putting the latter in inferior conditions.[11]

[9] For example, the provision requiring that 75 percent of the professors have the official title could not be fulfilled. The National Pedagogical Institute did not produce enough! Moreover, Catholic groups felt that the Institute made it difficult for qualified teachers in their schools to gain equivalency status. They were often refused entry into the Institute, and required to do the entire course of several years to obtain certification of equivalency. See a letter from a Maracaibo committee of Catholic parents: "Hablan los Padres de familia: Memorandum dirigido al Episcopado," in *SIC*, No. 98 (October 1947).

[10] Decree 321, quoted in M. Mudarra, *Historia de la Legislación Escolar Contemporánea en Venezuela* (Caracas: Tipografía Vargas, 1962), p. 205.

[11] *Resúmen de la relación presentada por el R. P. Carlos Guillermo*

73

The Church's strong reaction came as a genuine surprise to AD. Apparently, the Decree had been presented and approved within the government as a purely technical matter, and at the time no one seemed aware of its potentially explosive implications.[12] From the outset, AD leadership, and above all Rómulo Betancourt, tried to isolate the conflict, seeking a peaceful way out of the crisis. Betancourt apparently saw the Decree as a maneuver designed to embarrass him and force him into politically undesirable confrontations. He later asserted that "This Decree was the product of a disloyal machination by a group entrenched in the Ministry of Education."[13] To mollify the opposition, Betancourt forced the resignation of the Minister of Education and other high officials responsible for the Decree. These resignations came on June 9, and on June 17, in a conciliatory speech broadcast nationally, Betancourt argued that:

> The concern aroused over Decree 321, the wave of agitation arisen around it, would not have manifested itself had the discussion been posed from the outset in measured terms. It happened that I, accompanied by various members of the Executive Cabinet, was visiting Ciudad Bolívar on the very day in which the debate over 321 turned into a street brawl. I sincerely believe that this lamentable circumstance [his absence] contributed greatly to the fact that the discussion left its technical and pedagogical limits to become an ideological and political conflict. The interest of the Government, the goal of the Government, never was and never could be to place the

---

Plaza, S.J., Presidente Nacional de la AVEC ante la I Asamblea Nacional de Colegios Católicos, 1951 (Mimeographed), p. 3. This is hereafter referred to as *AVEC Memoria, 1951.*

[12] A contributing circumstance was the absence of Betancourt. He was in Ciudad Bolívar. As soon as he read the text of the Decree, while boarding a plane for Caracas, he remarked that there was going to be trouble (source: Interview B-13, July 16, 1968).

[13] R. Betancourt, *Política y Petróleo, op.cit.,* p. 493.

discussion in such terms. And much less to see it converted into a religious conflict.[14]

Throughout the crisis, Betancourt tried to limit and confine the formulation of the issue, seeking to convince both the Church and his own rank and file that the fundamental question was technical, not political. He further argued to his own partisans that compromise was not the same as appeasement, and that in a delicate situation such as that provoked by 321, with a government still in the process of stabilization, prudence had to guide official actions. Thus, Betancourt noted that:

> A vast sector of opinion which has surrounded the Revolutionary Government since the 18th of October finds itself concerned that this Government will cede to the pressure of reactionary forces or, to use the formula which has had such success: take one step back. But the Revolutionary Government guarantees categorically that it will not go back or stop in its path of democratic achievements. At the same time, however, it invites this sector to serene reflection through which it may distinguish the secondary from the fundamental and principal. Seeking a conciliatory formula in a problem is a method which prudence and a sense of responsibility always counsel; incompatible with simple stubbornness.[15]

In addition to forcing the resignations of those responsible for the Decree, Betancourt also issued a new Decree (344), suspending the application of 321's provisions.[16] But his attempts at conciliation were doomed to failure. The nature of the conflict as perceived in each camp precluded

[14] Radio speech to the nation by Betancourt on June 12, 1946, reprinted in *Trayectoria Democrática de una Revolución, Discursos y Conferencias* (Caracas: Imprenta Nacional, 1948), II, 17-18.

[15] *Ibid.*, p. 22.

[16] Decree 344 promoted some students without examinations, and postponed examinations for others until the second half of September of that year.

any successful attempt at isolation. General political positions and questions had absolute priority for both sides.

It is obvious that few on either side were aware of the potentially high cost of unleashing a religious-political conflict in the new context of the *trienio*. For the scale of social and political action had been immeasurably expanded, and touching off a conflict in the new system had results unimaginable in the days of Gómez—more people, more violence, more far-reaching consequences.[17] Newness meant inexperience and failure to recognize the political need for compromise with an intense opposition, no matter how much of a minority it was. Moreover, the seeming hegemony of AD (its overwhelming popular support plus military backing) made many in AD see their position as unchallengeable. Practical incentives to compromise were few and far between.

If the Church saw Decree 321 as the opening gun of an antireligious campaign, no less solid was the belief of many partisans of the revolutionary government that clerical opposition was merely the front for a counterrevolutionary drive by the Right, defeated but not liquidated on October 18, 1945. The battle cry of proponents of the Decree became: NOT ONE STEP BACK. One article in the Caracas press argued this way:

> In vain have attempts been made to pose the conflict in the limited area of student problems and grievances. In vain have attempts been made to make it appear as an argument for liceo students injured by an apparent inequality. Education is, in its nature, political. And moreover, for even the most ignorant, it is well known that politics penetrates fatally in all manifestations of public life. Against it [321], in an attitude of combative bel-

---

[17] They knew that the fall of the government was a distinct possibility, but there was no way of foreseeing the character of the repressive military rule that followed. In any case, the Church found it difficult to control the actions of its followers, and in this sense the costs and consequences of conflict were indeed unknown.

ligerence, the Venezuelan Reaction stands united like one man: the reactionary clergy, the Jesuits, COPEI in a menacing attitude, imperialism, the banks and usurers, the great landowners—the most anti-patriotic and anti-national elements of the country.[18]

As we have seen, in a conflict where participants are weakly organized, conflict itself may be hard to control and channel. Lack of organization means limited control over rank and file actions. The struggle over 321 is a good example. On the Catholic side, the bulk of action was organized and carried out by the students of the Catholic *liceos* of Caracas and other major cities, with no direct intervention by either the Church or COPEI. The Church and the teaching orders confined themselves to explaining student actions to parents and defending them before public opinion. This diffuse response to crisis reflected the real organizational poverty of the Catholic sector. AVEC, the only group formally representing Catholic education, had been formed just a short time before the Decree appeared. It was unable to mount a coordinated national opposition.

While the Church itself was organizationally weak, COPEI had also just gotten off the ground. I argued earlier that the definition of the issues, and the newness of the institutions involved (both the official state forms and the parties themselves) made the success of political appeals for moderation highly unlikely. Loyalties and commitments to institutional preservation simply did not exist. With this perspective, we can understand that COPEI would be both unwilling and unable to act as a political mediator, moderating the intensity and reducing the scope of conflict. COPEI was swept up in the wave of religious opposition to AD, and its identity and political character were insufficiently established at the time to make a difference in the course of conflict. COPEI was not significantly differentiated from the rest of the Catholic sector by virtue of being

[18] R. A. Freytes, "Ni Un Paso Atrás," *El Nacional*, June 8, 1946.

a political party with political concerns which might lead it to moderate conflict in the name of institutional stability.

The persistence of unresolved legitimacy questions implies that the institutionalization of conciliation procedures will be weak. Institutions themselves are in question. Hence, negotiating roles will not be created, and those that do exist will not be used. After the temporary suspension of 321, a commission was formed to draw up regulations for the eventual future application of the Decree. AVEC was invited to name a delegate to this commission. The invitation was itself an unprecedented gesture of conciliation, but attitudes on both sides made genuine compromise initiatives impossible. Neither side saw the commission as a vehicle for settling the dispute, and no delegate was empowered by his own "higher-ups" to seek or negotiate a settlement. A prominent member of the Catholic sector, when asked about the possibility or value of any contacts or negotiations at that time replied simply that "there was no spirit for it" (*no había ánimo para eso*).[19]

The suspension of 321 put open conflict on ice for almost a year. A new Minister of Education[20] was appointed and once in office devoted himself to neutralizing the conflict. However, he was replaced in March 1947 by Luis B. Prieto, a major spokesman for *estado docente*, a leading figure in the teachers' movement, and a top-ranking leader of AD. As the new examination period (July 1947) approached, Prieto indicated that he intended to apply Decree 321 fully this time around. Since the examination schedule was slightly different in different parts of the country, reactions were not synchronized, and a student strike—a refusal to take examinations under the new conditions—broke out in Maracaibo, finding immediate support in other large cities.

The context and significance of the strike will become clearer if we take a step back in time. Although open conflict had been shelved with the suspension of 321, bitter

[19] Interview A-16, February 14, 1969.
[20] Dr. Antonio Anzola Carillo.

argument continued. The issues were clarified and extensively debated in the sessions of the National Constituent Assembly which convened in February 1947 to write a new Constitution. The Assembly was dominated by AD, which held 137 out of 160 seats. But for the first time in modern Venezuelan history there were also delegates publicly committed to the defense of Catholic values and positions—the 19 delegates of COPEI.[21] Potentially religious aspects of the debate were reinforced by the presence of several priests elected as deputies.[22]

In educational matters, battle lines were drawn early as the FVM (in February 1947) and AVEC (in March 1947), submitted to the Assembly contrasting lists of educational "Principles" designed to orient the new Constitution. The FVM position followed the lines of *estado docente*, with vigorous emphasis on public control and orientation. To AVEC, these principles were unacceptable, giving too much power and discretion to the state. While AVEC was willing to recognize that education was a proper sphere of public action, it rejected claims to official monopoly. To AVEC, a monopoly which gave the state the right to orient the educational system simply gutted constitutional guarantees of *libertad de enseñanza*. Catholic schools would have to seek official authorization for all their programs, and "Once permission is obtained, they will have to accept the philosophical principles which the Thinker-State dictates from above. If they have personal points of view, they will have to sacrifice them and accept the ideological orientation of the State. For the State is infallible in educational matters!"[23]

The Constituent Assembly witnessed three debates concerning education. First, there was a general debate over constitutional articles dealing with education. Since they would reflect the social doctrine of the revolution, and pre-

[21] The other delegates were two for URD and two Communists.
[22] One for AD, the rest for COPEI.
[23] Carlos Guillermo Plaza, "Pliego de Peticiones de la Federación Venezolana de Maestros," *SIC*, No. 93 (March 1947), 650.

sumably guide the actions of governments for some time, these articles were naturally important to all sides. Second, debate flared up over Decree 321 itself, when the Assembly discussed approval of a report on the Ministry of Education's activities in the previous year. Finally, there was an important debate over a proposal (incorporated into the Constitution) providing authorization to make the training of teachers an exclusive function of public institutions.

In the first debate, controversy centered on two points: the definition of education as an "essential function" of the state, and the placing of any guarantees of *libertad de enseñanza* within "the conditions of organization and orientation" of future laws. This would of course make the guarantee contingent on future legislation and official interpretation. For AD, the Constitution had to define education as an essential function of the state since education was a social function. Private groups could have no rights more basic than those of society as a whole, embodied in the state. The collaboration of private interests was welcomed, but restricted to secondary roles. For AD, the new Constitution had to establish both the right of the state to control education and its duty to carry out programs of educational expansion. Only this way could the implementation of new programs be ensured. After all, compulsory free primary education had been decreed in Venezuela as long ago as 1870, with no visible results.[24]

From the Catholic point of view, these provisions were weapons aimed directly at the Church. The Church was the core of private education, and hence any restrictions on private education became, in effect, restrictions on religious education. The idea that the state should orient education was seen by Catholic leadership as the first step toward an indirect public monopoly, through the imposition of

[24] See R. González Baquero, *Análisis del Proceso Histórico de la Educación Urbana (1870-1932) y de la Educación Rural (1932-1957) en Venezuela* (Caracas: Imprenta Universitaria, 1962), especially Chapter 1 for an account of the 1870 law and its impact.

uniform national guidelines for content and methods of teaching.[25]

However, AD insisted on this point and argued that attempts at compromise were merely pretexts for surrender, and hence unacceptable. Compromise was identified with appeasement. Thus, J. M. Siso Martínez, speaking for AD, argued that

> . . . appeasement never has good results. We cannot appease in this debate in the National Constituent Assembly, and thereby sacrifice what is dearest to the Venezuelan people: the idea of education directed by the State, that the State give equality of opportunity to all the children of Venezuela, that it guarantee their education . . . this private *libertad de enseñanza* is nothing more than the remaining vestiges of the privileges of our oligarchies, who are the only ones who, in a given situation, can arrange not that their children be given an orientation in accord with the principles of nationality, but rather that they be given a sentiment of class superiority, a sentiment which should be abolished and which already is abolished in the minds of the Venezuelan people.[26]

The debate over Decree 321 itself came when the committee charged with evaluating the Annual Report of the Ministry of Education proposed full approval of the Decree arguing that "in its essential doctrinal aspect, Decree 321 is simply a progressive pedagogical measure and in no way merits the social, political, and educational importance which has been artificially given to it throughout the past year."[27] Attacks on the Decree came in familiar terms, emphasizing above all the factor of timing. The Decree was promulgated only a month before the examinations were

[25] A major practical problem here was the ideological image of the Pedagogical Institute and the Church's fears of contamination of its schools by Marxist professors.

[26] *Diario de Debates*, Venezuela, Asamblea Nacional Constituyente, session of March 10, 1947.

[27] *Ibid.*, session of September 24, 1947.

to be administered, and this effectively precluded any adjustment to its provisions. This, it was argued, revealed its real motive: discrimination against Catholic schools and students. Pbro. Sánchez Espejo,[28] one of the priest-delegates, argued from official statistics that only four *liceos* in the entire country (all in Caracas) could meet the condition of having 75 percent of their professors graduated from the National Pedagogical Institute.[29]

This debate offers some of the clearest expressions of the depth of division provoked by the Decree and of the general feeling on both sides that much more was at stake than a merely technical measure: for AD, the future of the entire revolutionary process was brought under attack by the opposition to 321; for the Church, the integrity of Catholic education and of the Catholic faith itself was attacked. Another priest-delegate warned the Assembly that "I am perfectly sure that if for the misfortune of the Nation, 321 were not reformed and changed in certain of its dispositions, the day of its application would create such a conflict for the Catholic Church in Venezuela, that the very Catholics of Acción Democrática would shudder."[30]

Belief that 321 was merely a disguised attack on Catholic education had been reinforced earlier by an amendment proposed (and later adopted) giving the state the power to make teacher training an exclusive monopoly of public institutions.[31] To the Church, such power, if taken up, would mean the liquidation of Catholic education. Its source of teachers would be choked off, and Catholic schools would be forced to use teachers trained in institutions whose ideological climate was repugnant to Catholic

---

[28] "Pbro." is a contraction of "Presbítero," the Spanish term for a parish priest (as distinguished from a member of an order like a Jesuit or Dominican).

[29] *Diario de Debates*, session of September 24, 1947.

[30] *Ibid.*

[31] The amendment was proposed by Jesús González Cabrera, formerly director general of the Ministry of Education. He was one of those forced to resign in the 321 crisis.

values. A committee of parents in Maracaibo complained to the Episcopal Conference in these terms: "It seems to us useless to reflect at length on the really grave impropriety of having some of these professors form part of the faculty of a Catholic school. Professors who, apart from the scandal of their very presence, might exercise a deleterious and destructive influence, destroying the very concept of Catholic education."[32]

This amendment was the subject of a special Memorandum to the Constituent Assembly from the Episcopal Conference, charging that aside from abridging the divinely sanctioned right of the Church to teach, such a provision in the Constitution would only deepen the social division already visible in Venezuela. The Bishops urged the Assembly to reconsider: "We greatly fear that if the Constitution is not changed in such an important point, far from bringing joy to Venezuelan homes, it will contribute to deepening the division, which unfortunately we have to lament in many sectors already. Even worse, it will sharpen the conflict already present in the educational sector."[33]

Acción Democrática rejected this call for reconsideration. The head of the AD's delegation argued that it implied that the delegates were like little children who did not know what they were doing.[34] Catholic delegates argued that if AD were to insist on constitutional provisions inimical to Catholic doctrine, then the Constitution itself, and the entire political system based upon it, would be fatally flawed. Pbro. Rojas put it this way:

I want us to learn the methods of civic struggle, and for this reason, even betraying interests which some might have believed me capable of representing here, I have worked with the majority, as a priest and as a friend, telling them a thousand times not to leave in this Constitu-

[32] "Hablan los Padres de Familia," SIC, No. 98 (October, 1947), 904.
[33] Reproduced in Diario de Debates, session of July 4, 1947.
[34] Ibid.

tion anything which clashed with Catholic doctrine so that we, as sincere priests, could freely and without any danger, put aside all political struggle. Because unfortunately we cannot here remain indifferent in the face of a party which argues for provisions condemned by the Church and by our own consciences. . . .

Thus, in every way, even exposing myself to the danger of betrayal, I have sincerely tried—let God be my judge—to keep Acción Democrática from retaining anything which might place it in opposition to Catholic doctrine, so that in Venezuela there might exist two political parties which could save this country from civil war, and before which we could be totally indifferent.[35]

This passage is crucial for it reveals the extent to which fundamental questions of political legitimacy were being aired. Rojas, looking toward a situation where priests and religious interests in general might be "totally indifferent" to the fortunes of any political party is saying that the ideal solution would be one where religious disputes were eliminated from politics. Only then could the "methods of civic struggle" prevail in Venezuela. From the Catholic perspective, until such issues and threats were removed from politics, conflict could never be limited or isolated—survival was at stake.

As debate grew hotter in the Constituent Assembly, a crisis flared up again in the country as the student strike broke out. In the face of an official refusal to negotiate a settlement, the scattered groups of parents supporting the strike felt they were getting nowhere. They saw the need for a unified national position, with the representation of Catholic interests at the highest possible level. Individual parents' groups requested the Bishops to take action, as all resources available at the local level had already been used without success. They appealed to the hierarchy for concrete norms to unify and guide the actions of schools, par-

[35] *Ibid.*

84

ents, and students in the crisis: "As a consequence of all this, we find ourselves in extreme conflict, facing the risk that hundreds of youths may lose one or more years of school, facing the menace that the present situation, if not contained with a firm and unbreachable barrier, may degenerate into frank and open persecution, into whose preliminaries we have already entered."[36]

AVEC felt constrained to call on the Bishops to take over direction of the conflict:

If the strike were not well resolved, there was a danger of the Catholic students scattering. Many spoke of continuing their studies abroad. The very cause of Catholic education was in danger. In view of the grave risks involved, AVEC, after long deliberations, felt it necessary to inform the National Episcopate and ask it to assume full responsibility for any future decisions. It was thought that perhaps the time had come for a general shut down of the private schools, until the conflict could be resolved. Such a step could not be taken without the express approval of the Episcopate.[37]

In response, the Bishops met in conference at the end of August 1947. They declared three days of National Prayer to seek divine aid and guidance, sent a Memorandum to President Betancourt, and after a month with no reply, issued a Pastoral Letter as a guide to the faithful in the crisis. In the Memorandum, the Bishops reviewed the evolution of the crisis, and expressed their conviction that "there is an entire plan, totally premeditated, which is being implemented gradually, tending to the complete suppression of Private Education, which is in its majority Catholic."[38] The

[36] "Hablan los Padres de Familia," 905.
[37] *AVEC Memoria, 1951,* p. 7.
[38] Memorandum of the Bishops to the President of the Junta Revolucionaria de Gobierno, reprinted in *Carta Pastoral Colectiva Sobre los Problemas Planteados a la Educación Católica en el País. Dirigida al pueblo con motivo de las Conferencias Extraordinarias, celebradas*

Memorandum further revealed the gravity of the threat perceived by the Church:

> The injustice committed against the Private Schools by Decree 321 is considered by us to be an attack made expressly against the Catholic Church in one of its most sacred rights and activities: Education. The conflict provoked by this Decree, with its latest consequences in the student strike, is seen by us as a conflict which affects the intimate life of the Church, the harmony and security of the Christian conscience.[39]

In the Pastoral letter, published a month later, the Bishops addressed themselves directly to Catholic educators. They stressed the importance of their mission and of the defense of Catholic principles in education:

> Beloved children, priests, monks, nuns, and laymen, who collaborate in education in all its phases, you are the organs of the Church's education. Hence it is natural that she defend, shelter, and bless you with special care. It matters not that they slander you. That only signifies that you really participate in the spirit of our Lord Jesus Christ, who prophesied: "in the world you will suffer combats, if they persecuted me, so will they persecute you." Rejoice, that for this reason, your names are written in the Kingdom of Heaven.[40]

In a separate letter to parents, the Bishops drove home the point that the threat to private education was really a threat to religious education and through it to the Catholic faith and the Church itself:

> We earnestly exhort all parents who consider themselves Catholics and who are seriously concerned for the religious education of their children, the hope of our beloved

en Caracas, de 25 de agosto a 30 de septiembre de 1947 (Caracas: Editorial Venezuela, 1947), p. 7.

[39] *Ibid.*, p. 8.　　　　　　　　[40] *Ibid.*, p. 18.

Venezuela, to be and show yourselves constant in not permitting, in any way, that the faith of our beloved children be torn away, and their minds directed on paths incompatible with our Catholic traditions,—the most precious heritage our forefathers left to us. Keep your children in the Catholic schools, though it mean painful sacrifice for you.

We equally exhort you, beloved students, to be strong in the defense of your rights, as befits citizens of a free country, and never permit the enemies of our Catholic Faith to attain their goals, dividing you into hostile groups, with fatal consequences for our cause, which is the cause of the Fatherland and of the Church.[41]

In addition to re-emphasizing the Catholic position and rallying the faithful to the cause, the Bishops took important organizational steps, creating a Permanent Commission of Catholic Education to act as official Catholic spokesman in all educational questions.

With the debates of the Constituent Assembly, the student strike, and the publication of the Pastoral Letter, the tension and conflict reached a peak. While the debates, broadcast nationally, brought underlying political issues into the open, the student strike was bringing many demonstrations into the streets. The strike failed in its immediate goal as the Decree was not suspended. Many students lost the school year and others went abroad to continue their studies. However, the fact that the crisis reached such a high point obviously had an impact on both sides as the provisions of the Decree were nullified in the Organic Law of Education passed in late 1948, which tried to sidestep the whole issue by restoring the *status quo ante* 321. The Church itself helped lower the temperature of debate, by forbidding priests to stand as candidates in the 1947 con-

---

[41] "Nosotros los Arzobispos y Obispos de Venezuela, a los Padres de Familia y Estudiantes Católicos de la República, Paz y Benedición," *SIC*, No. 98 (October 1947), 903.

gressional elections. In writing the new Organic Law, AD itself tried to eliminate points of potential conflict wherever possible. Presenting the Law in the Chamber of Deputies, AD's spokesman noted that:

> We all remember the alarmist editorials in the opposition press, above all the press of the right wing opposition. The Law arrived and to the surprise of those who expected some kind of infernal machine, full of articles attacking the principles and institutions they claim to defend, the Law of Education appeared rather as a project in which all points which might have occasioned serious conflict had been eliminated without thereby betraying the basic principles which must guide national education.[42]

Although the outward manifestations of conflict were somewhat muted in the last year of the *trienio*, it is worth noting that public and parliamentary debate over the new Organic Law of Education continued until just before the overthrow of the government in November 1948. The new Law itself had only a few short weeks of life before being annulled by the military junta.

THE TERMS OF CONFLICT: FORMULATIONS OF THE PROBLEM

At this point, it may be useful to retrace our steps, and point out some basic elements of the conflict as perceived by the participants. It is important to remember that AD was not prepared for a conflict of the kind that arose over Decree 321. For the party leadership, both the Decree and the ensuing dispute were ghastly mistakes. The party had not sponsored the Decree and was in general desperately anxious to avoid being drawn into religious conflicts. A prominent member of AD told me that,

[42] *Diario de Debates*, Venezuela, Cámara de Diputados, session of August 11, 1948.

The Decree was a deviation, an error. First of all, it was not even a party policy. It was proposed by a Minister not of the party. The Decree and the Minister himself lacked political sensitivity and skill, and thought only in terms of his anti-clerical interests. Approval of the Decree was a real mistake, but it was done more or less as a matter of course, a routine backing of the Minister in his initiative.[43]

Logically, then, when the conflict erupted, immediate concessions were made: the Minister of Education was sacked and the Decree suspended. In general, party leadership tried desperately to keep the dispute on technical grounds, denying its broader implications. But as the crisis took on a political tone, a threat to the entire revolution was perceived in the partisan advantage opposition groups were reaping from the conflict. The atmosphere of a young and enthusiastic revolution plus the relative youth and inexperience of the majority of those in power at the time contributed to a quick and sharp reaction to the anti-Decree campaign.

The inevitability of the conflict, however, lay not in any deliberate attempts by AD to seek or avoid it, but rather in the nature of the threat perceived by the Catholic sector— a threat whose spearhead appeared in educational reform. Even before the 1945 Revolution, the Church had opposed the principles and programs of Acción Democrática and that party's arrival in power naturally put the Church on the alert for possible danger. Decree 321 sparked a tremendous reaction, for it confirmed deeply held fears. From the outset the Church was prepared for a more extensive conflict than was Acción Democrática.

As we have seen, the determining factor in putting conflict irrevocably on political grounds was the fact that the Catholic sector perceived a bias in the political institutions of the *trienio*, a bias which distorted their true strength,

[43] Interview B-2-b, January 12, 1968.

thwarted all their initiatives, and left them powerless to secure acceptable solutions of their grievances within the system. When the same principles objected to in a mere Decree were later incorporated into the new National Constitution, the picture of exclusion for the Church and the Catholic sector in general was complete. Representing, so they thought, the "wishes of the Catholic majority," they were nevertheless unable to break AD's domination of all political institutions. The extreme institutional bias perceived by Catholic leaders helped launch the Church into direct political action, and fixed the conflict in political terms from the outset. The combination of perceived threat plus perceived exclusion and powerlessness within the system helped elevate the conflict to a procedural level, raising open questions of legitimacy. Catholic leadership felt that the rules of the system were being fundamentally changed to their disadvantage.

As we have seen, with a procedural definition of issues, the resolution of general political questions takes priority and conflict cannot be confined to lower-level arenas. Political conflicts require political solutions. In this case, the underlying procedural question was resolved by the military coup of November 24, 1948, which removed the immediate threat to Catholic interests. Remember the Catholic reaction to the coup: "God has saved us." Describing the effects of the coup on the status and actions of Catholic organizations, AVEC in 1951 noted that:

> AVEC no longer found itself—from the 24th of November on—facing a hostile Government but rather facing a regime which showed itself disposed to attend to our grievances and to offer us positive support. Consequently, a change of style of action was necessary: hostile public campaigns were replaced by direct negotiations with the authorities of the Ministry of Education and with the Junta of Government.[44]

[44] *AVEC Memoria, 1951*, p. 2.

CONCLUSIONS

The structure of the *trienio* political system—characterized by AD hegemony and a sense of powerlessness and exclusion in the Church—made the isolation of conflict impossible. Political questions of the survival and legitimacy of institutions took precedence, and thus a dispute over technical reforms in the examination system was rapidly expanded into a more general framework of conflict and opposition.

Once the survival of the Church and of religious values in general was put on the line, the actions of Catholic leadership helped magnify and extend conflict, rather than limit and confine it. Although organizational ties were not decisive in the conflict, the organizational weakness of the Church, when added to the pervasive hegemony of AD, profoundly affected the course of the conflict since it meant fewer buffers between the two sides. Those organizations which did exist at the time in education were all either secular (and anticlerical) or Catholic. Exclusion was mutual, and the idea of cooperation or compromise was unthinkable. An important participant in *trienio* struggles, and a leader of Catholic education since 1958, has recognized the relevance of this factor in an interesting way:

What happened after the 1945 coup was simple—AD expanded into a vacuum and won enormous backing among the electorate. There was almost no organization among the Catholic sectors, as COPEI was just getting off the ground. Neither was there any other base of political organization, or of organizations of any kind—not in other parties, not in the business sector, not in the Church—nowhere but in AD. Thus when conflict arose over 321, the clash was direct—there were no mediating organizations, no buffers to soften the shock. The real difference since 1958 lies in the general growth of pluralism in the country, which softens the clashes of institutions like the parties and the Church by providing a number of other organizations to work through.[45]

In this regard, the role of COPEI, in the *trienio* and after, is of crucial importance. A politically mediating role (like that played by COPEI after 1958) was impossible in the *trienio* context. COPEI lacked the strength and institutional identity to carry it off. Moreover, the political motivations and commitments to institutional preservation essential to such a role were weak. COPEI was literally bowled over by the tide of religious enthusiasm. Of course COPEI has never considered itself a confessional group, but rather a political party with political goals and programs. But the character of the crisis unleashed by Decree 321 and the very newness of its own structures meant that COPEI was easily absorbed into the religious-political struggle then dominating the scene. A prominent figure associated with COPEI describes the party's situation in these terms:

> At the time of the Decree, COPEI had recently been formed and was following a typical path for a new political party, with an essentially political orientation and appeal. But the promulgation of Decree 321 set off such an enormous emotional reaction in the country that many forces sought to line up with COPEI against the AD government. . . .
>
> The experience of the struggle over 321 taught COPEI some lessons, and opened our eyes to the fact that many people neither of the Church nor of the party were alongside us, shouting against the government, but were not really dedicated to the Church or to COPEI as a political party.[46]

The feeling that COPEI had been used by reactionary forces was instrumental in promoting a conscious role for the party after 1958—a conciliatory and mediating role. In

[45] Interview A-2-c, February 15, 1968.
[46] Interview A-16, February 14, 1969.

general, the religious and political conflicts of the *trienio* offer a clear example of the effects of lack of mutual guarantees among social groups. Neither side felt its survival or collective identity secure in the face of the other. The lack of felt guarantees short-circuited attempts to isolate and conciliate conflicts. The following chapter examines the construction of such guarantees after 1958, and related changes in the formulation of issues and conflicts between Catholic and secular groups.

CHAPTER 5

Catholics and Seculars: Toward the Isolation of Conflict

THE experiences of the *trienio* have weighed heavily on the Church and the political parties since the restoration of democracy in 1958. The memory of old conflicts and their role in undermining the *trienio* regime led the parties to explore avenues of accommodation with the Church, side-stepping, if possible, the sensitive subject of educational reform. A prominent educator, also a high-ranking member of AD, summed up the impact of past experience this way:

> I believe that the entire experience, any experience of such importance, creates an impact on the forces acting in it. If someone going along a path stumbles on a stone, the next time he will manage to go around that stone, and not hit it again. It is evident that this conflict, along with many others, was part of the reason for the fall of the government. I do not believe it was decisive but it did, in a certain degree, have an effect. Logically, then, experience has shown us that such conflicts have to be avoided, especially when they are not necessary.[1]

Chapter 4 described the fundamental philosophical-political positions of the Church and secular groups in educational matters, and the heritage of conflict in that field. This chapter analyzes changes in the structure and scope of conflict through examination of changes in the Church and AD, which led to a long series of negotiations over educational reform from 1965 to 1967.

[1] Interview C-16b, June 4, 1968.

94

EDUCATION UNDER MILITARY RULE

With the advent of military rule, the Church and Catholic education found an immediate change of climate within the government—a change favorable to their interests. Among the first official acts of the military government in 1949 was the promulgation of a Provisional Statute of Education, replacing the AD-sponsored Organic Law approved just before the coup. The Provisional Statute ordered two important changes: (1) two hours of religious instruction weekly, within normal class hours (the 1948 Law kept it outside the normal schedules); and (2) equality of status as teachers in secondary schools for graduates of University Faculties and graduates of the National Pedagogical Institute. This last provision, combined with the granting of a charter for the foundation of a Catholic University (which opened in 1953), allowed the Church for the first time to break the official monopoly on training secondary school teachers.

However, it is not in statutes, but rather in statistics, that the true impact of the dictatorship on Venezuelan education is best revealed. From 1948 to 1958 the rate of growth of public education dropped sharply. This, of course, indirectly favored private education, allowing it to regain much of the ground lost during the *trienio*. While the budget of the Ministry of Education had more than tripled from 1945 to 1948, in the decade that followed this Ministry's total expenditures rose from 119 millions to only 178 millions. (See Table 5.1.)

In primary education, the number of pupils in official schools less than doubled, while private enrollments multiplied more than three times. While the number of official primary schools actually declined, private primary schools increased almost fivefold. (See Table 5.2.) In secondary education, the rapid expansion of private schools was even more marked. While only 12 new public *liceos* were opened in the decade, almost 200 private *liceos* were founded. The

95

TABLE 5.1

Educational Budget: 1948-58*

Year	Amount
1948-49	119,052,739.31
1949-50	121,599,753.00
1950-51	122,147,425.00
1951-52	142,129,078.00
1952-53	145,999,146.00
1953-54	146,499,146.00
1954-55	149,713,910.55
1955-56	163,241,205.90
1956-57	168,947,647.00
1957-58	178,340,825.95

SOURCE: M. Mudarra, *Historia de la Legislación Escolar Contemporánea en Venezuela*, p. 284.

* Figures are only for the Ministry of Education. For these years, no data are available giving the expenditures on education of all different sources.

TABLE 5.2

Primary Schools and Pupils: 1948-58

Year	Schools		Pupils		TOTAL
	Public	Private	Public	Private	
1948-49	6,369	272	395,804	46,308	442,112
1949-50	6,636	320	443,533	53,301	496,834
1950-51	6,587	369	443,555	59,567	503,122
1951-52	6,786	462	463,816	72,396	536,212
1952-53	6,685	556	485,215	85,071	570,286
1953-54	6,381	633	501,679	94,703	596,382
1954-55	6,212	744	515,371	107,712	623,083
1955-56	6,111	989	526,737	120,058	646,795
1956-57	5,791	1,000	561,367	132,826	694,193
1957-58	5,606	1,070	608,428	143,133	751,561

SOURCE: *Memoria y Cuenta que el Ministro de Educación Presenta al Congreso Nacional de la República de Venezuela en sus Sesiones de 1968, Tomo II*, Table 1, p. 117.

The proportion of primary school pupils in private schools rose from 10.5 percent in 1948-49 to 19.0 percent in 1957-58.

TOWARD THE ISOLATION OF CONFLICT

proportion of *liceo* pupils enrolled in private institutions more than doubled. (See Table 5.3.) To cap off the progress of private education, charters were granted for two private universities, the lay Universidad Santa María and the Jesuit Universidad Católica Andres Bello. Political turmoil that closed the Central University in 1951-52 and the imposition of heavy matriculation fees for public universities further contributed to the stagnation of state universities and the rapid expansion of private institutions. (See Table 5.4.)

TABLE 5.3

Schools and Pupils in Secondary Education: 1948-58

Year	Liceos		Pupils				TOTAL
	Public	Private	Public	(Percent)	Private	(Percent)	
1948-49	50	49	16,253	(81)	4,045	(19)	20,298
1949-50	53	62	17,275	(76)	5,472	(24)	22,747
1950-51	52	83	16,467	(69)	7,324	(31)	23,791
1951-52	52	96	18,272	(67)	8,850	(33)	27,122
1952-53	52	96	18,606	(63)	10,987	(37)	29,593
1953-54	52	145	20,055	(60)	13,426	(40)	33,481
1954-55	52	172	22,050	(57)	16,869	(43)	38,919
1955-56	60	206	25,308	(57)	19,125	(43)	44,433
1956-57	61	236	28,742	(55)	23,678	(45)	52,420
1957-58	62	238	30,095	(55)	25,099	(45)	55,194

SOURCE: *Memoria y Cuenta que el Ministro de Educación Presenta al Congreso Nacional de la República de Venezuela en sus Sessiones de 1968, Tomo II*, Table 91, p. 307, and Table 92, p. 308. All percentages are rounded off to the nearest whole number.

Benefiting from the friendlier climate of military rule and the regime's slight interest in education, the Church rebuilt its strength and relative position to levels which equaled or surpassed those of 1945. In material terms, then, there was much to fear from the resurgence of a lay sector which for 10 years had been harassed and persecuted for its strong ties to AD and its vigorous opposition to military rule. Particularly alarming to many church officials was the apparent spread of extreme left-wing influence into the top echelons

97

TABLE 5.4

University Enrollments: 1948-58

Year	Official		Private		TOTAL
	No.	Percent	No.	Percent	
1948-49	5,117	(100)	—		5,117
1949-50	5,657	(100)	—		5,657
1950-51	6,453	(100)	—		6,453
1951-52	1,671	(100)	—		1,671
1952-53	4,758	(100)	—		4,758
1953-54	6,686	(94)	462	(6)	7,148
1954-55	6,529	(90)	717	(10)	7,246
1955-56	6,446	(88)	879	(12)	7,325
1956-57	7,573	(86)	1,261	(14)	8,834
1957-58	8,188	(80)	2,082	(20)	10,270

SOURCE: *Memoria y Cuenta que el Ministro de Educación Presenta al Congreso Nacional de la República de Venezuela en sus Sesiones de 1968, Tomo, II,* Table 224, p. 575. All percentages are rounded to the nearest whole number.

of the Ministry of Education. An official of AVEC at the time describes the situation:

At the time of the fall of Pérez Jiménez, a strong Marxist element in the country emerged into positions of considerable power, especially in the Ministry of Education. . . . The general atmosphere was one of unity of all forces and anyone not of the Left was immediately branded a *perez-jimenista*. The result was a general surrender of positions to the Communists. . . . At that time, there really seemed to be no room for Christians in the solution of national problems, especially in the Ministry of Education.[2]

CHANGES IN ORGANIZATION AND OUTLOOK

These fears were significantly abated when the Provisional Government which had followed the downfall of

[2] Interview A-8, January 15, 1968. Such fears were strongest in 1958, during the Provisional Government of Admiral Larrazábal.

Pérez Jiménez gave way to the elected government of Rómulo Betancourt. The Church, emerging from the dictatorship with bitter memories of persecution, was anxious to contribute to the stability of the new regime. Although concerned about leftist influence in education, the Catholic sector nevertheless took a number of initiatives which indicated a willingness to live and let live—to try out the new system as a framework for the expression and defense of Catholic interests.

As we have seen, among the democratic political parties (excluding the Communists for the moment), the common goal of stability and institutional continuity facilitated the extension of bridges across previously unbridgeable chasms of suspicion and distrust (see Chapter 3). The steps taken at the level of inter-party relations (Pact of Punto Fijo, coalition government, trade union coexistence, and the like) were soon reflected in other areas. Restraints on the expression of partisan hostility by the political parties contributed to a general shift in the social and political climate—a shift favoring initiatives of accommodation.

A significant step in this regard was the integration of teachers from Catholic schools, as a group, into the Venezuelan Federation of Teachers and the College of Professors of Venezuela. A high official of AVEC describes the decision to join in terms of the Church's need to establish and maintain greater contacts with other sectors:

> Before 1958, the Catholic educators had no contact whatsoever with the existing professional organizations. . . . In fact, there was largely a lack of organization, and the Catholic educators as a group were at the margin of these associations. They kept apart from the FVM because of the deep philosophical differences dividing them from the majority of the Federation. They preferred to avoid "catching something" from too much contact. Since 1958 there has been a general change of criteria. In promoting the affiliation of Catholic educators with these organiza-

tions we have sought to maintain a Christian presence in these organizations. As for philosophical differences, these of course remain, but our attitude is that we should affiliate. We can always talk about these differences.[3]

Within the secular teachers' organizations, political considerations clearly prevailed over continuing distrust and dislike of the Church to encourage limited initiatives of cooperation. Although from the Communist point of view, such initiatives were an unprincipled intrusion of Catholic influence into anticlerical organizations,[4] dominant forces in the FVM saw such cooperation as part of a larger process of drawing together. One official of the FVM argues that

> The real difference lies in the fact that experience has shown the country that it is useful for various sectors to get together around a table—that this can contribute a great deal to mutual understanding. The basic positions of the sectors, the fundamental points of view of the politicians, the Church, and the professional associations all remain the same. The difference lies in a general social experience in the country which forces sectors to talk before they begin to fight. Twenty years ago, we set out right away to war with them.[5]

The memory of past conflict is often an effective spur to accommodation. The desire to avoid future severe conflicts

[3] Interview A-6-b, January 13, 1968.
[4] A Communist educator, Alexis Márquez Rodríguez, on p. 196 in his book *Doctrina y Proceso de la Educación en Venezuela* (Caracas, 1964), complains that:

> At the same time, the Reaction entered through the unguarded door which the slogans of unity had left open in the Venezuelan Federation of Teachers, disregarding the principles—*estado docente, lay education*—which this institution had adopted as its ideological platform. In this assault on positions within the FVM, the Church in truth has shown no scruples of conscience. The anti-clerical principles of the Federation don't seem to matter while attempts to pentrate it are under way.

[5] Interview B-5, February 7, 1968.

may be crucial to the reconciliation of old enemies.[6] Initiatives of accommodation may also reflect a growing confidence that moves previously unorganized sectors to organize, and thus strengthen their hand in future contacts. In this way, increasing self-organization reflects and reinforces growing self-confidence, and an implicit acceptance of the new system's rules. The Venezuelan Church is a good example since moves toward greater dialogue and contact with lay sectors went hand in hand with a considerable strengthening of the Catholic organizational network.[7]

AVEC, which naturally had declined after the crises of the *trienio* went by the boards, was revived. Finances were reorganized, new regional chapters founded, and a systematic collection of internal statistics begun. Moreover, AVEC sponsored the formation of a national federation of parents' associations of Catholic schools (FAPREC). The idea of FAPREC had been raised in 1947 and again in the mid-1950's, but in each case political conditions impeded implementation. FAPREC was founded on February 6, 1958, with the explicit goal of defending Catholic education in times of crisis. One of its initial backers describes the purpose of the association as follows: "in a time of normal life, and not of crisis, it is better to have a national organization. Also, this type of organization gives more control over the actions of individual parents and parents' groups, thus making regular, orderly relations with the State much easier."[8]

The motives are themselves significant. A concern to prepare for existence in "normal" times and to ensure greater control over rank and file implies a new perspective of long-term dialogue and interaction—a perspective opposed in principle to the idea of total conflict and total victory. A concern for control, moreover, reflects the Church's interest

---

[6] A fuller discussion, in a comparative perspective, is provided in Chapter 8 below.

[7] A good account of the many new Catholic organizations is C. Acedo Mendoza, *Venezuela: Ruta y Destino* (Barcelona: Ediciones Ariel, 2 vols., 1966).

[8] Interview A-8, January 15, 1968.

in molding an effective, disciplined tool—something it could bargain with, and not merely unleash.

FAPREC grew rapidly and soon provided Catholic education with a formidable, nationwide organization capable of rapid mobilization in the event of crisis. The association was originally seen as part of a plan whereby Catholic education would have three representative groups: (1) AVEC, bringing the schools together; (2) FAPREC, federating parents' associations; and (3) CEFEL (Centro de Estudiantes Federados de Educación Libre), an organization of students in Catholic schools.

Growth in the organizational capacity of the Church was coupled with new strategies for the penetration of official institutions. In 1959, a program known as APRO-FEP Asociación Pro-Fomento de la Educación Popular) was founded, offering scholarships and residential facilities to Catholic students wishing to attend the National Pedagogical Institute. In his Report to the Tenth National Assembly of AVEC in 1962, Padre Jenaro Aguirre, President of AVEC, emphasized the crucial importance of the new association (APRO-FEP) for Catholic education:

> The most important work for the Church in the overwhelming educational problem in Venezuela is APRO-FEP. This is no mere slogan. . . . Even supposing that Church schools worked at full capacity, we would still have abandoned and surrendered to teachers of doubtful (when not pernicious) ideology, the great majority of Venezuelan youth. Even the University problem, of which so much is said, will never be resolved without first cleaning up Secondary Education. The Church can neither ignore nor abandon official education; on the contrary, it rewards a strong and effective Christian presence within *liceos* and other official institutions, such as normal or technical schools. . . . At the level of primary education, we must champion the Catholic normal schools and defend them like the apple of our eye. On the secondary

level, APRO-FEP, financing students of recognized Christian orientation for the Pedagogical Institute, helps solve the problem, while at the same time preparing competent personnel to fill the needs of the free [Catholic] schools.[9]

Self-confidence and increasing organizational capabilities stimulated attempts to compete on common grounds. In this regard, APRO-FEP is a major continuing effort to build strength in an institution hitherto conceded to the enemy. New organizational capacity and confidence were further reflected in a basic reorientation of the Church's energies toward bringing Catholic education to the poor and marginal populations of Venezuela's cities. In 1955, a program of mass, popular education was inaugurated under the name of Fé y Alegría (Faith and Joy), to bring general education and above all technical and artisan training to the urban poor—along with Catholic influence. After the fall of Pérez Jiménez, the Church, with support from private sources and from the government, began to build programs of technical education and artisan training on a larger scale. These initiatives were based on an explicit recognition of the importance for the Church, in an industrializing and highly mobilized society, of a popular orientation and increased contacts with the masses.

Speaking to the 1962 National Assembly of AVEC, Dr. José Luis Aguilar presented the case for a heavy investment of Catholic efforts in technical education. In a passage worth quoting at length for the profound changes it recognizes, Dr. Aguilar asked,

Why is Catholic Vocational Education so underdeveloped? . . . The basic reason, the source of my concern, is an explicit or implicit argument which must be changed. If the resources of the Church are limited, it is thought natural that these be concentrated among groups of the

[9] "Memoria y Cuenta de la Junta Directiva Nacional," *X Asamblea Nacional de AVEC, 19-23 agosto de 1962*, pp. 66-67.

greatest social influence: teachers and university graduates. Thus the upsurge of Catholic Normal Schools, Catholic *liceos*, and the Catholic University. But I believe that this argument is based on an outdated premise: namely, that teachers and university professionals are the persons of greatest social influence. . . .

In earlier times, the liberal professions supplied the real leaders of society. But nowadays, in spite of the fact that such professionals are ever more essential to the community, their influence has declined. . . .

The masses,—peasants, workers, office-workers, bureaucrats—persons of lower or middle status, through their union struggles and through the vote, have become aware of their own strength and tend not to let themselves be led but rather produce their own leadership. Thus, an apostolic effort aimed directly at these groups which are in the majority and which have in greater or lesser degree emancipated themselves from the guidance of other groups, offers greater rewards. In today's society, an Agricultural Technician or a Rural Homemaker has more influence on a rural community than an Agronomist or a Veterinarian; in today's society, a good middle-level technician has more influence on factory workers than Industrial Engineers, Lawyers or Economists who may be managers of the company.[10]

The Church's obvious concern with democratizing its educational system has helped break its class-bound image. Moreover, the move to popular education and mass organization indicates a recognition and acceptance by Catholic leadership of the new conditions of action and the new criteria of power in the political system. To represent and protect Catholic interests effectively, organization—mass organization—was clearly necessary.

[10] José Luis Aguilar, "Conferencia: La Iglesia y las Escuelas Técnicas," *ibid.*, p. 43.

The Church's efforts at democratization have contributed to improving the possibility of good relations between Catholic and secular educational groups; the latter for the first time see a Church interested in carrying out a program of social action which goes beyond mere alms giving. A leading Catholic educator and high-ranking member of COPEI commented as follows:

The most interesting phenomenon in the Church today, in my opinion, is the trend to popular education. There is a real social sensitivity in the Church today although the general orientation still tends to be towards the upper classes. This opening to the popular classes is the real key to the future of Church education. Its future lies in collaboration with the State in the extension of education to the poorer classes. From 1919 to 1947, with an exclusive dedication to the education of the upper classes, Catholic education grew only very slowly. Now, however, in the past ten years, with the general change in orientation, the Church has experienced a very rapid growth.[11]

COPEI's participation in the coalition government of Rómulo Betancourt (1959-1963) also helped smooth Catholic-secular relations. The same persons who had led the battles of the *trienio* now met in daily cooperation within the government. In a sense, the coalition both reflected and reinforced general social reconciliation, blunting the edge of partisan hostility and keeping down the intensity and emotional bite of political conflict.[12] The impact of this experience on individuals and organizations cannot be disputed. A prominent figure in Catholic education, who held governmental office under the coalition notes that,

It became quite clear to both sides, and both sides decided, that we had to sacrifice a little to the other. Also,

[11] Interview A-13, January 26, 1968.
[12] Coalition politics are a common response to internal subcultural fragmentation. See Chapter 8 below.

persons who had previously been totally opposed to one another in educational questions were thrown together, to work together, and they began to see (just what you would expect) that neither one was a complete devil, and that neither one was out to dogmatize the other, subject the other, ruin him, or wipe him out in any way whatsoever.[13]

These new experiences, combined with the friendly reception AVEC received in government offices, contributed greatly to improving relations, and to changing Catholic perspectives on the system. If benefits could be secured by working within the system—at a cost obviously lower than that of total confrontation—then perhaps old images of the system and its anti-Catholic bias had to be reconsidered. Initiatives of accommodation, meeting a favorable response, became self-reinforcing.[14] For its part, AVEC was careful to avoid engaging in polemics with the Ministry of Education. One AVEC official insisted that "I never go complaining to the Ministry on the basis of rumors or unconfirmed incidents. I only go on cases where I am absolutely sure, with evidence and documentation. This serious attitude has won respect for AVEC within the Ministry."[15]

These changes were coupled with the elimination of direct political action by the Church. The proliferation of Catholic associations helped remove the Church per se from politics: other groups could act in the name of Catholic interests and values. This fact alone is important in reducing the likelihood of direct clashes between Church and state. Moreover, the growing prestige and influence of COPEI—its very existence and participation in the government—provided tacit guarantees of survival and protection to Catholic interests. A prominent *copeyano* has argued that, "COPEI has contributed greatly to avoiding clashes

[13] Interview A-2-d, August 26, 1968.
[14] For a general discussion, see W. Gamson, *Power and Discontent* (Homewood: The Dorsey Press, 1968), Chapter 3.
[15] Interview A-6-2, January 3, 1968.

between private and official education, by acting as a shield for Catholic education, and by constantly promoting the idea of education as a *national* enterprise, one involving all sectors."[16]

In Latin America as a whole, the growth of Christian Democratic parties has absorbed political strategies within the Church and thus encouraged greater concentration on internal renovation, religious values, and community social action.[17] Venezuela is a good example. For as the public identification of the Church and COPEI has declined, both groups have undoubtedly gained in prestige and power. COPEI, building a firm, independent identity of its own, has helped legitimize the idea of "Catholic" action in politics.

Thus the Catholic sector in general, and particularly its educational institutions and associations, may be seen after 1958 in light of the following changes: (1) a more democratic image tied to the projection of Catholic education to the poor in an attempt to fulfill a genuine social mission; (2) an awareness within the Church that it was possible to work with old enemies and the realization that these opponents wanted above all to preserve social peace; and (3) an expansion of Catholic organization which (a) provided numerous points of contact with other sectors and a new competence in the give and take of bargaining, (b) developed a capacity for action and control of action unavailable to the Church in the 1940's, and (c) shielded the Church per se from direct involvement in politics. One Catholic leader describes the impact of these changes in almost textbook terms:

This pluralism—embracing not only strictly organized groups as such but also groups which in fact exist if not organized with a charter and the like—is a major factor of change in Venezuela. For one, it makes it impossible

[16] Interview A-13, January 26, 1968.
[17] See Vallier, "Religious Elites."

107

for any given party to impose its own criteria on all the rest. Also, it makes everyone—all groups and persons involved—more disposed to the reaching of accords, of genuine transactions and compromises. This is because it helps avoid radicalization of the forms of action by forcing everyone to take so many factors into account. This doesn't mean that radical differences in forms of thought are eliminated—*only forms of action.*

In addition, I think it provides a base for the democratic development of the nation. Because in reality it is difficult to maintain democracy when the groups acting are few and opposed to one another. Without some common base—of ideology, attitude, or simply methods of action, the democratic system is hard to operate as it is easy to fall into the temptation of trying to get everything by force. One sees the triumph of others with horror, and not as a part of a process of genuine exchange which can also run our way at times.[18]

New Perspectives on Conflict

Taken as a whole, these changes imply a new range of potential responses to conflict. On the Catholic side, there was sharp awareness of the possibilities of dialogue combined with a new self-confidence and organizational capacity. Were action to become necessary, action could be both of unprecedented scope and more carefully controlled than ever before. Capacity for control meant that in any situation the Church had something important to offer—the ability to refrain from conflict.

We believed that a violent reaction could have been produced in the country, a violent civic reaction to any Law of Education which seemed to threaten the Church. There could have been press campaigns, parades, student strikes, etc. In 1946 there was a conflict of this type be-

[18] Interview A-2-b, January 9, 1968 (italics added).

tween Catholic education and AD, and similar things
could happen again. The 1946 dispute was in fact a huge
conflict with very widespread ramifications, and we felt
that what we basically had to offer this time was peace.
Moreover, peace was what we wanted.[19]

The desire for peace was intimately related to the
Church's goal of becoming a truly national institution, ap-
pealing to all sectors, without regard to class or party:

> It does not suit the Church to enter political conflicts and
> acquire political ties, as this creates a religious-political
> attitude in others. For example, were I in AD, I would
> feel a barrier not only to other parties, but also to the
> Church, if the Church were fighting me.
>
> The Church feels that its mission is not limited to the
> adherents of any particular political parties in Venezu-
> ela. The mission Jesus Christ gave to the Church was for
> all men. Thus, both the Church and the parties had rea-
> son to avoid conflict. What we offered was the absence
> of conflict—the chance to avoid a conflict that was no
> good for either side.[20]

The general political climate of this period was characterized by the decision of President Betancourt to maintain
the best possible relations with the Church,[21] while tacitly
burying plans for major educational reform. Incentives for
compromise were powerful on both sides. In the end, all
had suffered from military rule, and feared a renewal of the
religious-political conflicts which many believed instrumental in laying the groundwork for the 1948 coup. This was
undoubtedly one factor moving the Church to self-organization. The old strategies of inter-elite accommodation, where
the Church could call on the military to defend its interests,

---

[19] *Ibid.*   [20] *Ibid.*

[21] See Chapter 3 above. Not only did the Venezuelan government
negotiate a modus vivendi with the Vatican, it also was instrumental
in securing a cardinalship for Venezuela.

could no longer be relied on to produce a satisfactory solution.

It is important to realize the full impact of political incentives on the Church. The only visible alternatives to the system were a return to military rule (from which the Church had, in the final analysis, suffered), or a Communist take-over through armed revolution, which would have meant the liquidation of Catholic life in Venezuela. These alternatives gave cause for great care and prudence, and provided the Church with a definite stake in the stability of existing political institutions. AD, once a socialist menace, now appeared as a bulwark protecting the Church from unknown dangers. An official of AVEC explained the need for prudence in this way:

> In encounters with the government, the Bishops must use their resources sparingly, as the possible consequences can be grave. In a direct clash between the government and the Church, the government might fall. As you know, in this type of conflict the Church has strong sympathizers in the military and other sectors of public opinion who may not like the idea of a military coup, but in fact prefer it to a situation in which the Church is persecuted. This is what happened in 1948, and it was in fact the whole conflict over 321 that finally broke AD. . . .
>
> Now this power of the Church can be good and can be bad. For, if the government falls, another Sunday can always come, and to have the Church in direct opposition to the State is a serious matter. This is what I often say to the hot-heads among us: it is unwise and imprudent to let things get to a situation where the government can no longer exist. I should add that since 1958 the government has also had the prudence to avoid conflict with the Church.[22]

[22] Interview A-8, January 15, 1968.

As a final introduction to the analysis of negotiations over the proposed Law of Education, let me emphasize that the Church had been moved by a genuine commitment to dialogue which naturally heightened the probability of compromise solutions and lowered the legitimacy of Holy Wars. In relation to the proposed Law, a Bishop with great interest in education told me that

> In the episcopate there was complete and unanimous consensus on the need to exhaust all possible means of peaceful negotiation. . . .
> The other possible line of action would have been one of struggle which is in fact inconceivable for the Venezuelan Church after the Vatican Council, which clearly directed the Church to dialogue.[23]

Thus, incentives to moderation were concentrated strategically throughout the system. Both sides feared the consequences of explosive conflict. Both sides took initiatives for conciliation. Both sides came to see that cooperation was possible, and built up a backlog of valuable experience in common enterprises. The Church no longer saw itself as a weak and persecuted minority. Its own new strength, COPEI's role in the coalition, and the obvious receptivity of the government all helped to soften the harsh edge of remembered conflict. The decline of AD hegemony, and the self-conscious dedication of its leadership to ensuring institutional stability and continuity, pushed AD to compromise.

The strength of general commitments to compromise and accommodation can be seen most clearly under fire. In a crisis, where issues of deep significance and emotional weight are at stake, how well do these potential capacities for conciliation stand up? To answer these questions, let us turn to a closer examination of the treatment of educational reform in recent years.

[23] Interview A-7, January 8, 1968.

THE TERMS OF CONFLICT: THE DECISION
TO NEGOTIATE

During the government of Betancourt, there was growing pressure for a complete reform of the Law of Education. The continued existence of a Law passed under the dictatorship was a constant irritant to many. The educational sectors of AD and URD sought a new Law, to be based on the ideas of the short-lived Organic Law of Education of 1948. By the end of Betancourt's term, these sectors were anxious to start work on a new Law. Meeting in November 1965, AD's Plenum of Educators reviewed the movement for a new Law:

> Two theses competed within the Party: a mere partial reform and an integral reform of the system, whose first step would be a new Law of Education. A thesis valid in the previous constitutional period [the government of Betancourt] no longer held the consensus of the Teachers' Organizations or of the Political Parties (of the Government and of the Opposition). In Acción Democrática we discussed this in full liberty with the *compañeros* of the Government and the Party Command, and *acción*—democratically we concluded both in the National Executive Committee and in the National Executive Committee meeting with the Cabinet that a preliminary draft be elaborated and presented to the Broad Base [the coalition government of AD, URD, and FND] after prior processing within the Party to the point where the project was considered feasible and ready for submission to Congress. This all took place in January and February of 1965.[24]

Earlier, the FVM had conducted a poll of its membership that revealed widespread sentiment for a structural reform

[24] *Informe del Secretariado Nacional de Educación de Acción Democrática, para el VII Pleno Nacional de Educadores, sobre "FVM y Nueva Ley de Educación"* (Caracas, November 13, 1965).

of the educational system.[25] Thus, in the key governmental parties and in the teachers' organizations they controlled, strong feeling arose that the time was ripe for a new Law. In addition, there was general conviction that a Law could be worked out and passed by Congress without provoking widespread conflict with the Church or anyone else. In an internal party document, Adelso González, then National Education Secretary of AD, argued that,

> It is no exaggeration to state that the draft proposal represents an effort for understanding and conciliation. And this is our great tool for disarming those who want to be warriors when war has not been declared. We must conduct a serene and constructive campaign on the fundamental aspects of the draft proposal. . . .
>
> The only war we must declare is war against fear and vacillation. We need to carry our message of dialogue and understanding to all sectors at every moment.[26]

A subsequent review of developments up to September 1965 noted as a major success for AD, "Establishment, as tactical and strategic guidelines for the political handling of the question, of: DIALOGUE, CONCILIATION, UNDERSTANDING, NEITHER TO PROVOKE NOR TO FALL INTO PROVOCATIONS."[27]

It is important to realize that pressure for reform came primarily from the parties of the coalition, and not from the government itself. Although education had expanded at a notable rate after 1958 (see Tables 5.5, 5.6, and 5.7), the government was anxious to concentrate on technical and quantitative improvements, sidestepping the potentially explosive issues of philosophy embedded in any general reforms of education. Thus, the parties' representatives in official positions remained aloof from proposals of general

[25] Interview B-5, February 13, 1968, with an FVM official.
[26] *Informe de la Secretaría Nacional de Educación Ante el Secretariado Nacional Ampliado*, July 24, 1965.
[27] *Resúmen del Informe del Secretario Nacional de Educación del CEN de Acción Democrática ante la XV Convención Nacional del Partido*, September 10, 1965, p. 4.

TABLE 5.5

Educational Budgets: 1958-67
(in thousands of *bolívares*)

Year	Ministry of Education	Total Education*	Education: Percentage of General National Budget
1957-58	178,341	342,172	12.3
1958-59	367,683	748,107	12.9
1959-60	461,092	816,962	16.1
1960-61*	541,051	877,950	16.0
1962	579,150	861,690	14.5
1963	638,322	988,042	15.9
1964	682,532	1,058,333	16.7
1965	842,260	1,271,097	17.5
1966	914,060	1,379,354	17.6
1967	1,015,216	1,489,668	18.2

SOURCE: *Memoria y Cuenta que el Ministro de Educación Presenta al Congreso Nacional de la República de Venezuela en sus Sesiones de 1968, Tomo II*, Table 20, p. 83.

* Figures for 1960-61 do not include data for July-December 1961 as start of fiscal year changed beginning with civil year 1962.

TABLE 5.6

Primary School and Preschool Pupils: 1958-67

Year	Schools		Pupils		TOTAL
	Public	Private	Public	Private	
1957-58	5,606	1,070	608,428	143,133	751,561
1958-59	6,577	899	775,586	141,178	916,764
1959-60	8,727	923	933,441	161,163	1,094,604
1960-61	11,043	914	1,080,714	163,234	1,243,948
1961-62	9,787	947	1,129,149	169,278	1,298,427
1962-63	9,985	971	1,159,564	180,099	1,339,663
1963-64	9,999	974	1,188,742	181,923	1,370,665
1964-65	9,824	1,013	1,227,663	194,296	1,421,959
1965-66	9,867	1,055	1,276,092	205,241	1,481,333
1966-67	9,759	1,094	1,328,310	212,926	1,541,236

SOURCE: *Memoria y Cuenta que el Ministro de Educación Presenta al Congreso Nacional de la República de Venezuela en sus Sesiones de 1968, Tomo II*, Table 1, p. 117.

TABLE 5.7

Liceos and *Liceo* Pupils: 1958-67

Year	Liceos		Pupils				TOTAL
	Public	Private	Public	(Percent)	Private	(Percent)	
1957-58	62	238	30,095	(55)	25,099	(45)	55,194
1958-59	94	222	45,675	(64)	25,690	(36)	71,365
1959-60	133	204	63,005	(72)	24,923	(28)	87,928
1960-61	145	212	78,621	(75)	26,380	(25)	105,001
1961-62	143	240	89,227	(73)	33,084	(27)	122,311
1962-63	150	315	95,416	(68)	43,971	(32)	139,387
1963-64	158	354	107,527	(69)	47,749	(31)	155,276
1964-65	169	370	120,709	(70)	52,727	(30)	173,436
1965-66	182	389	129,986	(69)	59,597	(31)	189,583
1966-67	195	406	147,171	(70)	62,650	(30)	209,821

SOURCE: *Memoria y Cuenta que el Ministro de Educación Presenta al Congreso Nacional de la República de Venezuela en sus Sesiones de 1968, Tomo II,* Table 91, p. 307 and Table 92, p. 308. Percentages are rounded to nearest whole number.

reform, and promoters of reform worked apart from the government. In other words, party rank and file were more enthusiastic about pushing reform than party elites, especially those involved in the government,[28] who would have preferred to go on burying the issue. This intra-party divergence becomes important later in the concessions actually granted to the Church. Party leadership later granted many concessions directly opposed to rank-and-file sentiment—all in the name of promoting compromise and avoiding conflict.

The first reform proposal (February 1965), came from the Ministry of Education, and provided for a partial, technical reform of the system, sidestepping the problem of a new Law and thus avoiding larger issues of philosophy or orientation. This proposal was well received by Catholic organizations and many of their observations were accepted as

[28] This is a general judgment. Obviously many high party leaders promoted the reform. But few of those sponsoring a new organic Law were actually holding positions in the government.

115

CATHOLICS AND SECULARS

modifications of the original text.[29] At the same time, however, AD and URD educators had been working on a proposal for a new Organic Law. This text was elaborated on the party level and then presented by the party sectors through the FVM and the CPV.[30] The FVM's 19th Convention authorized a general campaign for a new Law, and an FVM-sponsored draft was made public in March 1965. Catholic organizations responded with concern and suspicion. In a letter to the president, the Cardinal expressed the Church's views:

> I am full of fear, given the earlier declarations of members of the Federation, that this proposal will assert principles and dispositions that the Church could not accept in silence. They would bring on inevitable polemics, which, although deplorable at any time, could be particularly grave in the present situation. Alarmed by this danger, I have felt that my friendship for you obliged me to communicate my fears, in the certainty that should they prove well-founded, you would interpose your influence to keep this proposal from causing any deterioration in the relations of your Government with the Church—which would ultimately imply harm for the Nation.[31]

The call on President Leoni to interpose a moderating influence was reiterated by the Cardinal in an appeal to the

[29] Interview A-2-a, November 28, 1967.
[30] *Informe de la Secretaría Nacional de Educación ante el Secretariado Nacional Ampliado,* July 24, 1965, notes that the party freely chose to pursue a new Law rather than a mere partial reform, and that elaboration of the proposal was authorized by the highest levels in the party: "Later the proposal was transferred to the periphery and from then on work has continued through peripheral influence and pressures." The periphery refers to organizations like the FVM—nonparty organizations.
[31] Letter from Cardinal Quintero to President Leoni on March 10, 1965, published as "Anexo 1-bis," to the "Memoria y Cuenta de la Junta Directiva Nacional de AVEC," in *XII Asamblea Nacional de AVEC, 17-23 de diciembre de 1966* (Caracas 1967), pp. 129-130. This source is hereafter cited as *AVEC Memoria, 1966.*

116

nation for serene dialogue and discussion. Speaking on the eve of his departure for Rome to participate in the new session of the Vatican Council, Cardinal Quintero said:

> To our understanding, old sectarianisms which on other occasions have merely sustained useless and strident disputes, have now been superseded by a true civic maturity which allows for the rational and dispassionate dialogue which alone can produce a full and harmonious understanding. . . .
>
> Rumors of attempts to implant an official monopoly in education appear to us to be baseless, as much because such pretensions are barred by our Constitution, as because such an outrage could only occur in a totalitarian regime, and never in a democracy like our own.[32]

The Cardinal's position was the outcome of a long debate within Catholic education. Faced with an FVM-sponsored Law, AVEC's President Jenaro Aguirre met with President Leoni in March 1965 seeking political guarantees on the treatment of the Law. He later reviewed this meeting for AVEC:

> The President of AVEC was commissioned to have an interview with the President of the Republic in the first days of March, 1965. The conversation was based on the ideas outlined by the Cardinal in his letter. The President shared these fears. We can specify the conclusions of the interview as follows:
>
> —Catholic Education should be consulted and should make its views freely known on the essentials of the proposal;
>
> —a prior agreement should be reached before submitting the Project to Congress;

[32] "Alocución del eminentísimo Cardenal Quintero," March 1965, reproduced in *AVEC Boletín*, segúnda época, No. 33 (September-October 1965), 1-2.

117

—I am not prepared to promulgate a new Law of Education, the President assured, without the approval of the Cardinal.[33]

The next day, AVEC received copies of the FVM text, and a series of meetings was called among the major organizations in Catholic education—AVEC, FAPREC, Fé y Alegría, etc. A vigorous debate ensued on the proper course to follow. A minority favored an immediate public campaign against the proposed Law, seeking to kill it by raising the specter of overwhelming resistance. A majority, with full backing from the Church hierarchy, favored cautious entry into negotiations over the Law, arguing that nothing could be lost at this stage by negotiating. A key figure in this debate describes the difference of opinions as follows:

We called the members of this sector (mostly FAPREC and Fé y Alegría) to a meeting in the Archbishop's Palace. We asked them: what kind of modifications do you want in the Law? What are the technical differences that you want? What are the concrete problems you see? It became clear that their objections were of a general ideological and philosophical character and when they put forward these objections, it also became clear that they didn't know very much. We began to point out to them, first, that many of their objections were unfounded, and second, that there were a number of valid objections, real problems in the Law, that they had not seen at all.

As a result of this and other meetings, it became obvious that we knew a great deal about the Law and that they were not equipped to interpret its intricacies. The fact that they had not seen a number of problems increased their faith in us. Moreover, the obvious strong backing we had from the entire hierarchy induced them to hold off from jumping into the streets and to give us a chance to enter negotiations. Of course, as we told them,

33 AVEC *Memoria, 1966,* p. 68.

we could always have recourse to these methods of conflict, if necessary. But there was no need to jump into the streets right off the bat, particularly when there were good possibilities of reaching a genuinely beneficial agreement on a proposed Law.[34]

The pro-negotiation position had several basic arguments with which it sought to convince doubters: (1) that the resuscitation of religious conflict would be dangerous for the nation since its political institutions were not yet strong enough to withstand the pressures of a Holy War; (2) that this would have meant opening a second front against a government already heavily engaged with leftist guerrillas; (3) that open struggle was, in any case, always possible should negotiations fail; and (4) that the Church itself was anxious to avoid making politics an obstacle for religion.[35] Those favoring talks carried the day, and the Church named a Negotiating Commission to represent it in all discussions of the Law. Several days later, AVEC was invited to a meeting with the FVM.

The offer to negotiate and the acceptance of the idea, together form a phenomenon without precedent in Venezuelan history in this field.

At the first meeting of the two sides, the Church's Negotiating Commission laid out the basic points on which all future talks had to be based. The key demands were procedural. Catholic spokesmen insisted then, and throughout the long negotiations to follow, that a complete, binding agreement had to be reached before any attempt to submit the Law to Congress. Why?

Without a formal agreement, when the Law reached Congress situations of indiscipline could easily arise endangering all the work put into the Project. Leftist sectors in the Congress might accuse AD of abandoning its

[34] Interview A-2-d, August 26, 1968.
[35] Interview A-2-a, November 23, 1967. Many interviews confirm this analysis.

119

old principles and selling out to the Church. They might pressure some sectors of AD into changing positions. On the other hand, without a firm accord to cite to our own base organizations and rank and file, there could have been civic outbreaks, demonstrations in the streets, etc. . . . *A situation of this kind can easily get out of control, and this is just what we didn't want. The fact of an agreement was vital in controlling the passions of our own people.*[36]

Prior accords, with the Church and with other political parties, had also been a condition, within AD, of acceptance of the thesis of general reform proposed by sectors within the party. AVEC's preconditions for entering negotiations were neither accepted nor rejected in any formal sense, but the procedural safeguards sought by the Catholic sector were obviously acceptable to the parties.[37]

After several exploratory sessions, the Negotiating Commission insisted that talks be moved to a higher level. Negotiations would then take place between the Church's Commission and a group named directly by the coalition parties, and authorized to reach a binding agreement just as the Negotiating Commission was authorized to commit the

[36] Interview A-2-b, January 9, 1968 (italics added).

[37] The preconditions consisted of eight points: (1) specifying subsidies for free and semi-free private schools; (2) representation of private schools in technical bodies of the Ministry of Education; (3) transitional provisions for the requirement that all preschool and primary school teachers be Venezuelan nationals; (4) where the proposal said, "the State will create," add, "and authorize"; (5) that guarantees for private education be spelled out in the Law and not left to regulations; (6) that parts of the Ministry's partial reform be adopted; (7) that a prior accord, with adequate political backing, be reached to avoid unforeseen modifications in congress; and (8) that a graceful way of saving face (*una salida airosa*) be found for the Ministry of Education, so that the proposal not appear as a victory over the executive power. See *AVEC Memoria, 1966,* p. 69. The nature of these eight conditions—most of which were in the long run fulfilled—is interesting, especially the unprecedented concern of Catholic education for the prestige of its new-found ally, the Ministry of Education.

Church to agreements reached. The Catholic spokesmen asked the members of the different parties represented in the FVM to arrange for direct contacts with the parties.

The need for the three coalition parties to reach a common position (FND had no strength within the FVM and thus had not figured in the elaboration of the FVM text) imposed a six-month delay. The parties returned in September 1965 and were ready to negotiate; they had a new text, significantly modifying many points in the FVM draft which had proven objectionable to the Church.

It is important to remember that there was never any doubt on either side that negotiations would be resumed once the parties agreed on a common text, and furthermore that there was continuous pressure by the Church to ensure full agreement before submitting any proposal to Congress. Thus, in a letter to President Leoni on September 7, 1965, AVEC pressed the need for full, nonpublic negotiations before public or congressional debate: "Premature public discussion of questions where there are appreciable ideological differences and long-standing emotional burdens is not the most prudent way to avoid frictions and maintain the necessary serenity, without which it would be impossible to attain the balance which is the goal of all."[38]

In reply, the president ratified his earlier assurances that the government was not sponsoring any Law of Education, and expressed his belief that the triparty proposal was open to the fullest possible dialogue and accommodation.

Thus, on the eve of sustained talks based on the triparty text, both sides were fully committed to negotiations as the path to an educational reform, which, while not embodying one hundred percent of anyone's goals, could nevertheless be a compromise acceptable to all. By this time, the issue for Catholic leadership had changed from Law or no Law to the type of Law that could be achieved through patient bargaining and compromise. Furthermore, the commitment

[38] AVEC Memoria, 1966, Anexo 2, p. 131.

121

of elites to compromise was more than merely verbal. As we shall see, it was reinforced in the structure of negotiations, and in the strict control exercised within each sector over all actions related to the Law.

The initial concern for procedural guarantees reflects an attempt to remove the issue of survival from political discourse. Each side's preparations for negotiations revealed this concern in an emphasis on centralization, control of information, and privacy. Centralization meant limitation of the conflict to inter-elite contacts, insofar as possible. Centralization was reinforced by elite control of information about the conflict. Elites are the only source of information for their rank and file, and the claim of special expertise reinforces centralization. Centralization and control of information in turn enhance a drive to depublicize the conflict—to remove it from the public arena where passions might get out of control. Let me turn to a discussion of these facets of the conflict, examining changes in the content of issues and the mechanisms of elite control.

THE TERMS OF CONFLICT: REFORMULATION OF THE PROBLEM

The decision to enter negotiations was part of a basic reformulation of the problem of educational reform, a change common to lay and Catholic sectors alike. The idea of negotiations itself implies agreement on the nature of acceptable solutions, as it presupposes a range of solutions attainable within the framework of existing institutions. In this way, perceptions shift from survival and the threat of civil war to a common arena of technical discussion, bargaining, and mutual advantage. Redefinition of the problem in technical terms was a major goal of Catholic leadership. Remember that in the decisive meeting which set Catholic strategy, it was the Negotiating Commission's technical mastery of the Law combined with the open backing of the ecclesiastical hierarchy that carried the day for negotiations.

Once under way the talks were always conducted with a goal short of total victory. The Church's avowed goal was a Law acceptable to all, good for the nation, and not harmful to the specific interests of Catholic education. The Negotiating Commission constantly pushed the idea that compromise solutions were necessary and desirable. They argued that the Catholic sector, only one among many in a complex, plural society, could not seek purely sectoral advantage. When the Negotiating Commission produced a Memorandum commenting on the triparty text, they themselves described it as follows:

> The Memorandum produced a strong impact in various sectors. Above all, in our own ranks, excessively partialized and with a narrow vision of the problem, given the fact that many limited their campaigns to the traditional demands of *libertad de enseñanza*, subsidies, and the like, completely ignoring the other aspects, above all the more general interests of the Nation.[39]

A member of the Negotiating Commission describes its operational guidelines in similar terms:

> I realize that this may sound like a mere formula, a slogan, but our basic idea was this: in all matters where responsibility to national interests was of primary importance, even if these interests meant higher operating costs for the Catholic schools, these considerations of national interests were given priority. . . . There was never any hesitation in our minds on accepting what might be more difficult operating conditions for our schools, and indeed, less material benefit for the Church if, in our view, national interests demanded it.[40]

Within the parties (and the secular educational groups in general), the effort at compromise produced great strains. By admitting some of the Church's basic points as valid in

[39] *Ibid.*, p. 71.
[40] Interview A-2-b, January 9, 1968.

principle, and hence subject to negotiation over timing, extension, and quantity, party spokesmen had violated some of the most cherished tenets of *estado docente*. In AD's Plenum of Educators, held just after publication of the triparty text, a committee evaluating the annual report of the party's secretary of education complained that concessions on subsidies and on participation of private groups in public planning agencies were

> . . . in complete contradiction with the doctrine which in educational affairs the party has sustained since the very moment of its birth. The Commission wishes to observe that it is a betrayal of the democratic masses of the country to return to the old hand outs and feudal privileges. . . . For these reasons the Commission feels that this Plenum should dedicate its greatest and most careful attention to the important problem represented by these two articles.[41]

Here again, as within the Catholic sector, the role of elite restraint—holding back open dissent, pulling the rank and file into concessions and compromises—was crucial. From the outset, Church and party leadership were anxious to steer the discussion of reform in a technical direction. AD's National Executive Committee was deeply concerned to ensure a push toward the technical side.[42]

The drive to separate technical from philosophical and political considerations took form in the very structure of negotiations. After publication of the triparty text and the presentation of the Catholic Memorandum, the Church's spokesmen bent all their efforts to heading off any immedi-

[41] *Conclusiones y Tareas Derivadas del VII Pleno Nacional de Educadores,* November 13, 1965. The articles referred to are Articles 9 and 12 in the original triparty text, concerning, respectively, subsidies and participation in planning agencies.

[42] *Observaciones de Ultima Hora al Proyecto de Ley de Educación,* March 19, 1965. This is an internal AD document quoting observations made in the National Executive Committee meeting of March 5, 1965.

ate introduction of the Law into Congress, pressing instead for continued high-level talks. Given the parties' desire for rapid progress, it was decided to split the talks into two levels. Henceforth, negotiations went on simultaneously on separate "technical" and "political" levels. At both levels, the Church's spokesmen remained the same, while party representation was augmented on the "political" level by high national officials. This reorganization of the talks was designed to permit progress and agreement to proceed on technical points without being blocked by philosophical and political tangles. One negotiator describes the operation of the two-level talks in this way:

> There was no conceptual criterion for separating political and technical problems in the negotiations. Our practical guideline was that whenever either side felt they could reach a definite agreement without exceeding their authority, this was a technical matter. When either group felt that to accept the other's points involved too much responsibility, this became a political matter.[43]

This division of the talks is significant since it gave concrete form to the separation of technical and political aspects of the issues in the minds of elites. Whereas during the *trienio*, technical and political problems were irrevocably fused, here we see a self-conscious separation. Moreover, the higher political level now represented at the talks, and the greater power and prestige thus accorded the negotiators, facilitated the imposition from above of compromise solutions not wholly palatable to either side's constituency.

At this point, it may be helpful to summarize the actual extent of the concessions granted by each side. The Church felt that it had already yielded a great deal, in abandoning "total victory," shelving demands for a guaranteed educational subsidy, and agreeing in principle to requiring Venezuelan nationality for preschool and primary school teach-

[43] Interview A-2-b, January 9, 1968.

ers. Within the lay sector, the move from the FVM proposal to the triparty text also saw many important changes. These are summarized in Table 5.8.

If the reader compares the triparty text with the outline given earlier of the principles of *estado docente* (Table 4.1), the magnitude of change becomes truly striking. As we shall see, more change was in order before final agreement could be reached.

Talks continued through the first months of 1966, centering on the exact wording of the remaining points in contention. Catholic education clearly found the negotiations beneficial. Reviewing these early talks, the Twelfth National Assembly of AVEC (December 1966) pointed out that

> The meetings were conducted in an atmosphere of great cordiality and left us the impression:
> —of a great receptivity to our points;
> —of a clear awareness of the seriousness and importance of our points;
> —of the possibility of arriving at an accord, not totally satisfactory, but acceptable to our cause.[44]

However, because of crises in the governmental coalition (withdrawal of FND), talks were broken off and not formally resumed. The issue surfaced again in June 1966, when Dr. Prieto, facing down opposition from the Church and from elements in his own party, prepared to introduce a Law of Education into the Senate. The Church again bent all its efforts to head off the submission of any law without the binding agreements promised earlier.

On June 9, the Cardinal wrote to various AD leaders asking them to prevent discussion of the Law at this time. In addition, the Episcopal Conference, then meeting near Caracas, named a special commission of four Bishops to meet with the president and express the Church's worries. Reassurances were presented at all levels, but nevertheless

[44] *AVEC Memoria, 1966*, p. 72.

TABLE 5.8

Comparison of FVM Text and Triparty Text

FVM Text	Triparty Text
1. *Libertad de enseñanza* is guaranteed subject to "conditions of orientation and organization" specified by the Constitution and Laws (art. 8)	1. The phrase "conditions of orientation and organization" is deleted (art. 10)
2. All social services are free in public schools (art. 5, paragraph 2)	2. This provision is extended to private schools where education is tuition-free
3. A general guarantee to stimulate and protect private education with "moral and technical support as seen convenient" (art. 9)	3. Amplified to include subsidy for schools collaborating appreciably in the extension of education to the less-favored sectors of society; power is granted to extend it further to schools training needed technical personnel (art. 11)
4. A general article on planning (art. 13)	4. Amplified to specify a system of consultation of all sectors, public and private, in the elaboration and implementation of plans (art. 15)
5. Requirement that primary and preschool teachers be Venezuelans	5. Includes the following exceptions: (a) where there is insufficient Venezuelan personnel in the area; (b) for foreigners whose countries grant such teaching privileges to Venezuelans; (c) foreigners with two years teaching in Venezuela at the time the Law went into effect; and (d) a general provision that the regulations for the application of this article establish norms for gradual transition, keeping in mind "the general interests of education" (art. 77)
6. Provision reserving for Venezuelans by birth the teaching of materials "linked to nationality" (art. 94)	6. This is restricted to primary and secondary education (art. 78)

Prieto tried to submit the Law on July 1. Then and on the next day, a quorum was unattainable as members of AD and URD stayed away. After an intense struggle within AD, Prieto (then president of the party) secured a quorum and the Law was formally submitted on July 4, 1966. Presentation of the Law without the safeguards and prior accords sought by the Church created a potentially explosive situation. Both sides mobilized allies and prepared their organizations for a public battle over the Law.

The general developments we have seen so far lead us to expect, however, that in such a situation both sides, while preparing for conflict, would try to maintain strict control over rank-and-file actions and to depublicize the conflict, seeking above all to return to private negotiations. In this light, the Church took a number of steps whose orientation is crucial. On the day of the Law's submission in the Senate, a meeting was held between the heads of all the teaching orders and the Negotiating Commission. This meeting named a Coordinating Commission, composed basically of the members of the Negotiating Commission, whose task was to unify all sympathetic forces in preparation for a public campaign in defense of Catholic education, and to secure financing for the campaign.[45] AVEC and FAPREC met to plan joint strategies. The national coordination of Catholic forces was reproduced at other levels, as instructions were circulated for the formation of unified regional and local commands, embracing AVEC, FAPREC, CEFEL, Fé y Alegría, and the like. While the machinery of battle was being prepared, however, steps were taken to ensure high-level control and restraint. National officers of AVEC and FAPREC were on the phone day and night in early July persuading local groups of enthusiasts to stay off the streets.[46] The need for caution and moderation was stressed. In a circular sent to all the chapters of FAPREC on July 16, desirable strategy was described in these terms:

[45] *Ibid.*, p. 75.
[46] Interview A-1, November 23, 1967 with a FAPREC official.

Above all, we should make it clear that our immediate goal is to achieve, if still possible, *an agreement on basic points with the sponsors of Law.* In this regard, important contacts are under way, which may open the door to new high level conversations, with the goal of attaining a Law which if not satisfactory, would be at least acceptable for Catholic education in the present historical situation. Hence, we believe that for the moment, Catholic Education should abstain from attitudes which do not favor a climate of conciliation, dialogue, and understanding. *As long as there exists a possibility of agreement on basic points,* we feel that *aggressive* positions are unjustified, even under the pretext that they are legal, or constitute legitimate defense of our rights. . . .

We hope to be effective without being strident, adapting ourselves to the variations which may arise in the course of the problem. . . .

Let us prepare for all emergencies, but in a disciplined way.[47]

In public, Catholic spokesmen adopted a procedural orientation. On July 7, in a national radio and television broadcast, the Negotiating Commission presented a communiqué from Catholic Education "to the People of Venezuela." After reviewing the course of negotiations, the Commission called for continued talks, closing with a veiled threat of the dangerous consequences of failure to renew talks:

Catholic Education feels that to preserve social peace, in addition to proceeding to an agreement in a spirit of amplitude and conciliation, this agreement must be negotiated before falling into premature public discussions. Hence, it has maintained that the agreement be reached prior to the introduction of the Law into Congress.

With great effort, Catholic Education has tried to preserve social peace . . . it has suffered in silence a cam-

[47] *AVEC Memoria, 1966,* p. 75 (italics in original).

paign painting it as interested only in getting money, when economic aid was requested solely to help us attend to the needs of the poorer sectors of society. It has shown an evident spirit of conciliation, both in refraining from the pursuit of its maximum goals and in the actual negotiations. All to no avail, given the impatience and passion of some.

Nevertheless, the Church considers that it can be patient in the cause of peace, and generous in pardoning offenses. It remains preoccupied by the social upheaval which might arise, and convinced that agreement and conciliation could avoid it. Thus, despite all that has happened, the Church trusts that before consideration of the Proposal begins, common sense will impose itself, so that agreement may be reached, thereby freeing the Church from the need to resort, in legitimate defense of its rights, to the use of all methods of action in accord with the laws.[48]

This statement was designed to pressure the parties into reopening negotiations. Should the attempt have failed, Catholic organizations were ready for open conflict. But their distinct preference was for further discussions. A member of the Negotiating Commission describes the goals of the broadcast in this way:

We employed a very strong tone, without going into a detailed public discussion of the Law. We tried to avoid that approach as we felt that an article by article discussion in public would hinder the progress of negotiations. For example, we wanted to avoid allowing any politician to pick out a particular point and make himself champion of this point against the Church. So our public emphasis was on procedures, on the conduct of negotiations.[49]

[48] "Comunicado: La Educación Católica al Pueblo de Venezuela," *La Esfera,* July 8, 1966.
[49] Interview A-2-b, January 9, 1968.

The Church's desire to preserve negotiations as a framework for action and thus keep the conflict carefully limited and controlled was further emphasized in an important article published in *El Nacional* on July 16, 1966. In this article, Dr. Tomás Polanco argued that the interests of the Church itself should not be confused with those of Catholic education. After pointing out that often the schools had specific material needs not necessarily shared by the Church as a whole, Dr. Polanco closed with a plea for moderation and dialogue:

> Let us recall what the Council has proclaimed: NO ONE can legitimately invoke the authority of the Church in their exclusive favor, when what is at stake are solutions to problems of a temporal nature, even if these problems and solutions are connected with questions of a spiritual and religious nature. I esteem it inadmissible that organizations no matter how respectable, should speak in the name of the Church, when that function corresponds exclusively to the Bishops, who in this case have maintained a discreet attitude limited to studying the situation.[50]
>
> ... The theme of educational reform must be discussed with the greatest possible serenity, with a national spirit, with Christian comprehension of dialogue and not with a war-like spirit; let us recall that only a few months ago Paul VI returned the flags of Lepanto to the Ambassador of Turkey, saying "the religious wars are over."[51]

The negotiations themselves, of course, helped reinforce existing dispositions to compromise. The ongoing process of negotiations enhanced the prestige and authority of each group of negotiators within their respective constituencies. The rank and file on each side depended heavily on its

[50] Tomás Polanco, "Los Percances de un Proyecto de Ley," *El Nacional*, July 16, 1966. This article was published with the approval of part of the Hierarchy.
[51] *Ibid.*

spokesmen for regular information about the progress of the Law. This dependence was converted into strong control from the top over statements and actions relating to the Law. The constant reinforcement of elite authority, and the consequent strengthening of dispositions to compromise, helps explain why the negotiations were able to survive strains which in earlier times would have ruined them.

THE TERMS OF CONFLICT: INSTITUTIONAL ASPECTS

A basic hypothesis guiding this study is that resolution of legitimacy questions (and the establishment of mutual guarantees) leads to a tendency to concentrate conflict, limiting its expression to common vehicles where the consequences of action are easier to control. In this regard, a striking feature of Catholic-secular relations since 1958 has been their high degree of institutionalization. Setting aside philosophical differences to concentrate on common forms of action and their control constitutes institutionalization in two senses: (1) participants view their relations as normal, legitimate, and permanent—a framework within which acceptable solutions can be reached; and (2) specialized roles are created, roles explicitly charged with reaching a peaceful settlement. A corollary, of course, is that elites be prepared to call on the occupants of such roles to perform the tasks of conciliation.

The normality of relations between the two sectors was brought out at every turn. The constant emphasis by Catholic spokesmen on procedural aspects of the discussions itself reflects prior acceptance of the idea of ongoing relations as a vehicle for resolving disputes. Indeed, although the Church's insistence on nonpublic discussions until binding accords could be reached was at first rejected by the parties, it is worth noting that once the Law was introduced into Congress, it was never formally debated. Negotiations were resumed more or less where they had left off, and were

132

carried forward to a full and final accord between the Church and the AD-URD commission in August 1967.

The second criterion of institutionalization, the creation and use of negotiating roles, is fully exemplified here. From the outset, the Church's Negotiating Commission was authorized to seek and reach binding accords. The political parties, although originally promoting reform through the FVM, were obliged by the Church to intervene directly. This jump in the level of negotiations was crucial. For as the authority and political weight represented on each side grew, so too did the possibility of reaching an accord and making it stick, even over strong opposition within each sector. These consequences, of course, depend on the shift in elite perspectives already described. Whereas during the *trienio*, linkages to national levels of authority and organization served primarily to magnify and extend conflicts, redefinition of the issues at stake meant that such integration now helped isolate the conflict.

As we have seen, the Church gave its spokesmen the job of avoiding conflict. AD also charged its representatives with the specific task of avoiding open conflict. A prominent educator and high-ranking AD member has described the negotiators' role in this way: "Obviously the Law raises many sensitive issues. Our political goal was to avoid or minimize conflict on these points. Thus, in the negotiations, our representatives were instructed to make secondary concessions which might reduce the conflict, while trying to maintain the central ideas of the Law. This was the general task given to them."[52]

This general goal was augmented by a series of conditions insisted upon within AD before the party leadership would agree to consider sponsoring any Law of Education. Among these was securing the widest possible sponsorship for the Law, particularly from sectors outside the governmental coalition. This condition speaks eloquently of AD's

[52] Interview C-16-b, June 4, 1968.

133

recognition of its nonhegemony, and of a new understanding of the dangers of riding roughshod over an intense minority.[53]

The debate within AD which delayed Prieto's submission of the Law in July 1966 was concerned precisely with this question: had sufficient support been assured to warrant the risk of taking the Law to Congress?[54] The general secretary of AD explained publicly that Prieto and Adelso González had in good faith considered themselves authorized by the party to submit the Law after conversation and discussion with other sectors. The majority of the national leadership, however, felt it necessary to make a prior political evaluation of the degree of support available, and to fix the date and hour of submission with the greatest possible care. Such decisions could only be taken by a plenary session of the party's National Executive Committee.[55]

> However, as the President of the Party and of the Congress, *compañero* Luis Beltran Prieto, had already committed himself publicly before the Parliament and before the entire nation, to introduce this Law on a specific date, the National Command finally resolved to admit that the Law of Education be presented and that its discussion take place in the regular sessions beginning in October.[56]

Another way of appreciating the importance of the tasks given to the negotiators is to note the enormous control each

[53] As we have seen, this, of course, says nothing about relations with the Left, an *isolated* minority.

[54] The Law was originally presented with AD and URD as co-sponsors. But many lost their nerve. Jóvito Villalba, the URD leader, forced the URD signatories to withdraw their names at the last minute. The Law then went to the Congress with the AD signatures alone. FND refused to co-sponsor the Law since it had withdrawn from the government some time before.

[55] Jesús Angel Paz Galarraga, *Carta Pública del CEN de AD* (*Pre-Convención Nacional*), No. 7, July 5, 1966, p. 10. Such a CEN meeting was also needed to discuss the wisdom of presenting a Law of Education at the same time as the *Reforma Tributaria*—a controversial overhaul of the tax system—was being debated.

[56] *Ibid.*, p. 10.

team maintained over its own rank and file. Within the Catholic sector negotiations were tightly controlled, and any public statement or action by Catholic organizations required prior approval from the "official" negotiators. A member of the Negotiating Commission has pointed out that "From the very first, we never permitted the anarchization of the emission of opinion by any of our groups. All the output of information was centrally coordinated and there was in fact no case of rebellion against this policy."[57]

Even when extensive preparations were being made for a possible public campaign against the Law, these were based in the Negotiating Commission itself. Dr. José Luis Aguilar, a key member of the Negotiating Commission, was also secretary of the Coordinating Commission charged with preparing (and funding) a public campaign. The initially strong position of the "official" spokesmen of Catholic education thus became a source of further power as negotiation became an accepted relationship with the state—a normal feature of the landscape. Through bulletins, lectures, personal visits, and the like, members of the negotiating team kept their constituency informed. These information channels in turn served as means of control and reinforcement of the "official" position.

Within the secular associations, the parties often made agreements opposed to the expressed principles and interests of the rank and file—particularly in the teachers' organizations. It is important to remember that one of the motive forces behind the initial push for a new Law had been the general feeling among many educators that the Ministry of Education had been making too many concessions to "the Right," specifically to the Church.[58] But these groups soon found that their parties, after taking over direct man-

[57] Interview A-13, January 26, 1968.
[58] Among the concessions most resented were, for example, the drastic reductions in numbers of official normal schools (for training primary school teachers) without any pressure on private education to close inefficient or bad normal schools.

agement of the talks, had proceeded to offer concessions undreamed of at first. A high official of the FVM explained the differences in criteria between the parties and the professional groups in this way:

> The political groups later took over the negotiations with a political interest different from ours, and we naturally have reservations about some of the accords reached on a political level with the Bishops. Among our reservations are the provisions on subsidies, nationalization—the agreement is too lenient on the transitional period for foreigners—and supervision conditions.
>
> As an institution we reject this type of accord. We are very intransigent on these matters. In fact, we are completely sectarian in these questions. But nevertheless we never made a public issue out of our disagreements as we in the FVM believed that it was better to avoid promoting differences and thus creating hard and fixed positions in the country over these problems.[59]

Of course, the parties did not leave everything to the public spiritedness of the FVM, and exercised extremely firm control. Through their representatives in the teachers' organizations, they channeled and controlled the actions of these groups in accord with the parties' political goals. The existence of strong ties to the political parties is crucial. These linkages provided constant pressure on the negotiators, constant reiteration of general political considerations and of the need for moderation and compromise. Coordination was ensured by a weekly caucus of each political group within the National Directive Committee (CDN) of the FVM prior to the formal CDN meeting. Party discipline was imposed to govern the actions of the CDN members. In AD, the National Education Bureau had the job of guiding the actions of party members within the teachers' organizations. AD's national education secretary was entrusted with

[59] Interview B-5, February 7, 1968.

providing concrete instructions on the tasks of the FVM and on the proper relation of the FVM officers to party officials in the educational field.[60] Another device for ensuring full coordination was a weekly meeting of the president of the FVM (a member of AD) with the party's national education secretary. The expression of opinion on the Law was strictly limited and controlled through party channels. National leaders of AD in the field of education were forbidden to raise questions relating to the Law (or to other problems of the FVM or the party) in public assemblies of the FVM or the party at the base level. For such discussions, they were required to use the national organs of AD's teachers' movement (e.g., National Education Secretariat, National Bureau of Education, and National Plenum of Educators) or, as a last resort, the highest decision-making bodies of the party itself, including its National Executive Committee, National Political Committee, National Directive Committee, and National Convention.[61]

In this way, powerful bonds were forged, ensuring close coordination of party and sectoral positions, with a clear imposition of party criteria all along the line. The dominance of the party point of view is visible in the difference between the original FVM proposal and the triparty text of the Law. Considerable opposition to some concessions, even from high levels within AD, was overruled on the grounds of compelling political need.[62]

[60] Point 5, in the Conclusions of the Buro Nacional de Educación Ampliado (Especial), held on October 14, 1965, in the Secretaría Nacional de Educación of AD. These Conclusions refer to party policy and tactics within the national directive committee of the FVM.

[61] *Ibid.*, point 6 in the Conclusions.

[62] The observations and recommendations presented to the CEN of AD by a technical-political commission (José Angel Agreda, Mercedes Fermín, Luis B. Prieto, Adelso González, Octavio Lepage, and René Domínguez) were critical of many points in the triparty text. Protests were directed above all at provisions for subsidies to private education and the authorization requested by the Church for founding of private Pedagogical Institutes. Protests were extremely bitter, and foresaw the liquidation of public education if

The narrative presented so far carries us to the end of 1966. After the submission of the Law and its burial in Congress, the degree of centralization of the conflict in the negotiations became even greater. The risk of crisis had further reinforced elite concern for control, which as we have seen, arose from fear of the consequences of extended conflict. Centralization became even more marked as the Law was wrenched out of the public eye back into private discussion.

The level of authority and political weight on each side increased even further. For the first time, the ecclesiastical hierarchy participated directly in the talks. The Bishops took over the "political" level of negotiations. The Negotiating Commission remained as advisers on this level, continuing to function on the "technical" level. On the secular side, negotiations were completely taken over by the parties. In early 1967, a high-level commission of AD and URD was formed to carry on the talks. Its conclusions were fully ratified within AD, whose National Executive Committee then named a special Political Commission, composed of the very highest party officials, granting it sufficient authority to set the tactics and strategy to be followed on all aspects of the Law.[63]

Under these conditions, negotiations continued throughout the spring of 1967. In May, important agreements were reached on participation in planning agencies, nationalization of primary and preschool teachers, the conditions for chartering new universities, and equality of status between graduates of University Faculties of Education, Arts, and Sciences with graduates of the National Pedagogical

---

such articles were incorporated into the Law since then any group could establish schools and demand aid.

[63] *Conclusiones de la Comisión del CEN Sobre Nueva Ley de Educación*, February 9, 1967. This commission was made up of Prieto (president of AD), Paz Galarraga (then first vice-president), Gonzalo Barrios (general secretary), Carlos Andres Pérez (head of the parliamentary delegation), and Adelso González (national education secretary).

Institute.[64] Discussions continued until August 1967 when a formal, final accord was signed between the representatives of AD and URD and the Church.[65] The accord specified changes to be made in 21 articles of the Law submitted to the Senate in July 1966. Some important modifications of the triparty text are indicated in Table 5.9.

Thus, a process of carefully controlled negotiations over a period of almost two years had finally reached agreement, with the inclusion of legal provisions hitherto unimaginable in Venezuela—all in an atmosphere of cordiality and co-operation impossible in previous years.

The agreement was stillborn. The split in AD—with large sectors of the party leaving to back Prieto's presidential bid—left everything up in the air.[66] Sufficient support to guarantee implementation of the agreements could no longer be assured. Nevertheless, a precedent had been set. It was a precedent felt deeply by all sides—the possibility of initiating and sustaining extended talks over an issue as delicate as education, and of carrying the talks to mutually acceptable positions.

[64] Conclusions of the meeting of the AD commission with representatives of the Church, held on May 22, 1967. This is an old issue, particularly important for the training of secondary school teachers. See Chapter 4 above.

[65] Negotiations in this last stage were peopled with a true cast of notables: for AD, Prieto, Gonzalo Barrios, Paz Galarraga, Carlos Andres Pérez, Octavio Lepage, Carlos D'Ascoli, Manuel Mantilla, José Vargas (for affairs relating to Social Security), Carlos Marín Loreto (legal consultant to the Ministry of Education), José Angel Agreda, Mercedes Fermín, Adelso González; for URD, Jóvito Vallalba, Omar Rumbos, Vicente Guerra, Juan Hernández Parra, Dionisio López Orihuela; for the Church, Padre Jenaro Aguirre, José Luis Aguilar and Monsignor Alejandro Fernández Feo, Bishop of San Cristobal and president of the Episcopal Commission on Education. The political punch concentrated in the AD delegation is extraordinary.

[66] In the final agreement there were spaces for three signatures for AD: for Prieto, Adelso González, and Carlos Andres Pérez. The division of AD was already foreseeable, and the accord was a victory for Prieto within the party. Thus, Pérez did not sign.

TABLE 5.9

Triparty Text and Final Accord on Law*

Triparty Text	Final Accord
1. Gives subsidies for private schools collaborating appreciably in the extension of education to less-favored sectors of society with power to extend subsidy to schools training needed technical personnel	1. The requirement of *appreciable* collaboration is eliminated
2. Specifies a "democratic" system of consultation of all public and private sectors in planning agencies	2. The word "democratic" is replaced by "effective"
3. Provides for full coordination of secondary education and university studies with national plans—through planning agencies	3. Includes provisions to guarantee the autonomy of universities to set their own programs and standards within this general coordination

* The final accord is variously named: "Final Accord of AD and URD with Other Sectors of National Life," or "Final Accord of AD and URD with the Episcopal Commission of Education of the Catholic Church." I have seen texts with either heading.

So far, I have focused on three basic factors in the management of the conflict over educational reform. First, the general political climate provided political incentives for moderation and favored initiatives of accommodation. Love did not suddenly blossom between the Church and AD. Rather, their common commitment to political stability drove them to conciliate differences insofar as possible without bringing into question the institutional foundations of the regime. In a very basic way then, the potential scope of conflict was sharply reduced long before the issue of educational reform arose in explicit form. Second, the actual formulation of the issue was marked by a conscious attempt to put aside philosophical and ideological differences in the pursuit of a compromise acceptable in some measure to all. Total victory was discarded. Third, reformulation of the issues meant that the integration of initial contacts with high levels of power and authority could serve to control, delimit, and reduce the scope of conflict. In all three dimensions, the role of leadership is crucial. Let us now consider the changes in elite perspectives so crucial to changing the structure and scope of conflict.

THE TERMS OF CONFLICT: LEADERSHIP AND LEARNING

Among the most notable changes in Catholic political perspectives since 1958 has been a self-conscious move away from a position of sectoral defense toward a new awareness of the possibility and desirability of genuine transactions with other sectors—exchanges where no one gets everything, but everyone gets something, and no one is harmed.

The experience of a conflict of broad scope and great cost during the *trienio* was the key factor in influencing elites to avoid such conflict in the future, if possible. On the Catholic side, many of the leaders of the *trienio* opposition appear again after 1958 leading the negotiations and arguing for dialogue and conciliation. They entered the post-1958 period fearing renewed problems for the Church and for Catholic education. However, finding openness and receptivity, they discovered that gains could be made within the system, that the system did not work against them. Methods of action congruent with old expectations and perceptions became inadequate in the new situation. Key elements of Catholic leadership thus entered the situation created by a possible new Law of Education with their perspectives and expectations profoundly altered. Aware of changes in secular and official circles, and of the new opportunities at hand, these persons managed to take and maintain close control over the entire negotiation process, consistently steering it toward conciliation while suppressing outbreaks of open hostility in their own ranks.

141

While the fruits were borne in education, the change was general since it became clear to leaders on all sides that there were limits on what could be accomplished or claimed by anyone in politics—that politics means compromise. This is part of what I have called the growth of a procedural consensus in Venezuelan politics. The core of this consensus lies in the acceptance of common norms and institutions, and in the restraint of partisan hostility. Politics means compromise partly in order to allow people to live together without being constantly at one another's throats. Politics means compromise as it becomes apparent that "more for you need not mean less for me." Transactions and exchanges can replace victory or defeat as solutions to political problems. One of the most common phrases one hears in Venezuela in discussions of the *trienio* is, "we have grown up politically, we have matured as a country." A prominent Catholic layman, long associated with COPEI, put it this way: "Our political immaturity in the 1940's was above all the inability to see the limits of power, and of the need to act in politics according to reason, and not merely emotion."[67]

A leading educator summed it up for AD in similar terms:

The experience of dictatorship and exile helped to mature these groups of leaders [in parties] as it gave them experience in the political life of other countries. It opened our eyes to the fact that in politics events do not obey one's desires. Rather, they follow the real possibilities of power and organization which illuminate the limits of action. Learning the limits of action was a great lesson of exile.[68]

Among Catholic leaders, the new awareness of the potential for compromise and accommodation facilitated the integration of Catholic institutions into the norms and patterns of behavior of Venezuela's party system. It is not that

[67] Interview A-16, February 14, 1969.
[68] Interview B-4-a, January 31, 1968.

142

the Church came to form a political party: quite the contrary. Integration into the party system refers to the Church's recognition and adoption of the methodology of bargaining and give and take, of the importance of organization and organized mass support, of the propriety of leaving political roles and strategies to political parties. The development of new Catholic organizational capacities was accompanied by awareness that they were one sector among many, and therefore bound by the same norms of prudence and compromise that were becoming characteristic of the mainstream of Venezuelan politics.

CONCLUSIONS

In conclusion, it may be instructive to place this case in the context of some general considerations on the political impact of subcultural cleavages.[69] In a recent work on the emergence of competitive political systems, Dahl has suggested three factors which affect the possibility of building successful competitive political orders in fragmented societies. In his view, conflict between subcultures will be moderated to the extent that: (1) no ethnic, religious, or regional group is indefinitely excluded from participation in government; (2) a set of understandings (formal or informal) evolves, that provides a high degree of security to the subcultures; and (3) the regime is effective in meeting demands and solving problems as these are defined by the politically aware groups of the population.[70]

In Venezuela, all three conditions are fulfilled. In terms of participation, the experience of the governmental coalition, and the greater political balance reflected in the decline of AD's old hegemony, have been crucial in shaping the new relations of lay and Catholic sectors, and convincing all sides of the possibility of compromise and concilia-

[69] See Chapter 8 below for a fuller discussion.
[70] R. Dahl, *Polyarchy. Participation and Opposition* (New Haven: Yale University Press, 1971), Chapter 7, especially pp. 114-121.

tion. In terms of mutual guarantees, while these have little formal, constitutional codification in Venezuela, a sense of guarantee clearly exists. Further, the participation of Catholic institutions is solicited and welcomed in planning and decision processes. Here is the real significance of the Law's provisions on participation in planning agencies. Finally, the regime has been effective, both in general and specifically in its educational policies and relations with the Church. The regime opened the doors to cooperation and pushed its affiliates (such as the FVM) to follow suit.[71] In addition, AD governments increased official subsidies to the Church and helped finance expanded programs of Catholic technical education.[72]

The events described here shed some light on the impact of the resolution of legitimacy questions on patterns of political conflict. For, as these questions were settled, and issues of collective survival removed from politics, the setting of Catholic-secular relations changed dramatically. Moreover, while the Catholic sector was integrated into the political system, the system's own norms changed, as part of the general process of social reconciliation. Above all, this case demonstrates the primacy of resolving legitimacy conflicts. Their resolution is a condition of the isolation of any specific dispute. There must be a conscious, general commitment to isolate conflicts, to keep them from spreading and fusing. Such a commitment emerges as part of a more general social and political reconciliation. Only with the settlement of legitimacy conflicts can political motives of concern for stability and institutional continuity take root and help push all sides to concrete actions which build and support that stability.

[71] It is important to remember that accommodation with the Church did not mean abandonment of a general commitment to educational expansion (see Tables 5.5, 5.6, 5.7 above).

[72] Exact figures on this funding are hard to find since it is provided by a variety of ministries. There has been no centralization of such subsidies through the Ministry of Education.

CHAPTER 6

Students and Conflict

CONTEMPORARY Venezuelan students are heirs to a deeply felt tradition of political involvement and struggle. Before the emergence of modern political parties, student organizations often stood alone against dictatorship, repression, and political terror. The tradition of student political action has been modified by recent history, for as political parties developed and organized broadly based mass support, independent student power and hence the possibility of an autonomous role for student organizations, simply disappeared. Students became firmly tied, in ideological and organizational terms, to party organizations.

This is to be expected. For autonomous student power reflects organizational weakness in the rest of society. Where few political groups of any kind exist, any organized group has power and increased political impact simply by virtue of being organized. In such a situation, groups with a limited social base, such as students, may wield political influence out of proportion to their size. But the power of such groups declines with the rise of new political organizations with a broader social base. Students as a political group become tied into broader organizations; they remain visible and vocal, but no longer decisive.

Student politics are considered here as a case study in political conflict, with special emphasis on their integration with national organizations and patterns of conflict. As we shall see, the evolution of student politics in the 1960's cannot be understood apart from the more general conflicts arising out of the exclusion of the Left from post-1958 political arrangements. Party ties became extremely important in student politics because as the nation became polarized into civil strife and open guerrilla warfare, students (like other politically aware groups) lined up in terms of the general struggle.

These concerns dictate an analysis of student politics somewhat different from that which has dominated recent writings. Rather than ask which kinds of students in what types of setting are more disposed to political involvement and activism, I pose these central questions: given the activism of students and student organizations, how is this activism related to national patterns of conflict and opposition, and under what conditions do student organizations wield autonomous power, both per se and as a bloc within more general organizations such as political parties?

Student politics, then, are of concern in terms of norms of conflict, with particular relevance to the evolution of norms governing the isolation of conflict. Among the specific norms most important here are those concerning the use of organizations, the methods of action appropriate to student politics, and the issues appropriate to conflict in the universities. As we shall see, it is only with the defeat of the Left, and its acceptance of the more limited scope and methods of politics implied in post-1958 political arrangements (see Chapter 3), that the extreme fusion of student and national politics could be relaxed. In other words, for students, as for the Catholic sector, the ability and desire to isolate conflict was contingent on the settlement of more general conflicts over legitimacy. Once these conflicts were resolved in some way, the whole relation of students to political parties, the role assigned to students by political parties, and the issues, methods, and resources emphasized in student politics, changed. But I am getting ahead of my topic, and for a perspective on these questions, it may be useful to turn now to the origins of many contemporary situations—the experience of students in the resistance to Pérez Jiménez.

146

PRELUDE TO VIOLENCE

The party based division of students and student organizations begun in the 1940's was consolidated during the decade of resistance to military rule (1948-1958). During this period, *liceo* and university students were the visible spearhead of opposition to the regime. The crucial nature of party affiliation is revealed in the fact that every major instance of student confrontation with the regime found students led by a committee composed (wherever possible) of representatives of the major political parties. Student leaders considered themselves representatives of their parties, and provision was often made for replacing an arrested student with another from the same party.[1]

Inter-party unity characterized student opposition to military rule. At first, this unity encompassed only AD and the Communists.[2] Later, COPEI and URD were brought in. Unity was built from below in a series of joint actions beginning as early as February 1949, when the *comité inter-liceista* led by AD and the PCV directed antiregime actions in the two major *liceos* of central Caracas—the Liceo Andres Bello and the Liceo Fermín Toro. Unity was broadened in the petroleum strike of May 1950 when AD and the Communists called a series of sympathy strikes in *liceos* and universities in support of the oil workers. Cooperation in the petroleum strike, where COPEI and URD, although not officially backing the workers participated at the student level, led to the formation in August 1951 of a Democratic University Front, with representatives of all four parties.[3]

The regime soon provided an occasion for confrontation. In August 1951, the rector of the Central University was

---

[1] This account of student opposition to military rule relies on Doyle, *op.cit.*, Chapter 5, "The University Explodes."

[2] Then and later AD-PCV unity at the student level was often disavowed by AD party leadership in exile.

[3] Miguel García Mackle for AD, Hectór Rodríguez Bauza for the PCV, Luis Herrera Campins for COPEI, and José Vicente Rangel for URD.

sacked and replaced by a man whom the students regarded as a tool of the regime.[4] When classes began in October, the new rector was insulted and shoved by protesting students. A week later, an AD plot to assassinate the entire military junta was uncovered and several armed rebellions by AD groups were put down. The government seized the opportunity to link student disorders with the attempted coup as a pretext for asserting firmer control in the Central University. A general reorganization was decreed, and the administration of the UCV was placed in the hands of a Reform Council, named by the government. In February 1952, the Reform Council dissolved existing student organizations, expelled many students, and liquidated the vestiges of university autonomy. A University Strike Committee called two weeks of strikes and disorders, forcing the Reform Council to close the University.[5] It remained closed for almost two years, and hundreds of students and professors were expelled, arrested, and exiled.[6]

The closing of the Central University, coupled with fierce repression in the country at large, drove all opposition underground. Student political activity did not revive until early 1956, with a strike at the Liceo Fermín Toro in Caracas. From then until the overthrow of Pérez Jiménez, students played a key role in antiregime organization and action. Of the events precipitating the revolution of January 23, 1958, three milestones stand out: a Pastoral Letter of Msgr. Arías Blanco, Archbishop of Caracas (May 1, 1957), which put the Church in opposition; the student strike of November 21, 1957, which shut down the UCV and unleashed a chain of protests, turning many middle-class and professional groups against the regime; and the frustrated

[4] At that time, university authorities were named by the president. After 1958, provision was made for their election by the university community.

[5] In a decree dated February 22, 1951.

[6] See F. Febres Cordero, *Autonomía Universitaria* (Caracas: Imprenta Universitaria, 1959), for a detailed account of the 1951 crisis.

revolt of New Year's Day in 1958, which by revealing divisions in the armed forces, gave hope and renewed impulse to the opposition, whose activities grew in crescendo from then on.

Antiregime planning in the UCV began in early 1957, when a Frente Universitario was established, with representatives of AD, COPEI, and the PCV, to coordinate student actions in the elections scheduled for November 1957.[7] Formal liaison committees were established with the student wings of all political parties to ensure maximum coordination and mobilization. Other student organizations were formed independently in the UCV and the Catholic University, and after some difficulties, contacts were established between all the groups. In early November, the regime announced that the forthcoming elections would be replaced by a plebiscite designed to ratify Pérez Jiménez in office. Plans for a massive protest and strike began immediately. URD joined the Frente Universitario, completing the spectrum of party representation, and after several delays, the strike began on November 21.

Although the strike failed to block the plebiscite, it laid the basis for more extensive opposition actions. Once the

[7] The subsequent careers of members of the Frente Universitario are instructive. Américo Martín (AD) became a member of the National Command of the MIR on the division from AD, later passing on to be secretary general of the party. He was twice elected president of the student federation in the UCV, and became a leading guerrilla commander. At the time of writing, he was in prison. Germán Lairet (PCV) was a student leader and became a member of the Central Committee, the Politburo, and was for some time the FLN representative in Havana. As to their alternates, Hectór Rodríguez Bauza (PCV) was a student leader throughout the period of resistance, was elected deputy in 1958, and arrested with the other leftist parliamentarians in 1963. He is member of the Politburo of the PCV, and is now a deputy again. Hectór Pérez Marcano (AD) was president of the UCV student federation (1959-60), a member of the National Command of the MIR, and is now a leading guerrilla commander. The major *copeyano* member, José de la Cruz Fuentes, has not followed a political career.

New Year's Day revolt showed that Pérez Jiménez did not enjoy undivided military backing, opposition broadened. The Frente Universitario began to send teams of students into the lower-class barrios of Caracas (concentrated strategically on the hills overlooking the downtown area) for agitation and the distribution of antiregime propaganda. The incorporation of the barrios into the struggle, which meant the dispersion and exhaustion of the regime's police in daily battle throughout the hillsides of Caracas, was fundamental to the dictator's fall. Throughout the demonstrations and fighting leading up to Pérez Jiménez' flight, *liceo* and university students were in the vanguard, leading and organizing the protests.

When the regime fell, the Frente Universitario and students in general enjoyed great prestige. Moreover, the continuing disorganization and weakness of the regular party machines, added to the natural confusion that follows the fall of a government, gave effective power to the students. A student leader of the time recalls the role of student organizations in this way: "The political parties at that time were still recovering from the effects of the dictatorship and only beginning to organize again. They were still weak. Thus, because of the respect student organizations enjoyed, and the access they had to the government and the parties, people came to us with their problems from all sectors of society."[8]

A wave of violence against the police and the foreign communities (for their open support of Pérez Jiménez) led to a breakdown of police authority, and in fact, the regular police force was completely dissolved. Its place was taken by "brigades of order," organized by university students in about 550 patrol units, to maintain public order in Caracas. These patrols continued until the end of February, when a new police force was finally organized. A Communist youth leader of the time recalls the prestige of these brigades:

[8] Interview D-15, May 8, 1968.

After the 23 of January, the Frente Universitario is something like the FEV of 1936. Great prestige. The famous brigades of order were formed, and wielded a tremendous power, above all a moral power. The masses, on the barricades. If the police went, they stoned them. They hooted at the military. But when the students came, they immediately quieted down and said, "we will listen to what you say, what do you want?" This power lasted two months, until the parties returned to their level. . . . Then part of the moral power of the Frente passed to the parties, given the fact that its members were also militants of the parties.[9]

Student prestige received a final touch as student organizations, in close coordination with the parties, were crucial in mobilizing public pressure to defeat two attempted coups against the Provisional Government, in July and September of 1958.

By the end of 1958, when Rómulo Betancourt was elected president, student politics can be characterized as follows. (1) The student movement was firmly organized on party lines, and party loyalty and identification was strengthened by the experience of underground resistance. (2) Since the parties remained weak after ten years of repression, student organizations filled the gap and took on exaggerated and unreal importance. (3) The mobilization of the barrios against Pérez Jiménez, and the successful defeat of the July and September coups, reinforced the image of student power. (4) Thus the Frente Universitario looked powerful, much like the FEV of 1936. But the power and the resemblance were artificial since they rested on the temporary disorganization of the parties. As the parties recovered, the power of students per se had to decline. (5) But the image of power remained, and weighed heavily in the planning and execution of the Left's strategy of armed insurrection after 1960.

[9] Interview D-27, June 25, 1968.

151

ORIGINS OF VIOLENCE

After the fall of Pérez Jiménez, the slogan in the university, as in the nation, was inter-party unity. The first elections for student organizations were held on a unity basis, with single slates of candidates composed of representatives of all parties. The party definition of student elections was visible from the outset.[10] At that time, the student organizations at the university-wide level were still considered genuine federations, and their presidents elected indirectly by the presidents of the different student centers (e.g., of the Faculties of Law, Medicine, Engineering, and the like). Hence its name, the Federación de Centros Universitarios (FCU). This indirect system prevailed for the first two elections, after which a method of proportional representation (with party-list voting) was imposed to ensure the presence of all major parties on the Executive Committees of the Centers and the FCU. These procedures gave a final party stamp to university elections.

The new electoral system was formalized on the eve of AD's first major division, when the MIR emerged, dominating the student movement but with little other organized support. The MIR claimed the sympathy of youth, but in fact made few inroads into working-class or peasant youth, which remained firmly embedded in organizations loyal to AD. From the beginning, students had a central role to play in the strategy of the MIR. A founder and high-ranking member of the MIR describes this role:

In the first years of the struggle, this is to say, right after 1960, the universities were to fill two roles. In the first

[10] The first president of the FCU in the Central University was a member of AD. He was elected on the basis of a prior inter-party agreement that allocated the presidency to AD and the vice-presidency to the Communists. Party influence was such that when the Communist candidate was elected, because of the presence of some independents, the election was repeated in order to fulfill the pact. (Interview D-27, June 25, 1968, with Communist youth leader of the time.)

place, the university was to provide leadership cadres for the party's activities in the barrios, the factories, and in the countryside. As the MIR was the dominant force in the universities, it had many student leaders and a good deal of its National Command was made up of students. In the Youth Bureau and other high level organisms, the number of students was quite high. Given these circumstances, from the beginning our National Command felt that the university was the seedbed of leadership, a reserve which had to spread out throughout the country to guide the struggles of the party in the barrios, factories, and in the countryside. . . .

The other role the party reserved for the universities was that of contributing, more than any other sector, to the agitation which the party considered fundamental to the development of our struggle against the regime of Betancourt. . . . What the MIR and the PCV did in 1960, 1961, and 1962 was to cultivate agitation among the students, using this as a kind of guide, a symbol and fixed point for the rest of national opinion.[11]

The weight of students within the MIR was reinforced by the image of student power carried over from the resistance against Pérez Jiménez. The MIR theses on the political role of students were systematized by Humberto Cuenca in an important book on the revolutionary role of the university. Cuenca argued that in revolutionary struggle, students corresponded to an intellectual proletariat: "They must be essentially revolutionary, and provide a link between soldiers, peasants, and workers whose alliance is crucial to the Latin American revolution. The bonds between the barracks, the cities, and the countryside can be woven together by students."[12]

Given the key role of students in giving force to the revo-

[11] Interview E-1, May 21, 1968.
[12] H. Cuenca, "Prólogo Clandestino," to his *Ejército, Universidad, y Revolución* (Buenos Aires: Ediciones Movimiento, 1962), p. 9.

lutionary process and defending it against reactionary coups, Cuenca argued that Latin American universities should provide military training for all students:

> The university is the institution most hated by militarism, which reserves its most aggressive blows for it. Therefore, the Latin American university must prepare to defend itself with arms, not only with intellectual force. All our universities should organize student brigades, according to the conditions of each country. . . . Revolutionary military instruction, given in a dignified and stimulating way, is indispensable to the liberation of all Latin American peoples.[13]

Cuenca and many in the MIR leadership saw the students as a revolutionary vanguard. The original intention of the MIR, however, had never been to rely so heavily (in theory or in practice) on students. Its founders had conceived of the MIR as a socialist party with an urban working-class base. Political circumstances inflated the student role. One founder of the MIR put it this way:

> The intention of the MIR was to project itself to the masses using students as activists, but never intending that these groups should constitute the vertebral column of the party. Our goal was to organize among the working classes, above all the urban working classes. But as the party began to suffer reverses, the role of university sectors, both as activists and sources of funds, naturally increased as the party sought shelter in these sectors.[14]

The crisis of the MIR thus threw students into the center of national politics, propelling them into open conflict and confrontation with the government of Rómulo Betancourt. In general, the impact of the MIR on national politics was enormous. Many saw it as a potent new force on the Left,

[13] H. Cuenca, *La Universidad Revolucionaria* (Caracas: Editorial Cultura Contemporánea, 1964), p. 100.
[14] Interview E-2, November 9, 1968.

with great appeal to the urban masses, above all in Caracas and Maracaibo, the nation's two largest cities. The MIR was born in the shadow of the Cuban Revolution, and the example of Cuba convinced the MIR leadership that revolution was possible:

> The impact the Cuban Revolution exercised on the majority of us, people of little political experience and a lot of youthful enthusiasm . . . had a determining effect, in the sense of orienting our political perspectives of the possible and desirable. These influences, plus the attitude of Betancourt and the conditions we believed to exist in the country for a successful popular insurrection led us to initiate a series of agitations in the student movement and the barrios of Caracas with the goal of creating a climate of confusion which would facilitate a military coup by our sympathizers in the armed forces. This, joined to a popular uprising would overthrow the government.[15]

Almost immediately after organizing, however, the MIR found itself limited, harassed, and kept off the streets. As we have seen, a basic operational guideline of the Betancourt government was to require permits for street demonstrations. Permits were hard to get. Less than two weeks after the formation of the MIR, constitutional guarantees were suspended for 15 days in response to an attempted coup. This meant that the MIR and the PCV were unable to hold public meetings and were denied access to radio and television to comment on the attempted coup.[16] On June 24, 1960, after an unsuccessful attempt to assassinate Betancourt,[17] guarantees were again suspended, this time

[15] Interview E-7, March 19, 1969.

[16] Betancourt was accused by the Left of using right-wing coups as a pretext for moving against the Left. They compared his policy of suspending guarantees and relying on force to that of the Provisional Government, under Admiral Larrazábal, which had relied on mass mobilization against coups.

[17] The attempt was financed by Trujillo, dictator of the Dominican Republic.

155

for 130 days. A leading Communist describes the impact of these restrictions on the MIR:

> For the first time since 1958, people who wanted to condemn a military conspiracy were denied the right to speak. . . . Thus all the visions we had of a powerful ally on the Left, able to speak and organize among the masses—all that was crushed after only ten days. We and the MIR requested permits for meetings and these were denied, on the pretext that the situation was delicate and that we would only confuse it more. And the MIR began to realize that its only remaining weapon was its weekly newspaper, *Izquierda*.[18]

It was the status of *Izquierda* (Left) that touched off the bloody events of late 1960, in which the political role of students received its first sharp definition. The crisis was sparked by the arrest of many of the MIR leaders for an *Izquierda* editorial which the government saw as an open call to insurrection. The editorial actually read as follows:

> Our movement gives voice to the will of the people: change the government. Now the people must tell us how to achieve this goal: by elections or by revolutionary action. Henceforth we will fulfill our duty as *revolutionaries* by telling the people that so far there has never been a system where the dominant classes and their gendarmes have willingly turned over state power to the oppressed masses and their parties. And state power is the tool with which true revolutions are made. The people have the last word![19]

The arrest of the *Izquierda* editors, among them several student leaders, sparked a wave of violent protests. Despite attempts by the university authorities to limit political clashes on campus, the scale of violence obliged them to suspend classes and things quieted down until late Novem-

[18] Interview D-27, June 25, 1968.
[19] *Izquierda*, October 14, 1960.

156

ber when disturbances broke out again on November 21, Day of the Student. These continued, mixing with the violence of a telephone workers' strike, until November 28 when constitutional guarantees were suspended once again. The Central University was surrounded by troops who exchanged fire with student snipers. University authorities then closed and evacuated the UCV and classes did not resume until after the new year. Constitutional guarantees remained suspended for 496 days, until April 6, 1962.

The violence of late 1960 fixed the relation of the Left to the government and clarified the role reserved for students within the overall revolutionary strategy of the PCV and the MIR. A founder and high-ranking member of the MIR describes the role of the students in these and subsequent confrontations:

> As the university combined the sharpest contradictions with the greatest political awareness, logically the party considered it a primary field of battle. Within our tactical plans, the universities were to play the role of vanguard, of spearhead, the sector which engaged in the greatest conflicts and agitated the most. . . .
>
> In our opinion, since the government of Rómulo Betancourt would respond by accentuating the repression, persecuting the entire popular movement of which the MIR was then the vanguard, we foresaw great clashes in the university, with Betancourt trying to put down the student movement by force. Then, the student movement, with its radicalism, firmness and proud heritage of opposition to the government would provide the match to ignite the entire nation.
>
> This was our tactical scheme at the time, and events conformed to it. The university was the focal point of struggle from 1960 to 1963, and held the government of Betancourt in check. Vanguard, detonator, spark: the university filled these roles marvelously in those years.[20]

[20] Interview E-1, May 21, 1968.

If the Left's stance was fixed by the 1960 violence, so too the position of the government crystallized in the crisis. All through 1960, the Left had been calling for a reorientation of the government. The crisis indeed provoked a change, but not the one sought by the Left. Persons most favorable to the Left, and opposed to a policy of police repression of student political actions, resigned from the government.

In response to student violence and the ensuing repression, the Minister of Education (Dr. Rafael Pizani) resigned. His resignation is of great importance since it marked the end of a lengthy effort to isolate the universities and schools from political violence by negotiating pacts between the parties to keep extreme propaganda and violent acts out of educational institutions. In October 1960, Pizani tried to arrange a pact, offering job security for teachers who were members of opposition parties (no political firings) in return for guarantees by the parties to depoliticize the schools. As one might expect, only AD (with little to lose) backed the scheme, while the Left insisted that the schools were an important and legitimate front of antiregime activity. Students were shock troops; classrooms and campuses one front among many in the struggle against what was seen as an illegitimate regime. Pizani, feeling that his position was untenable, tried to resign then and there, but was persuaded to wait. The violence of late November prompted his resignation. With his departure from the government, the hard line within the cabinet, favoring firm repression of disorders by students or anyone else, won out and characterized official policy from then on.

After 1960, the Left faced conditions similar to those it had endured under military rule: gradually its members were expelled from trade unions, its press was censored and driven underground, and its parliamentarians arrested. As the Left suffered defeat after crushing defeat in other arenas, the university in general and students in particular gained political importance. This relation between defeat in other arenas and the growing importance of students is significant, for it repeats, in reverse, the long-term relation between the growth of mass organization and the decline of student power. In the nation, student power is maximized under conditions of institutional disarray and confusion: the aftermath of the death of Gómez or the fall of Pérez Jiménez are good examples. Within a party, student power is maximized as the organization declines in other areas. If a party retains student support while failing elsewhere, it is only natural that it entrench itself in the university, and put a growing proportion of resources into ensuring control of student politics. Student leaders, of course, may then convert this situation into greater power over party policy.

As the parties define their position in terms of a legitimacy conflict (a "war of national liberation," for example) there is growing pressure to line up all arenas in terms of support for the party in the general struggle. The relation perceived by students and party leaders between issues and conflicts in the university and issues and conflicts in the nation will be very strong. General patterns of opposition structure issues and conflicts at all levels. National conflicts are projected into the student arena and student conflicts are defined in general political terms. The student arena then becomes a sort of Spanish Civil War in microcosm, a proving ground where all sides can test new tactics, slogans, and alliances. Powerful linkages between student politics and national politics also lower the chances of evolving and maintaining any regular processes of conciliation within the arena of student politics. Conflicts are defined in terms external to the university; hence, conciliation within it is difficult. Moreover, loyalty to, and concern for the university as an institution in itself are naturally weak: party criteria and party loyalties take priority.[21]

[21] A good example is the attempt of a group of politically independent professors to succeed where Pizani had failed, by securing agreement among the parties to withdraw from the university. Limited agreements were in fact reached, but as might be expected, they could never overcome the powerful integration of all elements of the university community into national political conflicts. A detailed

By the end of 1960, all major parties had formulated a relatively clear role for student political action. The government and AD sought to isolate the university from politics. The Left depended on the university in its revolutionary strategy. To round out the picture, the position of the Christian Democrats must be described. After 1958, COPEI rose from the position of a skeletal organization of limited appeal into a powerful position of rapid growth which made it the largest individual force in the universities, although outvoted by the combined Left. In 1958, COPEI's youth wing had only a few hundred members, and its organization was effectively limited to Caracas. By 1963, it counted over 100,000 members and a national organization reaching into all the universities and most of the *liceos* of Venezuela.[22] In the Central University, although the *copeyanos* were a substantial force, they were overwhelmed by the violent offensive of the Left.

> We were never really prepared for this kind of violence and it crushed us badly. There is no answer to such tactics when used by a majority. A violent reply only increases the total violence which is what we naturally wanted to avoid. . . . We never had a clearly planned and organized strategy of response in the universities. The violence took us by surprise and kept us constantly on the defensive, off balance, seeking above all to survive.[23]

The strategy which finally developed reflected *copeyano* determination to avoid being pushed out of the universities. *Copeyano* students tacitly withdrew from the FCU, falling back on the Centers in the Faculties they controlled, and

---

account of these efforts (with the texts of each party's reply and the "norms of university conduct" formally agreed upon) may be found in René De Sola, *Balance Inconcluso de Una Actitud Universitaria* (Buenos Aires: Ediciones Casasola, 1962), pp. 287-303.

[22] Interview D-2, July 5, 1968, with a *copeyano* student of the time.

[23] Interview D-5, June 5, 1968.

using these as a base for building strength in other Faculties. This effective parallelism, with the Left going one way and COPEI another, never reached the point of a formal division of the student organization and establishment of rival national federations. The Christian Democrats have consistently refused to abandon the existing student organizations, hoping to win control through elections.

Given the strategic importance and prestige of student politics, no party is likely to withdraw permanently. While the Left entrenched itself and COPEI refused to pull out, AD too, despite its proclaimed scruples, doggedly kept on trying to recover lost ground. Throughout the 1960's, AD ran its own slates in student elections at all levels. For example, in the UCV, *adecos* have run their own candidates every year since 1960, except for 1962 when they backed COPEI. In other universities, AD also ran on its own, often retaining a respectable force.

STUDENTS AND THE DECISION TO LAUNCH
AN INSURRECTION

Students were crucial in the strategy and tactics of the Left after 1960. The implications of this role for the use of student organizations and for the scale and direction of student political action are most clearly visible in the genesis and immediate consequences of the MIR-PCV decision to pursue revolution through armed insurrection. As we have seen, the general defeat of the Left made continuing control of the student movement loom larger, and student leaders were able to take on greater power within their parties. A founder of the MIR (then a strong proponent of armed struggle) now feels that the Left was dazzled by its great appeal to students and thereby blinded to the lack of mass support (urban or rural) for an insurrection:

The line of violence and insurrection made us lose support in the masses, and naturally the student leader-

161

ship in universities and *liceos* gained influence within the party, as they appeared as the only genuine leaders, the true revolutionaries, those who never retreated or knuckled under. . . .

One of the factors which made us believe that conditions existed for an insurrection was our complete domination of the student movement. We saw the reality of the country through the eyes of *liceo* and university students, and we forgot that in the working class and the peasantry we had no support—there was absolutely no mass solidarity with the idea of insurrection.[24]

In the developing strategy of the Left, the role of the university as a strong point and source of shock troops was fundamental. As the rhythm of armed action rose, and the first scattered guerrilla units began to appear, students became even more important as a firm vanguard. A MIR leader described this role as follows:

As the repression grew, the role of the university became even more important. As you know, when the masses clash with a regime which responds with force and maintains itself, fear, demoralization and desertion often occur. The masses will advance against a government when they win some immediate successes, and the regime shows symptoms of vacillation, decomposition, or confusion. But when the masses . . . come up against a government which employs all repressive means firmly and successfully, skepticism and fear pervade them, and they retreat temporarily, seeking protection.

At this time, it is more vital than ever to have a firm vanguard, of steel, able to continue fighting so that fear does not infect the rank and file. . . . The MIR and the Communist Party had to entrench themselves in the universities, using the actions of the students, who were

[24] Interview E-7, March 19, 1969.

firmer, more courageous, to counter the demoralizing effect which official repression was producing among the masses.[25]

Continued violence within the university and conflict between students and the government[26] put great pressure on the university authorities of the UCV who resigned en masse on January 27, 1962. The resignations were an attempt to pressure the parties into restraining political action and violence among their students. Once again, the authorities contacted all the parties, asking them to withdraw from the university. Each party responded with a formal statement and the documents were all published in the national press.

For the Left, withdrawal was clearly out of the question. The Communists argued that the government was to blame for the violence—for trying to destroy political freedom in the universities as it already had in the nation as a whole. Hence, any solution for the violence had to come from the government, and not from the students or the parties of the Left. The MIR was even more explicit:

The present university situation reflects a general crisis in the nation, produced by the anti-national and anti-democratic behavior of the present regime, a crisis affecting all Venezuelan institutions. A struggle has been joined because the government, just as it has attacked other institutions, wants to turn our highest institution of learning into a submissive university. It is disturbed by the

[25] Interview E-1, May 21, 1968.
[26] In the month of January 1962, according to an official communiqué, 19 persons were killed and 110 wounded in street fighting. A total of 1,053 persons were arrested throughout the nation. Américo Martín, of the MIR, president of the FCU in the Central University, was arrested as were other leading university figures associated with the Left. Primary and secondary schools were shut down on January 20, to avoid injuries to students, and the UCV followed suit, closing on January 24.

163

present university, where the people's struggle for liberation finds resounding echo.[27]

For AD, the resignations of the university authorities provided an occasion for further definition of the party's position on the need for separating student organizations from national political conflicts. AD argued that direct political action by students was unjustifiable in a stable, democratic regime, and incompatible with the academic functions of the university. Political action should be concentrated in explicitly political vehicles. Party spokesmen put the argument clearly:

> Under dictatorships, when all paths of dialogue and political action are closed, our universities like all cultural and scientific institutions, justifiably assume the defense of democracy. The history of our universities is rich in struggle against armed barbarism. But in democratic regimes, political and ideological currents have sufficient channels in the parties, and in turn, these find sufficient scope for action in the citizenry, the parliament, and the mass media. Direct political action—given the tension and antagonisms it arouses—is incompatible with the atmosphere of serenity, reflection, and civility which must prevail in educational institutions.[28]

The events of early 1962 crystallized what might be called the "Left-student" and "official" images of the university. Student leaders denied responsibility for the crises, throwing the blame on official provocation. They argued that students had the right and duty to respond in kind to official violence. This position was the concrete expression of a doctrine embodied in the FCU motto: "Struggle and Study" (*Luchar y Estudiar*). In an important synthesis of this doc-

[27] In *El Nacional*, February 18, 1962, signed by Simón Sáez Mérida, general secretary of the MIR.
[28] In *El Nacional*, February 18, 1962, signed by Rául Leoni, Jesus Angel Paz Galarraga, and Amado González, respectively president, general secretary, and secretary of education of AD.

trine, a Communist student leader argued that students were inescapably woven into national politics, explicitly rejecting the thesis of concentration and compartmentalization espoused by AD.

Merely to study is to deny an unavoidable obligation, whose fulfilment is both necessary and possible. Those who call on students to withdraw from politics are really trying to remove a powerful force for national transformation. . . .

They want to make politics into the private business of the "insiders"; those who control power, those who monopolize the media, those who direct determinate "machines." And just as exclusive dedication to classes is demanded of students, workers are told to concentrate on their work, peasants to devote themselves entirely to cultivation. . . .

No genuinely national interest can be invoked to justify students' abstaining from a prominent role in politics. Because they are the heralds of progress and national liberation, and these are the goals which Venezuela must conquer.[29]

The regime clarified its stance in a full-page advertisement in the national press on February 15, 1962, entitled: "The National Government Replies to the Communiqué of the Communists and Their Satellites in the Central University." After reviewing the recent violence, and noting that the government had respected university autonomy by never sending troops on campus, the communiqué accused the Left of violating the spirit of autonomy:

Within the University City crimes have occurred, crimes subject to laws beyond the shelter of university autonomy. University autonomy can under no circumstances provide immunity for criminals. The University City of Caracas

[29] Freddy Muñoz, "FCU, Estudiar, Luchar: Un Lema que Define Una Conducta," *Cultura Universitaria* (October 1963-March 1964), 158-159.

165

has been used by outside groups and by those who call themselves students or student leaders as a general headquarters for crime, with the goal of converting our primary center of higher learning into a base for terrorism and insurrection. . . . The university has become an arsenal, a veritable fortress for insurrection against the democratic system, a rebellion conceived in, and wholly executed from the offices of the Federation of University Centers.[30]

University authorities were subjected to great pressure to enact stringent control measures within the university, but this pressure was consistently rejected, on the grounds that the university had to remain open to all groups. Although the resignations were eventually withdrawn and classes were resumed, the underlying crisis was not so easily resolved. Tension, violence, and the entrenchment of the Left in the universities became even greater as large-scale guerrilla warfare emerged.[31]

Universities became of even more critical importance for the Left after November 1962 when student organizations in the *liceos* were suspended for an indefinite period.[32] Draconian regulations were promulgated and enforced to restrict violence and political activity in the schools.[33]

[30] "El Gobierno Nacional Replica al Comunicado de los Comunistas y sus Satélites en la Universidad Central," *El Nacional*, February 15, 1962.

[31] The difference between the "official" and the "Left-student" image of the university clearly falls along these lines. The government wanted student politics to be *student* politics, limited in scope and relevance to explicitly student concerns. The Left replied that facing an illegitimate and repressive government, student concerns could only be those of national liberation. These opposed images of the university help explain why student politics in the 1960's cannot be understood apart from the conflicts arising out of the Left's challenge to the entire political system.

[32] *Liceo* student centers were suspended after the shooting of a teacher, Daniel Ramírez Labrador, during a political demonstration in his school, the Liceo Juan Vicente González, in Caracas.

[33] Remember that this came along with the government's dismissal of many leftist teachers.

166

Access to school buildings was strictly limited to the students and staff of that particular school. School principals were given broad powers of expulsion for political activity, indiscipline, or undue absences. One principal threw out the entire executive committee of the student center. A student government in exile was established.[34] The *liceo* student organizations had been important sources of agitation and future leadership, and their suspension, which lasted until mid-1966, was a damaging blow to the Left.

STUDENT ROLES AND THE USE OF STUDENT ORGANIZATIONS

So far, I have emphasized the role political parties attribute to students and student political action. It is worth pointing out that the party perspective is fully shared by student leaders. A recent study of conflict and consensus in Venezuela included a sample of university student leaders. The results highlight the salience of political roles for these leaders. Student leaders demonstrated one of the highest rates of political participation of all sample groups. In the six months prior to being interviewed, 77.2 percent had attended a political party meeting, 98 percent had discussed politics with a friend, 36.6 percent had engaged in a strike, and 67.5 percent had done active work for a party or candidate.

Of all groups sampled, student leaders were second in attendance at political meetings, second in work for a party or candidate, and first on participation in strikes. The great importance of political roles is highlighted by the sources of information about politics upon which respondents relied. Among sources regularly employed, student leaders listed the commercial press (83.2 percent), political party newspapers (64.4 percent), and political party meetings (63.4 percent) in the top three positions. But when asked

[34] The expulsions were for physical violence against teachers. Interview B-10, August 21, 1968, with Ministry of Education official.

which source was most trustworthy, 52.7 percent named political party meetings, followed far behind by the commercial press, named by only 14.2 percent.[35]

These responses reveal the importance of party organization as a source of information and a channel of communication for student leaders. What is the impact of such powerful party identities and loyalties on the role of student organizations in national politics? If conflict is defined in essentially political terms, and different arenas and levels of action are fused on unitary lines of opposition, then the problems treated by student organizations, the methods of action favored by student leaders, and the communications structure of the arena will all depend on the status of the conflict dividing society as a whole, and not on particular issues that apply to the university alone.

As long as political conflicts are defined as questions of institutional legitimacy, conflicts at lower levels will be locked in step. As pressure grows to choose sides in the nation as a whole, the party definition of student roles will grow, and communication and information within the arena will be increasingly limited to party channels. Direct contact and cooperation between political groups is low.[36]

The problems emphasized at the student level become exclusively political, methods of action are conceived in terms of their relation to national conflicts (e.g., tactical support of or opposition to the guerrilla movement), and communications are funneled through the channels of party organization. However, if the general legitimacy questions are resolved, then political organizations can relax the rigid fusion of arenas: they can define a functionally specific role

[35] CENDES, *Estudio de Conflictos y Consenso, Série de Resultados Parciales, No. 4 Muestra de Líderes Estudiantiles* (Caracas: Imprenta Universitaria, 1967), p. 63, Table 3.

[36] Communication is increasingly through party channels. For example, direct contact between student organizations at different universities is rare: contact is between members of the same party at different universities, and is usually arranged through party organizations. See Chapter 7 below for a full discussion.

for student organizations, emphasizing student problems and grievances; they can de-emphasize methods of action involving students in open political confrontation with the government; and intra-university cooperation can have a chance to work.

Consider the consequences of a legitimacy conflict for student organizations. For the Left, the use of student organizations was determined by the general strategy of insurrection. The role given to student organizations was primarily political: to aid and support the "war of national liberation." A MIR youth leader argues that,

Since the emergence of what we might call the most important historical event since Independence, that is, the appearance of armed struggle as the certain path to winning political power, naturally changes have occurred in all legal organizations. I don't mean that it was necessary to put all legal organizations—the FCU, the CUTV, etc.—on a war footing. But it was necessary to maintain a more firm, more effective attitude, and contribute more to the general line of the popular movement: armed struggle.[37]

UNIVERSITY STUDENT ELECTIONS

The importance of students to the parties, and the unreality of university politics—in the sense of a lack of correlation between the balance of forces in the university and in the nation—are revealed by comparing the course of student elections with the political evolution of the nation as a whole. The dimensions of importance and unreality come out in the strong left-wing control of student organizations compared to their miniscule strength in the nation. We have already seen how and why the Left entrenched itself in student organizations. The effort was rewarded in the votes.

[37] Interview D-17, July 17, 1968.

169

During the 1960's, university student elections were polarized between the Left (the MIR, PCV, and a shifting group of minor parties) and COPEI. Table 6.1 summarizes the results of student elections in the three most important public universities.[38]

Figures 6.1, 6.2, and 6.3 offer a graphic view of the difference between party strength in the universities and in the nation. As you will see, AD's student vote came close to its national vote only in 1967, when there were no elections in the Central University. Excluding the UCV, of course, means taking over one-half of the nation's university students out of the picture. Since the MIR never participated in a national election—founded after the 1958 election, it boycotted the voting in 1963 and 1968—I have made what is probably an overgenerous estimate of its initial vote potential.[39] Abstention from student elections (total

[38] Figures for 1960 and 1961 are for the UCV only. Data were unavailable for other universities for those years. Figures for 1967 exclude the UCV, which held no elections in that year. The results are totals for the elections for president of the FCU in the Central University, the University of the Andes, and the University of Zulia. Figures are rounded off to the nearest whole number percentage. This Table is intended as a summary, and results are given only in percentages. Percentages do not come to one hundred because of rounding and the presence of a number of invalid votes in some years, notably 1960, 1961, and 1962. Detailed election results for the Central University, the University of the Andes, and the University of Zulia, for the 1960-68 period are given in Daniel H. Levine, "Patterns of Conflict in Venezuela" (Ph.D. dissertation, Yale University, 1970), Appendix II, pp. 361-383.

[39] To give the most generous estimate possible of the national strength of the PCV-MIR, I have used for 1958 the PCV congressional vote (6.23 percent) which was almost twice the vote for president (3.23 percent). The 1968 Communist vote represents the votes going to the UPA congressional candidates. No presidential candidate was run on the UPA line. For the MIR, I have projected their vote by multiplying the number of congressional seats the party controlled by the vote quotient needed for a seat. The full quotient undoubtedly exaggerates the vote potential. I took the PCV vote as a base— 160,791. With this vote, the PCV had 7 deputies and 2 senators. The quotient for senator is approximately 3 times that for deputy. Hence, dividing the PCV vote by 7 plus 6 (2 senators), yields a quotient of 12,368. At the outset, the MIR had 15 deputies and 1

TABLE 6.1

Elections for President of Student Federations, National Totals
(in percentages: 1960-68)

Party	Year								
	1960	1961	1962	1963	1964	1965	1966	1967[a]	1968[a]
MIR-PCV	59.6	51.4	50.8	51.5	50.0	49.7	46.8	40.6	60.1
COPEI	38.9	37.8	43.7	39.7	33.7	37.0	40.3	37.2	38.2
AD	—[b]	9.8	2.1[c]	5.4	11.8	11.7	12.9	20.5	1.7
Other	—	—	3.4[d]	3.5[d]	4.4[e]	1.5[e]	—	1.6[f]	—
Total Votes N =	8,837	11,018	19,439	18,181	17,751	20,730	23,475	8,479	28,596

[a] Although the MIR and PCV ran separate slates in these years, their total votes are together here for comparability
[b] In 1960, UCV elections came just before the MIR split and hence, the votes for AD were MIR votes
[c] Allied with COPEI in the UCV and ULA
[d] PRN in 1962 and 1963
[e] FND in 1964 and 1965
[f] VPN in 1967

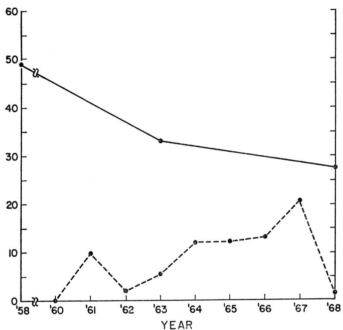

FIGURE 6.1

Acción Democrática National
Vote and University Vote
(in percentages)

——— PERCENTAGE NATIONAL VOTE (PRESIDENT)
------ PERCENTAGE UNIVERSITY VOTE (UCV, ULA, LUZ)

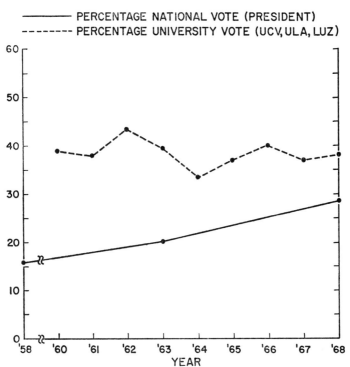

FIGURE 6.2

COPEI National Vote and
University Vote
(in percentages)

——————— PERCENTAGE NATIONAL VOTE (PRESIDENT)
--------- PERCENTAGE UNIVERSITY VOTE (UCV, ULA, LUZ)

FIGURE 6.3

The PCV-MIR National Vote and
University Vote
(in percentages)

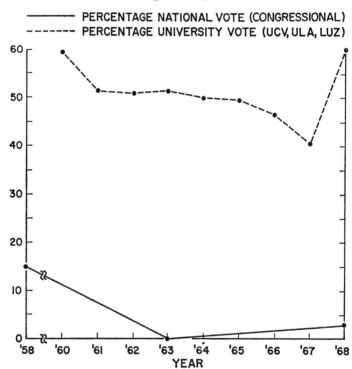

enrollment less total vote) has averaged about 30 percent in recent years. The lowest abstention came in 1961 (23 percent) and 1962 (19 percent), when the sharp national crises made university elections especially salient.[40] The graphs provide data only for the three major parties. URD, which took over 30 percent of the national vote in 1958, 17.5 percent in 1963, and 11.85 percent in 1968, has never run its own candidates in any university.

CONCLUSIONS

Many analyses of the political role of students attribute activism to generational factors of immaturity, rebelliousness, or irresponsibility. Students, it is argued, are shielded from assuming the consequences of their actions. Hence, they develop a style of political action which is ideological and utopian, given to total solutions and the rejection of compromise.[41] The irresponsibility argument, like others that rely heavily on generational factors, is inadequate. It reduces political factors like organization and ideology to a residual status, making political action dependent on a vague and elusive level of maturity.[42] But if ideology, organization, and political discipline are to be taken seriously for other groups, why not for students, where their importance is so obvious?

Students in Venezuela have a clearly defined political role. This is true both from the perspective of the parties and from the point of view of student leaders, who define

---

senator, and hence 15 plus 3 (the 1 senator), which multiplied by the quotient yields a total vote projection of 222,624, or 8.63 percent, which added to the Communist vote gives a total of 14.86 percent for 1958.

[40] Abstention data are not given in Table 6.1 since figures for enrollment are not available for the latest years.

[41] For an example of this kind of analysis, see William Hamilton, "Venezuela," D. Emmerson, ed., *Students and Politics*, p. 378.

[42] For example, see Robert E. Scott, "Student Political Activism in Latin America," *Daedalus* (Winter 1968), 83.

their roles in political terms. The definition of a party role for students and student organizations reinforces the powerful linkage of arenas and levels of action as issues, methods, and possible solutions in student politics are set at a supra-student level—within the political parties. These linkages imply that student organizations, and students as political actors, find their role primarily in their relation to more general legitimacy conflicts. To understand the full implications of this relationship, the following chapter examines the integration of students into party organizations.

CHAPTER 7

Students and Conflict: The Role of Political Parties

A USEFUL way to grasp the full meaning of party-student linkages in Venezuela is to take a close look at the place provided for students within regular party organizations. Through an examination of these structural ties, this chapter will describe the organizational bases for the fusion of student and national politics. The impact of these ties on the structure and scope of conflict, and the pattern of change beginning in the mid-1960's, will be explored through the study of several key issues.

The organization of youth in general, and students in particular, is of concern to every party. Students are the party's future elite, its seedbed of leadership. Moreover, strength among students and success in student elections confer prestige and a youthful image on the party.[1] All political parties in Venezuela begin to enroll members in their youth wings in the first year of secondary school—that is, at ages 12 to 14. Some even begin with primary school students, although this is still rare. In COPEI, for example,

> We begin to organize students in the *liceos* beginning from the first year, that is, from twelve to fourteen years old. This organization is carried out through the party

[1] In addition, students have often been the most disciplined and solid base of support for party leadership. For example, a high PCV leader told me that as differences with the MIR and Fidel Castro grew sharper, the role of youth in support of party leadership was crucial: "The attack was very strong, backed up by all his [Castro's] great prestige. But we were able to hold the youth on our side. Thus, of course, we could not be broken, nor could the party be divided." Interview D-27, June 25, 1968.

organization, and the party tie remains paramount throughout the students' career. Here in Venezuela, the fact of party membership is fundamental and cannot be denied. Everything is built on this foundation.[2]

Enrolling in a party youth wing is the beginning of a lengthy experience in party work, ideological and doctrinal training, and specifically student activities. The parties try to combine work in the youth wing with general party work in order to provide their rank and file with a broad range of political experience. COPEI sponsors a series of formal courses on doctrine for potential leaders, along with strong emphasis on practical party work.

In addition to formal training, the party uses study circles, above all in the interior of the country, where the university students conduct them. Study circles are held at the local level, and are designed to test the capacities of local youth leaders through a series of discussions and a program of active participation in party affairs. There is a sort of hierarchy of courses in this respect, and as one rises in this hierarchy, he is given greater responsibility in the party—progressively higher posts on a local, regional, and national scale. . . .

Our youth leaders take part in all aspects of party work, from organization and speeches in the barrios of Caracas to fund-raising or the distribution of propaganda in the interior. We deliberately provide a variety of experiences within the party because we want to form our membership not in a closed circle with no perspective other than the university, but rather with broad experience and understanding of all kinds of party activity and national problems.[3]

Party organization, then, begins early, and every attempt is made to reinforce the salience of the party tie whenever possible. Student elections in secondary schools are

[2] Interview D-5, June 5, 1968.   [3] *Ibid.*

held on party lines. Moreover, most parties reinforce their control by trying to direct their *liceo* graduates to universities where the party needs strength or has particular leadership gaps to fill. The Christian Democrats, for example, encourage students to enroll in public universities, rather than private institutions whose political importance is much lower.[4] For other parties, like the MIR, the process is more elaborate, as careful attempts are made to place potential leaders in key universities. According to a MIR student leader in the UCV:

This depends to a great extent on the situation in the different universities. As to leaders, we always try to orient potential university leaders to universities where we need them most. We have tried to concentrate the majority of our forces here in the UCV, as the UCV is the most important of all our universities, and has strategic importance given its location in a key city of almost two million people.[5]

Finally, some parties encourage their rank and file to enroll in the university of their region, pursuing in this way a balanced distribution of forces rather than a concentration of strength in any one institution. A national youth leader of the MEP describes his party's policy:

We are beginning to establish an orientation policy to direct our rank and file toward particular universities. This will be done through a series of organizational bridges which will encourage *liceo* students of each region to enroll in the university of that region. Our policy is not to concentrate our forces in one university, like the MIR or the PCV, but rather to concentrate students of a given area in the university of that area. . . . In addition, we also try to orient students entering *liceo* to particular schools. All the parties do this. For example, in Caracas

[4] Interview D-4, April 8, 1968, with *copeyano* student leader in the Central University.
[5] Interview D-16, May 14, 1968.

179

COPEI has seven big *liceos* where it is strong and well organized. Three of these are Church-run, and four are public.[6]

Early organization, extensive orientation, and the high visibility of student politics even at the secondary school level mean that many students are, in effect, university political leaders before they enroll in the university. In Venezuelan universities, each *curso* (students in the same year in the same field, following a common program) elects a delegate to represent it and handle any problems or grievances that may arise with professors or with the administration. From the very first year, these delegates are elected from competing party slates, usually made up of former *liceo* leaders.

The intensive effort at party organization and the involvement of student leaders in party affairs gives deep significance to party membership. If we look at the political careers of the presidents and vice-presidents of the FCU in the Central University, the importance of party ties for the students, and of student leadership as a springboard to party leadership, stand out. All the leaders elected for AD (or later for the MIR) from 1959 to the present are now either national leaders of the MIR, commanders of guerrilla columns, or both.[7] Freddy Muñoz, the first Communist president of the FCU, was arrested shortly after his election, and then imprisoned for four years on charges of military rebellion. He was exiled in late 1968 and returned to Venezuela

[6] Interview D-19, April 17, 1968.

[7] Hectór Pérez Marcano, president of the FCU in 1959-60, was a founding member of the MIR National Command, and is now a guerrilla commander for the MIR. Rómulo Henríquez, the FCU president in 1960-61, is now a professor in the UCV and member of the MIR National Command. Américo Martín, the FCU president in 1961-63, was general secretary of the MIR and commander of a guerrilla front. He is now in jail. Julio Escalona, president of the FCU in 1964-66, was national secretary of the MIR Youth. He left the UCV in the middle of the academic year of 1966 to join a guerrilla front in the eastern mountains.

in 1969. He has been a member of the Political Bureau and in 1971 joined the Movimiento al Socialismo (MAS), product of the latest split in the Communist Party. The other Communist presidents, Juvencio Pulgar and Alexis Adam, both hold high positions in the party organization and were key figures in the structure of UPA.[8] The *copeyano* vice-presidents have also had political careers of national importance.[9]

It is important to remember that in Venezuela's universities, no contradiction is perceived between the roles of student leader and political party representative. Student leaders fill both roles simultaneously. The strength of party ties, indeed, implies that political and ideological bonds normally outweigh generational solidarity as a motive for action. Students of different parties have more in conflict than in common. The results of this are visible in the parallelism characteristic of Venezuelan student life: the *copeyanos* going one way, and the Left another. In the UCV's University Council, the three student delegates (one each elected for COPEI, the MIR, and the PCV) rarely present a unified student bloc. There is no prior coordination of positions between student representatives. Voting in the

[8] Juvencio Pulgar, the FCU president in 1966-68, has been a student leader in the UCV since 1958 in a variety of positions. He was national secretary of organization of UPA, and was elected deputy in the 1968 elections. Alexis Adam, president of the FCU from 1968 to 1970, was national youth secretary of UPA, a candidate for deputy in 1968, and is a member of the Central Committee of the PCV.

[9] José de la Cruz Fuentes (1959-61) is not active in politics. Hilarión Cardozo (1961-63), has been a deputy since 1963, and in 1963 served COPEI as coordinator of electoral strategy. He is a member of the national committee of COPEI and was named Governor of Zulia in 1971. Alvaro Páez Pumar (1963-64), has been a deputy since 1963 and is a member of the national committee. Joaquín Marta Sosa (1964-66), was a member of the regional committee of COPEI in Miranda from 1963 to 1965, and then a member of the national directorate of the JRC. Abdón Vivas Terán (1966-68), was national secretary of the JRC. Delfín Sánchez (1968-70) is still a student in the UCV, and is a member of the national directorate of the JRC.

181

Council more often reflects political blocs, joining students with deans of their party. I have spent many mornings in the antechamber of the University Council, and it is remarkable to see the three student delegates, each in a different corner of the room, each surrounded by aides and fellow party members, each with his own group of reporters.

The coordination of students with party organization is normally a two-step process. Students are enrolled in the party's youth wing, which in turn is one of the component structures of the party. Most parties have a variety of national organizations—a trade union wing, a women's front, a teachers' movement, a youth wing, and the like. These functional groups usually have national structures which parallel the regular party structure and which are integrated with it at all levels. Thus, for example, district, regional, and national youth organizations are represented on the executive committees of the district, regional, and national party organization. The national secretary of a youth wing would be a member of the national executive committee of the party.

The Christian Democrats ensure coordination in two ways. First, the youth wing (JRC) coordinates with the party through its elected representatives in the party leadership at all levels and through a variety of specific agencies. For example, there is an electoral secretary of the party and an electoral secretary of the JRC. Within the youth wing, student affairs are handled through a university department and a department of secondary education. In addition, the regular party organization (as distinguished from the JRC) names a coordinator of university affairs, whose task is to ensure cooperative action between the *copeyano* students, faculty, and employees at different institutions. Although organizational details differ, the basic procedures are common to most parties.[10]

[10] The only party to provide a structurally autonomous organization for its youth movement is the PCV. The Communist Youth is a totally separate group, enrolling its own members and handling its

182

Party control increases where the national impact of decisions is greater. Thus, student actions in the Central University are coordinated with party organizations at a national level. Politics in the Central University are of national importance, and hence coordination takes place at the highest possible level of party authority. For example, the Communist Youth has two separate university bureaus, and two separate bureaus for secondary education. The first is for the Caracas area (the UCV and the Caracas *liceos*), and is directly responsible to the National Secretariat of the Communist Youth. The second set of bureaus depends, in organizational terms, on the respective regional committees. Decisions and policy for students of the Caracas area are thus handled by the national party leadership. In several parties, the youth secretary for the Caracas area has special status, reflecting his greater political importance. When I asked a high official of the MEP's Caracas Youth Section who was responsible for party affairs in the different universities, he replied by naming students of each of the three provincial autonomous universities, and for the Central University: "me."[11] He is not a university student.

In provincial universities, students are coordinated through regional party structures. At the University of Zulia in Maracaibo, where COPEI controlled student organizations from 1962 to 1968, the vast majority of contacts between student leaders and the regular party organization were at the regional level.[12] A *copeyano* leader at the Uni-

---

own finances. Linkages with the parent party, are, of course, strong, both in ideological and personal terms. Leaders of the Communist Youth are often members of the Central Committee and even of the Political Bureau. But the Communist Youth itself is a distinct organization.

[11] Interview D-20, July 16, 1968. During the interview the respondent was on the phone with his representatives in the University of the Andes, giving them instructions on how to handle negotiations over electoral alliances.

[12] Interview D-28, February 6, 1969, with *copeyano* leader in Zulia.

versity of the Andes describes the situation in this way: "Here in Mérida the dependence of the fractions on the local party is greater than in Caracas. . . . COPEI is more controlled here than in Caracas, and the same is true for the PCV."[13]

In this way, coordination is strongly institutionalized in the party structure. Coordination between students at different levels also works through party organization. *Liceo* students are organized and their actions oriented through special party bureaus of secondary education, and not through contact with university students of the same party.

These bureaus are usually elected, in a hierarchical process of internal party democracy. Each level elects delegates to the next, leading to a national youth conference. Depending on the party, this body either elects a general secretary, or suggests candidates for that position to the national party leadership. This pattern is reproduced within the universities, where each party maintains an organization (a "fraction"). Elections begin with base committees at the *curso* level, which elect delegates to local committees (schools), who in turn elect commands for each Faculty. The Faculty commands meet to elect an overall university command, with a general secretary, who is the key figure in the daily management of party affairs among students. Each party holds regular all-university conferences, in which the entire membership can discuss problems of the university, the party, and the nation. The university-wide structure of each party ensures coordination of students with other university groups affiliated with the party, such as professors or workers who are usually, though not always, organized in a parallel fashion. For example, COPEI, while it has designated persons responsible for coordinating the actions of *copeyano* professors, has not yet formally organized these professors into fractions. Hence, these coordinators are named by the party, and not elected by the professors as an organized group—as is the case for students.

[13] Interview D-9, September 10, 1968.

This elaborate control apparatus is designed to ensure that student decisions agree with overall party strategy and tactics. No party, however, need control everything its students do—it simply is not all relevant to party needs. As we have seen, party coordination operates and party discipline is imposed primarily on issues with a large public impact— strikes, elections, major demonstrations and rallies, and the like. In these matters, students lack independent power of decision, and the criteria of the party hierarchy prevail. For example, participation in student elections, above all in the UCV, is of national importance. Thus, great attention is devoted to the selection of candidates and to electoral strategies, tactics, and alliances. In the early 1960's, the joint Left slate in student elections was chosen as follows:

> The national commands of both parties always participated. The following procedure was used: the university bureau of each party, the PCV and the MIR, consulted with the commands of each Faculty and with students of each Faculty as to possible candidates for FCU and for the Executive Committee of each Faculty's Student Center. Once the list was complete, the University Bureau presented it to the National Youth Bureau . . . the National Youth Bureau would study this list and approve or modify it as necessary. Then the "purified" list went to the National Political Command [of the MIR]. If the National Political Command agreed, it called on the National Political Command of the Communist Party to begin negotiations. . . . The two party commands then made the final choice of candidates.[14]

Student organizations, then, are rarely autonomous bodies: they act and react in party terms. In no case is it reasonable to expect, *a priori*, deep differences between students and their parties. After all, they chose to be members of that party. Party affiliation is of fundamental importance,

[14] Interview E-1, May 21, 1968, with founder and former high officer of the MIR.

and student political action must be seen in the context of party. To ignore party means asking the wrong questions, and ultimately leads to a misunderstanding of the dynamics of student politics. In this vein, a recent analysis of Venezuelan student politics misses the point by considering student actions apart from party membership and identification. William Hamilton argues that students tend to assume the role of "critic":

> The role of critic is of course quite consistent with the image of the political student, but there is reason to doubt that students have much real influence in the process of program formation in the parties. In the first place, all the major parties, including COPEI, have elaborate and well-established ideological programs. Changes in these programs are made through formal procedures in which the relative influence of the youth wing is small. In the case of the parties actually responsible for governing, their primary concern must be with the necessities of day to day policy decisions; this concern is reflected in the fact that AD student leaders claim little or no programmatic influence for themselves.[15]

A more reasonable conclusion might be that AD students claim no influence because they have no strength within the party, nothing to bargain with, no leverage. Since 1960, AD's youth wing has been shattered by a succession of divisions, each one drawing off a majority of the students then associated with the party.[16] The case of COPEI is also relevant. Although *copeyano* students are strong, the party, like AD, is powerful in many areas, and hence the relative position of students within the party cannot be dominant. In contrast, we have already seen how the influence of students

---

[15] William Hamilton, *op.cit.*, p. 377.

[16] The MIR took the vast majority of AD students in 1960. The bulk of those remaining were captured by the ARS group in 1961. Then, in 1968, the MEP split took almost all the student strength built up through years of hard work in *liceos* and universities.

grew in the MIR and the PCV, as these parties were gradually decimated outside the universities. Clearly, the crucial variable is the political weight of students within their parties, and not some mythical "maturity" to be attributed to *adeco* students, by virtue of the sobering effects of governmental responsibility. In any case, AD, like other parties, exercises a strict control over what few students it still attracts. A high official of AD's National Youth Bureau describes the autonomy AD grants its student wing: "There is not a single decision of any importance—elections, alliances, candidates, attitudes to strikes, etc.—which is taken by university or *liceo* groups on their own. All these are reviewed by the National Executive Committee and its specialized bodies such as the National Youth Secretariat."[17]

The Impact of National Change: Communist "Rectification" and the Universities

The loyalties binding students to political parties provide a structural basis for the fusion of conflicts. Different arenas and functional spheres are bound together on party lines. Hence, conflict anywhere carries, in potential, conflict everywhere. Party structures and party loyalties, however, provide only a potential basis for fusion. They are insufficient in themselves to guarantee this type of conflict. In other cases, we have seen that as long as general legitimacy questions remain unsettled, the isolation of any specific arena is difficult and improbable. With this in mind, it is clear that the isolation of conflicts among students depends on the prior resolution of legitimacy questions in the nation.

If general legitimacy conflicts were resolved, we might expect profound changes in the use of party-student linkages. A party might pursue a more functionally specific role for its students, playing down previous concentration on students as the vanguard of revolutionary struggle. Basic

[17] Interview D-21, August 13, 1968.

187

changes would then occur in the kinds of problems treated by student organizations, the methods of action deemed appropriate, the relative power of students within parties, and the perceived relation of student conflicts to national patterns of opposition.

A case in point is the impact on student politics of Communist "auto-criticism" and "rectification." As we have seen, this process began in 1964 with doubts about the strategy of protracted armed struggle, and ended with total withdrawal from guerrilla warfare and renewed efforts at electoral competition. As the Communists began to reconsider the value of armed struggle, their view of the university began to change. A Communist youth leader describes this reassessment:

> Strong debate began, above all in the Communist Party, in 1964. What role should be given to the university? What can the university do? What is the purpose of the university? Is it merely appendage—is it a party, or of the parties? Or does it have a specific mission to fulfill, aside from that of political vanguard? In this way, two basic functions were outlined: that of political support, the duty to agitate, to be a vanguard; and the specific mission of being a center of culture and learning.[18]

These two roles had always been present in the university: "I don't mean to say that they did not exist before, but rather that in the period of civil war, from 1962 to 1964, for reasons of historical necessity, or because of the blindness of one or another group, the cultural role had been obscured, and the specific function of the university had disappeared under a purely political covering."[19]

Looking for a way out of the blind alley of armed struggle, the PCV came to reject the idea of vanguards of any kind "making" the revolution. Students, who had filled the

18 Interview D-27, June 25, 1968.
19 *Ibid.*

vanguard role, found their position sharply reduced, both in revolutionary theory and within the councils of the party. A Communist professor (also a high-ranking party official) described his party's reorientation as total:

> We have realized that a vanguard is simply not enough, and that a long and difficult effort of basic organization among the working classes is needed for success. In projecting ourselves once again toward the popular masses, we are now reducing the relative weight of students in the whole of our actions. This weight will be lower because: (1) given the objective conditions of a milder repression in the country, other forms of action can be carried forward freely, which has not been the case up to now; and (2) there has been a conscious decision by the National Command of the party to act openly and to seek the broadest possible basis of support. This means a great extension beyond the university.[20]

The MIR naturally rejected the PCV's new line on national and student affairs as a betrayal of revolutionary principles. To *miristas*, the correct line remained the fusion of student organizations with armed struggle. The "sure path" to national liberation remained guerrilla warfare; the "sure path" in the university continued to place students in the forefront of revolutionary action and confrontation with the government. The MIR students were soon fighting on two fronts: against the government on the one hand, and against revisionism and conciliation in the Left, on the other. A MIR student newspaper *Joven Patriota* (*Young Patriot*) put it this way:

> There is no struggle, be it political or purely for the presentation of student grievances, which does not find our student organization in the front lines, not only opposing imperialist infiltration of education, and the drive to liquidate student organizations, but also in the struggle

[20] Interview C-24-b, June 11, 1968.

against conciliatory positions which try to castrate the traditional combativeness of the students, restraining their struggles and thus putting the student movement at the service of a policy of accommodation to the interests of the ruling classes. . . .

Can the combative student movement be expected to agree that the "correct line" is the abandonment of armed struggle? Can the students be fooled by a "correct line" of hanging onto the tail of the dominant classes, begging for legality and adapting to the "requirements" of the government for participation in the "free democratic process"?

The false revolutionaries are mistaken if they think they can lull the student movement with their siren songs and ideological contraband. The students know that the true correct line is: STRUGGLE TO VICTORY.[21]

The MIR-PCV differences on the student level first surfaced in the Central University elections of 1966. Several years before, the two parties had signed a pact providing for alternation in the presidential candidacy of the joint slate of the Left. Although a Communist, Freddy Muñoz, was elected in 1964 and re-elected a year later, most of his term in office was spent in prison, and his alternate was a *mirista*. Thus the MIR had, in effect, held the presidency since 1960. Hence, the Communists argued that it was their turn to have the presidential candidacy. The MIR refused to go along, alleging that Communist "revisionism" (i.e., withdrawal from the armed struggle) had altered political conditions and invalidated the original pact. The MIR demanded a consultation of the "masses," to let the student body decide who should represent the Left.

This consultation took advantage of the two-stage nature of Venezuelan university elections. Elections are first held

[21] *Joven Patriota, Organo Nacional de la Juventud del MIR*, IV Epoca, No. 1 (June-July 1968). "Struggle to Victory" (*Luchar Hasta Vencer*) is the motto of the FALN.

for delegates to Faculty Assemblies, student representatives on Faculty Councils, and to the *Claustro*, the body that elects university authorities. Students get one delegate for every 40 enrolled students, and these delegates are elected from party lists. Then, normally about a week later, elections are held for the student organizations themselves, for the Student Centers of each faculty, and for the FCU. According to the MIR proposal, the parties would compete in the first round, and the one getting the most votes for *Claustro* would lead the unity slate against COPEI in the second round.

The Communists agreed reluctantly to these conditions. In the end, however, they won the vote, and the Left ran a Communist for president and a *mirista* for vice-president. The 1966 elections mark a turning point in the Central University (and by extension in student politics for the nation as a whole) as the Communists, once in control, set about implementing their new line. Communist leaders see this election as an about-face in the FCU's style of action. The MIR students agree completely, naturally viewing the changes in a critical light, as a betrayal of the revolution:

> The principal characteristic of these changes is precisely the reflection of revisionism on the university level, the fact that most student struggles have been and are limited, restrained, and liquidated by them. . . .
>
> The revisionists fear any deepening of struggles. They are always seeking some pretext, some argument to oppose these struggles. . . . All the recent history of the student movement shows that whenever a proposal is made to deepen the struggles, the PCV has argued for caution, waiting for better conditions, for the best opportunity, the proper moment, and the like.[22]

The changes the PCV has imposed in university affairs reflect its altered stance in the nation. The Communists

[22] Interview D-17, July 17, 1968.

realized that their entrenchment in the universities and overreliance on a student vanguard had been self-defeating. To escape from that trap, to survive and participate once again in national politics meant reorienting student organizations and moreover using them as a springboard for new contacts on the national level. In the universities, the PCV had imposed a new style of action. Communist leaders felt that, under the control of the MIR, the student organizations had become isolated. By refusing to deal with any one who did not back armed struggle, the MIR had cut student organizations off from potential allies and from fruitful contact with the masses. Moreover, they believed that many students had been alienated by the purely political stance of the FCU. Thus, after gaining control of the FCU, Communist student leaders put heavy emphasis on the resolution of concrete grievances and the widening of FCU contacts with other sectors and organizations.[23]

There has been a corresponding change in tactics. The Communists' basic goal was to avoid provocation and repression, and one means to this end lay in reducing the violence and relative importance of student political actions. The Communists sought to put politics back into strictly political channels (e.g., parties and elections) and returned organizational emphasis to broader social strata—rebuilding trade union or peasant strength, for example. In this vein, the PCV now avoids tactics which lack a payoff in mass terms. Thus, the tactic of paralyzing the national educational system through strikes or protest actions is set aside:

> We can paralyze the entire educational system of the country at all levels whenever we choose. But the fact is that we have realized that the policy of using the educational system in this way has been a policy without benefits. The tactic followed in the years of 1960 to 1963 of

[23] Interview D-23, November 13, 1968, with a member of the post-1966 executive committee of the FCU in the Central University.

192

paralyzing education very often *brings no political bene-fits and does not affect the relations of power in any way.* Rather than give results, it merely ended causing us more problems. Now we are trying to restrict the activities of the *liceistas* largely to the presentation of student griev-ances. Our goals in the *liceos* are less immediate action and pressure, than building a reserve of militants for the future while extending the base of our organization in all areas.[24]

As we have seen, the methods of action students employ are in line with the national tactics of their party. Party discipline is often imposed to restrict the methods that mem-bers of the student wing may use. A brief description of several strikes and student actions will help illustrate the operation of party discipline and bring out even more clear-ly the difference between parties in the methods of action they authorize. Changing methods, resources, and styles of action all reflect changing norms of conflict.

A good example is the student battle against the Regula-tions on Repeating Students (the RR). The RR were pro-mulgated in the Central University in 1964, and limit the number of times a student may repeat a given subject be-fore being required to leave the university. Before 1964, there were no guidelines on this matter, and a student could remain enrolled indefinitely. The RR established that any student who had to repeat more than one subject twice could not enroll in the same school again for four years. He could, however, enroll in another school within the University.[25] However, if once again he had to repeat more than one subject twice, he would be barred from any school in the University for four years.

[24] Interview C-24-b, June 11, 1968, with high official of the PCV (italics added).

[25] It should be remembered that admissions policy in Venezuelan universities is handled at the level of individual schools and faculties. The RR were an attempt to institute some kind of university-wide standard.

The first attempt to implement the RR was met by a "General and Indefinite Strike," supported by all major parties—one of the few instances where all political interests felt equally threatened. The strike lasted almost two weeks, but since the authorities refused to yield, it was called off and the RR, at least in theory, were applied on an all-university basis.[26] As a practical matter, the RR have never been applied on a uniform basis throughout the University. Some Faculties enforce the regulations and some do not, and to my knowledge the University Council has never sanctioned noncomplying schools or Faculties.[27]

Nevertheless, the RR remain a potent issue, as many students regard them as unfair and purely punitive. Since the theoretical imposition of the RR, significant differences have emerged, above all within the Left, over the best way to continue the struggle. The Communists have favored small-scale actions, yielding small but concrete gains. The MIR has argued for massive mobilizations to force university authorities to yield. A Communist propaganda flyer emphasizes these strategic differences:

[26] The theoretical application of the RR has been a cause of relief to many North American scholars who have written on Venezuelan student politics. Seymour Lipset, in "University Students and Politics in Underdeveloped Countries," *Comparative Education Review*, 10, No. 2 (June 1966), 132-162, saw it as an example of diminished student power. Hamilton, *op.cit.*, believes that "largely because a significant segment of the student body believed the rule a necessary step in the improvement of the University, it appears finally to have been successfully implemented" (p. 382). There is absolutely no evidence to support this proposition.

[27] In December 1969, after another crisis in the UCV (with an extended military occupation), a proposal for reforming the Law of Universities was introduced in the congress, co-sponsored by AD and COPEI. Among the proposed reforms is a strict definition of "regular students," those counted for enrollment and voting purposes. The following kinds of students were excluded from this category: (1) repeating students; (2) those who although having passed all their subjects, have still not taken a degree; and (3) those who are enrolled in a program totaling less than half the courses of a normal program. See *El Nacional*, December 24, 1969.

194

Our position has been and will continue to be struggle for victories and not defeats, victories no matter how small or partial, seeing them as part of a process which sensitizes and involves the bulk of students now absent from the struggle. . . .

To avoid massive confrontations for the moment, without discarding them as a resource, is what the very dynamics of the struggle counsel. We need hard work to prepare for confrontations in the best possible conditions, where we have a good chance of victory. Any defeat, no matter how small, undermines the fight against the RR and strengthens its supporters.[28]

A second case is another "General and Indefinite Strike," this time at the University of the Andes, in May 1967. The ULA Faculty of Medicine tried to impose a numerical limit on admissions (*cupo* in Spanish).[29] Students have long argued against the *cupo* as a denial of constitutionally guaranteed rights to study. They have pressured universities to accept all *liceo* graduates who wish to enter. A General Assembly of Students, again with all parties represented, agreed to strike. In the words of a MIR leader, "At first, everyone agreed, including the PCV. But later, they became afraid and as the struggle began to deepen, they started to limit and undermine it, to the point that once they, along with COPEI and AD, began to attend classes again, to break the resistance of the students, we had to call off the strike. This meant the establishment of the *cupo*."[30]

The national leadership of COPEI directed its students

[28] *Luchar Contra el RR, Si. Pero Hacerlo en las Mejores Condiciones y Sabiendo Utilizar Oportunamente Las Formas de Lucha Más Adecuadas.* Mimeographed propaganda flyer of the University Bureau of the Communist Youth. (My copy, no date.)

[29] The Faculty of Medicine in the University of the Andes argued that by admitting fewer candidates, it could graduate a larger absolute number of doctors, by being able to give each one a better education.

[30] Interview D-17, July 17, 1968.

195

to stay away from the mass demonstrations organized by the MIR. The Communists also shied away from such tactics, calling for a "new style" of action, one which would achieve settlement without confrontation, through private, high-level talks with the university authorities and political forces. The Communist's "new style" merited this comment from one leader of the MIR: "The 'new style' of which the revisionists speak consists precisely of this: they avoid mobilizations of the masses and try to treat problems through conversations and negotiations, leading to solutions imposed from above, rather than through mobilizations of students and energetic public demonstrations of the kind we have always promoted."[31]

Since the strike, conflict between the PCV and the MIR has grown more pronounced, and differences in political style more salient. These are the kinds of differences one might expect between a party committed to revolutionary war and another party trying to get out of revolutionary war and back into the mainstream of the political system. For the former, no university or student issue can be seen in a limited context. They serve above all as pretexts for mobilization and politicization. For the latter, settlement of problems on the university and student level becomes both feasible and desirable, as the linkage between student and national politics is consciously played down. The MIR accuses the Communists of revisionism, cowardice, and defeatism. To *miristas*, the Communist "rectification" is nothing more than a tacit acceptance of the rules of the game of bourgeois-democratic politics as played in Venezuela. The PCV for its part labels the MIR as a band of terrorists, "anarco-adventurers," and "petit-bourgeois radicals," glorifying violence for its own sake and driving the Left to total defeat and liquidation.

A final example of these differences comes from one of the most severe crises the Central University has faced in mod-

[31] Interview D-18, September 6, 1968, with a MIR leader in the University of the Andes.

ern times, the official closure of the UCV and its occupation by thousands of troops and police on December 14, 1966, an event known among Venezuelans as the *allanamiento*.[32] The *allanamiento*, which lasted almost four months in all, is fundamental for the subsequent political status of the universities, and for the general role of students in politics. The events of those months present a complex and often confusing panorama, worthy of book-length treatment.[33] The discussion that follows is selected and limited, using the *allanamiento* mainly to highlight inter-party differences over methods and styles of action.

In the fall of 1966, there was a sharp upswing in guerrilla activity and urban terrorism. Responding to the wave of violence, a prominent COPEI Senator, Dr. Edecio La Riva Araujo, gave two speeches denouncing the use of the Central University as the general headquarters and arsenal of the guerrilla movement. He argued that university autonomy had been turned into a shield for subversive action, distorting the administrative and intellectual core of autonomy until it constituted an effective guarantee against police action, making the UCV campus a refuge for criminals and a secure base for terrorist operations—everything from car theft to bank robberies and assassinations.

These denunciations, combined with a series of terrorist acts culminating in the assassination of a high military official and a near-miss attempt on the life of the chief of the Joint General Staff on December 13, 1966, prompted the government to suspend constitutional guarantees and order military occupation of the UCV the following morning.

The government was determined to make a permanent change by modifying the legal status of university autonomy. Official spokesmen argued that the maintenance of

[32] The word *allanamiento* refers literally to a police search. Thus it normally requires a warrant issued by a judge.

[33] The only attempt at a complete analysis of the *allanamiento* is J. Sanoja Hernández, *La Universidad: Culpable o Víctima?* (Caracas: Fondo Editorial Venezolano, 1967). This is a good general review from the Communist perspective.

public order in a university is a governmental function, and tried to distinguish administrative and academic autonomy from the inviolability of university grounds.[34] Another Decree issued on December 17 provided that maintenance of public order in a university should be the responsibility of the state and that roads within the university be public thoroughfares. Up to that time, police needed a specific search warrant to enter the campus, and traffic through University City was restricted and controlled by University police. These Decrees restricted the effective sphere of autonomy to University buildings, laboratories, classrooms, and offices, and permitted the police to enter the campus at any time, with no further formalities.[35]

The political parties lined up as might be expected. AD of course supported official actions,[36] arguing that autonomy had been prostituted by the extreme Left, converting the UCV into a tactical strong point of revolutionary war. AD described the UCV as one point of a subversive triangle, the other two being the rural guerrilla fronts and Castro's Cuba.[37] COPEI was deeply divided. While the bulk of the

[34] Article 6 of the Law of Universities states that the university campus (recinto) is inviolable. This had traditionally been interpreted as barring police entry without a specific warrant.

[35] The UCV suffered another allanamiento from October 1969 to January 1970. This crisis led to proposal and enactment of far-reaching reforms to the Law of Universities. The major reforms were: (1) prohibition of the re-election of the rector (and provision for executive removal of rectors who fail to comply with the provisions of law); (2) imposition of stricter auditing procedures on university budgetary operations; (3) tightening the legal definition of "regular" students (see note 27 above); and (4) redefinition of the meaning of autonomy along the lines pursued by the Leoni government in 1967. These reforms were approved by Congress and rejected by the UCV authorities. The Congress then named a provisional university council, headed by the Minister of Education. The rector, Dr. J. M. Bianco, resigned in protest, and in late October 1970, the UCV was occupied once again by the police and National Guard. At the time of writing (early 1971), it remains closed.

[36] There was some dissent in the youth wing, above all in Caracas.

[37] Jesus Angel Paz Galarraga, "Universidad Autónoma y Democrática," La República, February 3, 1967.

party, and especially its high command, supported the *alla-namiento* as a legal and politically necessary move, many *copeyanos* felt that the government would use the intervention merely as a weapon with which to inflict a political defeat on the University.

For the Left, military occupation of the UCV was a damaging blow, both for immediate tactical reasons and in the long-run as well. The Communists argued that the *allana-miento* was illegal and that subsequent decrees regulating university autonomy violated the spirit and letter of the Law of Universities. Communist spokesmen also attacked the MIR and the Douglas Bravo group,[38] who by their provocative acts of unnecessary terrorism, had stimulated the government to a damaging and seemingly indefinite occupation of the campus. In an underground edition of *Tribuna Popular*, the PCV posed the case in these terms:

> The present situation is marked by grave dangers for the university. These range from capitulation without resistance to the plans of the enemies of the university and of progress, to the adventurist and leftizing excesses of those who see no other way out than engaging again in methods which the revolutionary movement, and specifically Marxist-Leninist doctrine, condemn, and which so far have been the pretext used by the government and the national and foreign reaction for striking against the democratic and autonomous structure of our national universities. Both dangers must be fought courageously, without vacillation, but with care; firmly, but with the flexibility that circumstances require. A revolutionary, above all a revolutionary fully dedicated to intellectual tasks, cannot be dogmatic and inflexible.[39]

January and February of 1967 were spent in negotiations between the government and the university, and in public

---

[38] The Douglas Bravo group was then in the process of challenging the orthodox PCV leadership and splitting off from the party.

[39] *Tribuna Popular, Organo del Comité Central del PCV*, VI Epoca, Avance No. 7, February 28, 1967. (My copy.)

199

and private discussions of the proposed Partial Regulations of the Law of Universities, some key provisions of which are described below. On February 20, troops left the campus and classes resumed. Immediately, massive antigovernment rallies were held protesting the *allanamiento* and the proposed Partial Regulations. The rallies were organized primarily by the MIR, and ended in the destruction of a fence that the government—at the request of University authorities—had built to separate the University Hospital from the rest of the campus. The fence was originally intended to allow the hospital to continue functioning and receiving patients, regardless of political upheavals in the University as a whole. But it had become a primary symbol of governmental occupation, and students (led by the MIR) proceeded to tear it down. COPEI and the PCV opposed this action as an unnecessary risk and provocation, and those *copeyanos* or Communists who participated were either suspended or expelled from their party. To the MIR, the Communist attitude was just one more example of the PCV's unwillingness to go beyond verbal forms of action in opposing the government. The destruction of the fence and the general atmosphere of tension and violence led the University authorities to suspend classes on February 24, and the UCV remained closed until March 13, when classes finally resumed in a climate of continuing tension. From this time on, debates within the Left over proper methods of struggle have dominated student politics.

Argument centered on how to combat the new Partial Regulations of the Law of Universities, which altered the legal status of the universities and imposed limits on propaganda permissible on the campus.[40] The MIR favored ener-

[40] The conditions of political propaganda were stipulated as follows:

In university classrooms and facilities or during the course of any activity carried out with teaching goals, and excluding the free study, academic analysis, or exposition of philosophical doctrines, no activity or propaganda for political parties or favoring doc-

getic mass actions to mobilize popular support for the student position: through visits to factories, barrios, and the like, in a general antiregime campaign. To *miristas*, the negotiations which led to the resumption of classes in February had masked the abject surrender of the University to the government. Only the firm action of students (destruction of the fence) had prevented total betrayal. In a statement published on March 10, 1967, the MIR student leaders analyzed the situation as follows:

> The government "collaborated" by withdrawing troops and police from the campus; seeking to remove concrete motives for student protest but reserving the right to send them again whenever necessary. A sector of the press collaborated with a great display of stories emphasizing the "great normality in the UCV" prior to the reopening, laboratories working at full steam, professors preparing classes, and the like.
>
> It was all a plan to suffocate student protest, blindfolding public opinion and the students. But none of this resulted. The students, demonstrating a high level of patriotic and university awareness joined the struggle and demolished the plans of the conciliators and of the government.[41]

One of the tactics proposed by the MIR was a series of short strikes and stoppages, combined with a refusal to take examinations. Those who favored taking examinations were attacked as cowards and traitors. The *miristas'* greatest scorn was reserved for the argument that such tactics might

---

trines contrary to the principles of nationality, democratic order, or which offend morality and good customs, may be carried out.

Article 3 of Decree Number 753, published in the *Gaceta Official de la República de Venezuela*, February 17, 1967 (No. 28.262). The Decree itself is dated February 14, 1967.

[41] "Remitido: Julio Escalona, Jorge Rodríguez, Carlos Muñoz, y José Enrique Mieres Opinan Ante los Estudiantes y el Pueblo de Venezuela," *El Nacional*, March 10, 1967.

cause loss of the academic year. This was labeled "save-the-yearism." They believed that any vacillation caused by fears of losing the academic year would lead to defeat:

> Insistence on an absolute incompatibility between saving the academic year and fighting against the Partial Regulations and for an autonomous and democratic university, hinders the development of a victorious movement. It is insincere with the students, and consciously or unconsciously aids the "save-the-yearist" offensive, not to state clearly that the struggle may require supreme sacrifices and that students must accept these as conditions of victory.[42]

The MIR position is significant since it reveals a desire to retain strong linkages between levels of struggle, both in terms of the definition of issues (as legitimacy issues, with efforts directed against the regime) and methods of action (emphasizing confrontation and violence). Factors specific to university life, such as the danger of losing the academic year, take a back seat to general problems of conflict and opposition. Struggle in the university must involve direct confrontation with the government, drawing as many sectors as possible into a broad front of revolutionary opposition.

The Communists rejected such tactics, fearing to provoke renewed military occupation of the Central University. As we have seen, they had become reluctant to push students into actions demanding unnecessary danger or sacrifice. To the Communist student leadership, the FCU's desire to move the struggle outside the confines of the campus while strengthening it within required avoiding internal complications. The Communists, in a now-favorite phrase, denounced the MIR strategy as "anarco-adventurist," involving needless and damaging provocations. They characterized the MIR philosophy as *"the worse—the better"*:

[42] *Ibid.*

They try to pose every student action in terms of all or nothing. . . . If the university is occupied, all the better, as the government will be discredited. If the government intervenes, and students and professors are expelled and harassed, all the better, this way there will be more who struggle. . . .

To think that a movement in retreat will benefit by provoking blows from the enemy is not to realize that this only serves to demoralize the movement.[43]

For the Communist Party, the fundamental goal of auto-criticism and rectification was to get out of the guerrilla movement and break the political isolation of the Left. The universities had a key role to play in this strategy. After opening up student organizations in 1966, and rejecting violence and confrontation in the *allanamiento* and other crises, the PCV began to use the student arena as a source of new contacts on the national level, looking toward eventual participation in the 1968 national elections. A national Communist leader describes the PCV's university strategy:

We prefer not to stand out in the voting, and would rather unite with other forces against COPEI and AD . . . the phenomenon of alliances is politically more interesting than merely getting more or fewer votes. It yields no immediate advantage, but the policy of alliances is for the future, and for other things, not merely students. This also reflects on the policies of the political parties themselves. . . . Our success has been, along with our allies, in breaking the isolation which the dominant classes have tried to impose on the Communist Party. This is indispensable for us.[44]

The new Communist line got its final touches in the 1968 UCV elections. The PCV and the MIR completed their

[43] Pedro Ortega Díaz, "Las Elecciones Universitarias," *Documentos Políticos*, No. 11, May 31, 1968, pp. 9, 11.
[44] Interview D-27, June 25, 1968.

break by running separate and opposed slates in both rounds. The Communists led a "Progressive Front," joining with the PRIN, several micro-parties, and some independent groups. The MIR supported a "Patriotic Front," headed by a member of the Christian Left (recently expelled from COPEI), and also incorporating the followers of Douglas Bravo, the guerrilla commander recently expelled from the PCV.

The electoral campaign was a bitter one, marked by notable differences in style and focus between the two leftist slates. The MIR concentrated on ideological issues and problems, trying to stimulate discussion of international, national, and university problems, insisting on their close and necessary interrelation: cultural imperialism, guerrilla warfare, Vietnam, the *cupo*, and other issues. The Communists, on the other hand, ran a campaign based heavily on dances, games, and exhibits. One of the key elements in the new Communist campaign was the use of discothèques. I offer this only as an example of how much things have changed in Venezuelan student politics. One of the MIR leaders in the University of the Andes complained to me that "The Communist Youth tries to use hippy methods to capture votes. Thus, in the last elections here they applied the technique of discothèques they had used in the UCV. For us, the use of discothèques is simply incompatible with revolutionary principles and revolutionary methods of action."[45]

The 1968 UCV elections were a disaster for the MIR. They got only 3,780 votes for *Claustro*, dropping further to 2,467 in the second round. These 1,300 votes went almost entirely to the Communists, whose total rose from 7,304 in the first round to 8,432 for president of the FCU. The COPEI vote was relatively stationary, moving from 6,447 for *Claustro* to only 6,875 for the FCU.

The MIR's defeat in the Central University—more sig-

[45] Interview D-18, September 6, 1968.

nificant politically than victory in any other university[46]—
seems to reflect a trend in student politics, with the bulk of
students accepting the new Communist line with all its implications: abandon guerrilla struggle and violent confrontation, reorient student organizations and reduce their political salience, and move toward electoral participation in
the nation. The *miristas'* own explanation of their defeat is
significant, for it reveals starkly the extent to which, for the
MIR, everything is tied to the fortunes of war, the outcome
of the guerrilla struggle. A MIR student leader reflects at
length on the electoral results:

> In effect, it might seem a contradiction that organizations
> like our own, which we consider truly revolutionary, have
> experienced in practice a kind of stagnation, at least in
> the UCV, and they, nevertheless, have experienced an in-
> crease. This truth cannot be denied. To what can we
> attribute this? There is one important, overriding reason,
> and that is that the national perspectives of the MIR, the
> strategy the MIR outlines, is a strategy of sacrifice.
>
> We are saying something very simple which is at the
> same time very complex. We are saying that the perspec-
> tives for taking political power are difficult in the short
> run, that what is needed are supreme efforts, sacrifices,
> concentration on our work—not only for immediate short-
> term solution of our own urgent problems, but also for
> more general goals.
>
> Here the only way to capture political power is by the
> path of armed struggle. And to say armed struggle is to
> say a difficult and complex path. . . . We have outlined a
> strategy of protracted warfare and tactics which allow us

[46] The results in the University of Zulia and the University of
the Andes are also interesting. In Zulia, a coalition of everyone (from
Right to Left, excluding only AD), managed to wrest control of the
FCU from COPEI after 7 years of social-Christian domination. In
the University of the Andes, a MIR-led slate defeated both COPEI
and AD, as well as a slate made up of the PCV, MEP, and a host
of minor parties.

not merely to resolve concrete, short-term problems, but also to discover through practical experience, that such solutions are themselves mere palliatives for the problems we confront.[47]

The significant fact is that although the PCV now dominates student organizations as never before, the relative weight and importance of students within the party has been consciously reduced, as the new line is implemented at all levels. Seeking reincorporation into the general political system, the Communists have adapted to its rules. By lowering the political salience of students, rejecting vanguard theories of revolution, and concentrating their efforts on renewed mass organization and elections, the PCV tacitly agrees to the fundamental criteria of power imposed since 1958: mass organization, organized consent, and votes.

CONCLUSIONS

In Venezuela, many speak of projecting the university toward the masses, of taking it out into the streets (*sacar la universidad a la calle*). It is a slogan with many meanings. To the Communists, breaking out of isolation is crucial. To take the university into the streets has meant to show the nation that the PCV is still alive, and that with the vigorous support of students, the party can recuperate and advance. To the MIR, taking the university into the streets has meant using it as a spearhead, a vanguard in the legal political struggle, its fortunes tied to and its actions wholly coordinated with the illegal armed struggle.

These differences reflect fundamental changes in the structure of Venezuelan student politics in recent years. Changes in the structure of conflict in the nation as a whole—the resolution of legitimacy conflicts—have led the PCV to relax the rigid fusion of conflicts characteristic of the early 1960's.

[47] Interview D-17, July 17, 1968.

The crucial change is normative. The party abandons a style of action which rigidly fuses issues, conflicts, and solutions in all arenas, and seeks instead an autonomous, *sui generis* role for its university cadres. The organizational linkages which provide the concrete basis for fusion of course remain. They are a permanent feature of the political landscape. What changes are the norms of political conflict, as the defeated party accepts the prevailing guidelines as to conflict behavior, and abandons its direct challenge to the overall legitimacy of political institutions.

I argued earlier that the imposition of a party system in Venezuela has meant the concentration of political action in specifically political vehicles: parties become the principal vehicles for the expression of political conflict. They monopolize politics. With this in mind, it seems clear that in the broad sweep of Venezuelan development, the power of students as autonomous political actors has declined. Student power is essentially a traditional form of power. It is at its height when other social forces are unorganized or in disarray. But when mass political parties emerge and take hold, and the distribution of power comes to depend on popular organization and elections, it is only natural that the power of students per se should lose relevance.

It is ironic to consider, then, that the most self-conscious revolutionaries are those who remain wedded to a traditional power base. A fine epitaph for any discussion of student politics in Venezuela has been provided by Domingo Alberto Rangel, founder and first general secretary of the MIR. Rangel recently wrote that the Venezuelan Left has been kidding itself for years, thinking it had the support of youth while its influence never spread beyond the narrow circle of *liceos*, technical schools, and universities: "The parties of the Left in our country have no ties with youth. This statement will surprise many. But it is true. The Left enjoys prestige among students, but is unknown among working-class youth, or the youth of the barrios. Our young

207

proletariat and the barrio youth only sporadically experience the impact and attention of a party of the Left."[48]

The MIR calls its ex-comrades "revisionists," and accuses them of abandoning revolutionary principles to seek a place within the "rules of the game" of bourgeois politics. The MIR is of course correct. But the MIR is being liquidated, both nationally and among students, while the rules of the game—the procedural norms, criteria of power, and the institutions they reflect and support—have emerged strengthened from a lengthy and severe test.

[48] Domingo Alberto Rangel, "El Destino de las Izquierdas," *El Universal*, December 5, 1968. Many scholars have made the same mistake, speaking of the alienation of youth from the existing political parties when what they mean is the alienation of students. A good example is F. Bonilla, *The Politics of Change in Venezuela: Volume II*, 113, where the author discusses the alienation of youth from the elite.

CHAPTER 8

Conflict, Organization, and Change

THE preceding chapters have looked at a complex set of experiences. At this point, it may be useful to move toward synthesis, bringing a more general and unifying perspective to the analysis of Venezuelan political processes. One way to approach this integrating task is through examination of the alternative political models presented to Venezuelans in this century. These have been four in number: a Gómez-type regime, a military-technocracy, a revolutionary system, and the democratic-reform model embodied in the present party system. These alternatives may be compared on four dimensions: basic criteria of power, fundamental organizational vehicles for control and mobilization, basic methods of political action and power transfer, and dominant social attitudes to conflict and opposition. (See Table 8.1.)

The Gómez regime was not a traditional political system. Its power and legitimacy did not stem from traditional criteria of custom, inheritance, or divine sanction. It was basically a government in business for itself, using the power derived from a strong export sector (oil) to impose its will on a weak domestic economy and fragmented social structure.[1] The Gómez system was maintained by pure force. But force itself was weakly institutionalized, for the entire system pivoted on the dictator himself, not on the military institution per se. The currency of power was control over terror and violence. The organizational vehicles of control were the army and the state machine. The funda-

---

[1] Such regimes are referred to by K. H. Silvert as "mercantilistic authoritarianisms." See his "Leadership Formation and Modernization in Latin America," *Journal of International Affairs*, 20:2 (1966), 318-331.

TABLE 8.1

Alternative Political Systems in Venezuela

| Systems | Dimensions | | | |
	Criterion of Political Power	Key Organizations	Basic Political Methods	Attitude to Conflict
Gómez	Force	Police-army	Terror	Reject
Military-Technocracy	Force	Army	Intra-military consultation	Reject
Revolutionary	Mass mobilization	Single party	Mass mobilization	Reject
Democratic-Reform	Votes	Multiple mass parties	Elections—bargaining	Accept

mental method of political action was official terrorism, and the response to conflict and opposition was simple and straightforward: repression.

In a military-technocracy like the "New National Ideal" of Pérez Jiménez, power lay in the military institution. Conflict and opposition were vigorously suppressed as democratic politics were officially considered a drag on material progress and efficiency. The organizational vehicle for control and mobilization was the army. Political action hinged on bargaining and consultation within the military institution. Pérez Jiménez fell from power partly because of his failure to live up to (even these) norms. As his regime degenerated into open terrorism, and even military officers became subject to arrest and torture, the dictator's fundamental base of support, a unified military, rejected him.

The revolutionary model, embodied in the program of the guerrilla movement,[2] would presumably have converted Venezuela into a one-party state, more or less on the Cuban model. Power would then rest in the single party, and be allocated in accordance with conformity to revolutionary

[2] The program of the FALN is outlined in P. Medina Silva and N. Hurtado Barrios, *Por Qué Luchamos* (Caracas: 1963).

goals and policies. The organizational vehicle for control and mobilization would of course be the single party. The fundamental method of political action would be mobilization through the party machine—continuous mass participation at all levels. Conflict and opposition become by definition counterrevolutionary, and hence fit subjects for repression.

In the democratic-reform model, the currency of power is organized mass consent—votes. The organizational vehicle of mobilization and control is the mass political party, but party competition is built into the system so that the wide variety of functions and powers assumed by the single party in a revolutionary system does not hold. Rather, the basic method of political action and power transfer is electoral competition. Strategically placed groups with a shallow social base (such as students) lose power as a premium is placed on mass organization. This is the only model of the four which provides social and institutional room for conflict and opposition, building them into its operating rules.

In this century, Venezuela has moved from a regime of the Gómez type, through a period of increasingly institutionalized military control (from López Contreras to Medina Angarita and Pérez Jiménez, with a brief respite from 1945 to 1948), to a situation of stable democratic institutions. Attempts to reimpose military rule have been defeated, as has the drive for revolution through guerrilla war. This sequence of developments raises some important questions. Why has Venezuela's political system changed in this particular way? To what extent is the Venezuelan experience parallel, comparable, or generalizable to that of other nations? The argument so far has emphasized the emergence of a new set of rules governing political behavior—a method for the management of conflict. But why was it possible to impose a new set of rules? What are the social and political conditions of success in so risky an enterprise?

211

A careful look at the evolution of Venezuelan social structure and political organizations may yield some clues. Three dimensions are central to understanding the development of the present political system: (1) the nature of social structure and the relation of forces predating the emergence of modern mass political parties; (2) the pattern of conflict resulting from the encounter of existing power groups and institutions with new challenging groups; and (3) the way in which such conflicts were managed, if at all. These dimensions are closely interrelated, as the form of conflict management of course varies according to the origins and content of the conflicts themselves. The first two are more restricted in scope, as the content or the issues of conflict depend on the particular historical experience of a nation. The management of such conflicts, however, has often taken a common form in widely varying instances. To assess and generalize about the Venezuelan pattern of conflict management, two factors must be taken into account: the content of the settlement and the consequences of the settlement for subsequent patterns of conflict. Posing the problem in this way moves analysis beyond the detailed examination of any one national history (preexisting social structure—the encounter of new organizations with existing power groups—and the nature of ensuing conflict) to the more general problem of how a society deals with its conflicts and builds institutions to control them.

As we have seen, Venezuela before 1936 was in many ways a social and organizational vacuum. Important changes began under the Gómez regime, and the work of administrative and political unification was accomplished through terror and violence. But the social structure remained weak. As used here, the "strength" or "weakness" of a social structure has referred to the number and kinds of bonds tying people to existing groups and institutions. In these terms, Venezuelan social structure (especially rural) was weak. Destruction of the landed aristocracy in the civil wars of the nineteenth century meant that political leadership rested not in a stable socioeconomic elite, but rather in a shifting succession of regional military leaders. Moreover, many of the institutions which normally reinforce the social hierarchy were also weak. Religious sanctions were negligible, as the Church barely existed in the countryside, apart from the Andean states of Táchira, Mérida, and Trujillo. Political loyalties which might have carried over were shattered under Gómez—the Liberal and Conservative Parties simply disappeared.

In this context, the impact of oil was primarily to depress traditional agriculture and drive (or pull) people off the land.[3] Although oil never employed more than a handful of the migrants, it acted as a magnet for the discontented. People from all regions and social strata were on the move. In this way, economic incentives to mobility further weakened the already loose social ties of the countryside. This portrait of a society on the move, yet with a tight political lid holding down organization and action, has several important consequences. First, many are available for new social commitments, loyalties, and identities. Second, the weakness of traditional ties combined with the intensive experience of change magnifies the impact of new organizations once the lid is removed. Faced with novel experiences, pressures, and possibilities, migrants lacked new orientations to help them manage and understand their problems. Under Gómez, no one went to the urban or rural proletariat to carry the message of full citizenship, personal and group rights, and class consciousness, or even the possibility of collective organization to represent those interests and secure those rights.[4]

[3] See J. D. Powell, op.cit., pp. 1-4.

[4] A good example of the effects of mass organization in opening up multiple channels of political action where previously there had been no recourse from the decisions of local elites is the experience of Guatemala from 1944 to 1954. For a complete analysis, see R. N. Adams, *Crucifixion by Power: Essays in Guatemalan National Social Structure, 1944-1946* (Austin: University of Texas Press, 1970), especially Chapters 2 and 3.

The relation between weak traditional ties and powerful penetration by new organizations is crucial. A key premise of this entire book has been the great strength of organizational loyalties and discipline. Given the initial strength of organizational loyalty and identification, the coordination between action on different levels of an organization, and between members scattered through a wide variety of arenas (e.g., students, peasants, shopkeepers, workers, etc.) will be high. The organization per se assumes a key role in people's lives. Consider the case of Acción Democrática. A common explanation (among Venezuelans) of AD's lengthy hegemony is that the *adecos* stepped into a vacuum. Being first, they had a headstart which took years to overcome. Initial loyalties were reinforced and consolidated during the *trienio* by the promise and reality of general reforms and specific, concrete benefits (agrarian reform, union oganization, higher wages, medical and educational services). Once established, these loyalties persisted as loyalties to the party, and required less direct reinforcement.[5] This helps explain why the party was able to survive underground as well as it did, and moreover, why it was able to emerge relatively unscathed from a series of bitter and far-reaching divisions in the 1960's.

LEGITIMACY CONFLICTS: A COMPARATIVE PERSPECTIVE

Throughout this book great emphasis has been placed on legitimacy conflicts—their structure, content, and impact on other conflicts in the society. Legitimacy conflicts were inevitable in Venezuela after 1936. The encounter of existing power groups with a new set of political resources and organizations is bound to raise fundamental questions

[5] For an interesting analysis of the way in which political support, once established, can be maintained with decreasing rewards, see R. Merelman, "Learning and Legitimacy," *American Political Science Review*, 60, No. 3 (September 1966), 548-561

about the form of institutions, and the proper means of generating and allocating political power. In Venezuela, the shock of novelty was all the greater because official repression had so long been able to shut off any political expression of the new social forces being created. The same elements that contributed to a deep and powerful penetration by new organizations also fed the fires of extreme conflict. For new groups, organizational loyalties reinforced the commitment to struggle. The organization itself became a symbol, a rallying point for action. Political battles over legitimacy, after all, involve more than verbal differences: the organization's own identity and survival are on the line. On the other hand, for weakly organized traditional groups, like the Church, lack of organization meant inability to control the consequences of action. Without a regular net of Catholic organizations and lay spokesmen, the Church was forced to enter the conflict directly, and make extreme appeals to mobilize its potential (but unorganized and hence hard to reach) supporters.[6]

Legitimacy conflicts are social earthquakes. The challenges posed and the threats perceived are extremely far-reaching. Because they involve the form of institutions and the general framework of inter-group relations, such conflicts tend toward totalization: all kinds of specific lower-level disputes are subsumed in the general issue. Given these characteristics, the resolution of legitimacy conflicts might be expected to produce at least the following results: (1) agreement on institutional forms and procedures sufficient to allow conflict to be considered normal and legitimate (the agreement to disagree becomes possible); (2) relaxation of the strict correspondence between levels of action since involvement in any given dispute no longer requires participation in generalized conflict; and (3) the feasibility of isolating conflicts. In this way, the possibility of creating regular procedures for the conciliation of con-

[6] See J. Coleman, *op.cit.*, for an analysis of conflicts which discusses the impact of lack of organization in these terms.

215

flicts flows from the settlement of one overriding kind of conflict.

In the analysis so far, two sets of factors have been emphasized: organizational and normative. The nature of organization is important in determining the extent of organizational fusion in a conflict. The concept of organizational fusion describes the super-imposition of roles, the degree to which an organizational net structures memberships and loyalties so that the same sets of persons meet in conflict in all arenas. The effect of organization in reinforcing cleavages in this way makes conflict more severe by involving all of a person's roles and identities. In Venezuela party affiliation provides the structural basis for this integration of roles. But the potential for total conflict inherent in this pattern is not always activated. In fact, the development of common procedural norms has permitted the relaxation of these ties, thereby enhancing the likelihood of limiting conflict and controlling its consequences.

At this point, formulation and perception of the issues at stake becomes crucial. Formulation of issues may be described on a continuum from separation to fusion. Separation offers the possibility of delimiting conflicts and isolating them from one another, both conceptually and in practice.[7] Specific conflicts can then be raised and resolved without necessarily involving all other questions. Fusion implies that all issues are perceived to be inescapably woven together. Thus, no single problem can be raised or considered in isolation—each is seen to involve all the others. Consider a typical case of fusion. A perceived threat to the basic values and collective survival of any group will provoke a conflict of great intensity and scope. A powerful or prestigious group, confronted with new social forces, political organizations, and methods of action alien to its experience, is unlikely to accept the limitation of conflict to any given specific issue until the broader questions of its proper

[7] In other words, isolating the issues in the minds of participants and separating actions in different conflicts.

relation to these new forces, organizations, and criteria of power (in a word, questions of political legitimacy) are resolved. When legitimacy questions are at stake, and the form and content of institutions in question, then conflict runs rapidly up the hierarchy of arenas until political institutions themselves are involved. In this way, questions of political legitimacy take priority, short-circuiting the resolution of issues in other arenas, tying their outcome to the fate of the overall conflict.

Organizational fusion and the nature of issues give a distinctive scope to conflict (see Chapter 1). Organizational fusion bears on the objective scope of conflict, the structural ties which bind arenas and levels of action together. Perception of issues sets the subjective scope of conflict, the way perception of issues determines commitments to conflict. Attention to the subjective scope of conflict helps us understand that parties to a conflict may perceive their actions in totally different ways: while A prepares for a limited skirmish, B may see a Holy War developing.

One common term, "institutionalization," requires definition. As used here, institutionalization has meant two things. First, it refers to the subjective orientations of the actors: do they perceive interaction as regular and routine, implicitly accepting the maintenance of a common permanent arena for conflict as legitimate and desirable? Second, it refers to patterns of overt behavior: to what extent have specialized roles emerged, roles explicitly charged with negotiating a peaceful settlement, and to what degree are elites prepared to call on the occupants of such roles to perform the tasks?

Both organizational fusion and issue formulation incorporate parallel dimensions of separation and fusion. Taken together, these yield two polar types of conflict: one tending to the isolation of disputes, reflecting restraint on (or the absence of) cumulative cleavages; and another tending to the polarization of disputes, where cumulative cleavages are activated and reinforced (Table 8.2). Working with these dimensions, systems of conflict emerge—systems

TABLE 8.2

Conflict Systems

		Issue Formulaion	
		Separation	Fusion
Organizational Fusion	High	Strong conciliation system *a*	Radical conflict system *a*
	Low	Strong conciliation system *b*	Radical conflict system *b*

with differing potentials for conciliating conflicts and varying degrees of constraint on their fusion (Table 8.3).

A strong conciliation system is one in which some procedural consensus has been reached, and issues of legitimacy and collective survival removed from politics. The settlement of such issues permits the institutionalization of procedures for the conciliation of specific conflicts. The system as a whole offers incentives to the isolation and conciliation of conflicts. In a radical conflict system, on the other hand, procedural and legitimacy questions dominate politics. Incentives work primarily to polarize conflicts.

Types of strong conciliation systems and radical conflict systems are distinguished according to whether organizational fusion is high or low. For strong conciliation systems, this distinction is intended to differentiate between polities whose social and political cleavages are cross-cutting and those whose cleavages are cumulative and reinforcing.[8] My fundamental research questions have been directed to the latter—to the problems and processes of building institu-

[8] Respectively, for example, the United States and the Netherlands, or Austria. A recent study by Verba casts doubt on conventional assumptions about the effects of cross-cutting cleavages in moderating political attitudes and conflicts in the United States. See S. Verba, "Organizational Membership and Democratic Consensus," *The Journal of Politics*, 27:3 (August 1965), 467-497.

TABLE 8.3

Empirical Elements of Conflict Systems

Empirical Elements	I Conflicts Tending to Isolation	II Conflicts Tending to Polarization
1. Perceptions of the scope of conflict are	Increasingly limited	Increasingly extensive
2. Problems of legitimacy and procedure are	Settled	In question
3. Agreement on proper institutional location of conflict is	Present	Absent
4. Role of opposition is	Legitimate	Rejected
5. Organizational integration is	Flexible	Rigid
6. Organizational integration then serves to	Delimit and confine	Magnify and extend
7. Action of elites is to	Limit conflict	Magnify conflict
8. Creation and use of negotiating roles?	Yes	No

tions to manage (not eliminate) conflict in systems marked by deep and cumulative conflicts. For radical conflict systems, the basic line is drawn between systems where one or more of the parties is weakly organized (what I have called conflicts of traditional defense) and those occurring in highly organized and complex social structures (what might be called conflicts of revolutionary war).

As an example, consider the school issue. Subsidy and control of education (and the status of religious education) has been a major conflict in the development of Western nations. Control of education however, has been merely the tip of the iceberg, the surface expression of a deeper opposition. Conflict has been joined to determine which institu-

219

tions, political or religious, should have the right to orient social values, and to set forth the moral bases of legitimate political authority and social unity.[9] Understanding the depth of conflict built into the school issues helps explain why its resolution has been so central to the consolidation and stabilization of political systems throughout modern history.

In Venezuela the school issue has been resolved as a conflict over legitimacy. Opposition concerning education no longer implies all-out conflict over the proper bases of the political system. Reformulation of the issue in the early 1960's transformed it into a problem amenable to compromise and mutual adjustment. Settlement of the school issue in this sense was one facet of the consolidation of a legitimate and effective political system after 1958. The counterpart, of course, was the defeat and incorporation of the military on the Right and the liquidation of the guerrillas on the Left. With the effective elimination of both extremes, the range of political resources and methods permissible in Venezuela was sharply reduced. Limiting the number and variety of political resources is central to the building of legitimate institutions.[10] Once the range of acceptable political resources has been limited and the scope of permissible political actions clearly defined, then bargaining itself becomes a more realistic goal, and limited reforms can be attempted. In this sense, Venezuela has gone far along the way to establishing what Huntington has called a "civic polity": "The distinguishing characteristic of a highly insti-

[9] For a general discussion of these conflicts in Western European development, see S. M. Lipset and S. Rokkan, eds., "Introduction," to their *Party Systems and Voter Alignments*; K. H. Silvert offers a useful discussion focused particularly on conflicts between religious and political institutions in these terms. See his "Conclusions," K. H. Silvert, ed., *Churches and States: The Religious Institution and Modernization* (New York: American Universities Field Staff, 1967), especially pp. 216-217.

[10] C. W. Anderson, *Politics and Economic Change in Latin America* (Princeton: D. Van Nostrand Company, Inc., 1967), p. 90.

tutionalized polity . . . is the high price it places on power. In a civic polity, the price of authority involves limitations on the resources that may be employed in politics, the procedures through which power may be acquired, and the attitudes that power wielders may hold."[11]

In terms of styles of inter-group relations and policy content, the pattern of accommodation worked out in Venezuela after 1958 bears a striking resemblance to the experience of many European political systems where resolution of the school issue was central to political realignments and the creation of coexistence politics between ancient enemies. Good examples in this regard are France (after the school subsidy law of the early 1950's) and the Netherlands (where the resolution of the school issue provided the foundation for the present delicate system of inter-bloc compromise).[12] In many cases, deep subcultural cleavages, centering on religion (Austria or the Netherlands) or on language (Belgium or Switzerland) have been contained through structures of accommodation which essentially provide guarantees of survival to threatened groups.[13] The experience of

[11] S. Huntington, op.cit., p. 83.

[12] On France, see B. E. Brown, "The Decision to Subsidize Private Schools," B. E. Brown and J. B. Christoph, eds., Cases in Comparative Politics (Boston: Little, Brown and Co., 1965), pp. 113-147, and W. Bosworth, Catholicism and Crisis in Modern France (Princeton: Princeton University Press, 1962), especially Chapter 8. On the Netherlands, see A. Lijphart, The Politics of Accommodation, especially Chapter 6.

[13] On Austria, F. Engelmann, "Austria: The Pooling of Opposition," R. A. Dahl, ed., Political Oppositions in Western Democracies (New Haven: Yale University Press, 1966), pp. 260-283, and A. Diamant, Austrian Catholics and the First Republic (Princeton: Princeton University Press, 1960). On the Netherlands, A. Lijphart, op.cit., and H. Daalder, "The Netherlands: Opposition in a Segmented Society," R. A. Dahl, ed., op.cit., pp. 188-236. On Belgium, V. Lorwin, "Belgium: Religion, Class, and Language in National Politics," R. A. Dahl, op.cit., pp. 147-187. For a general discussion of European states in this regard, see H. Daalder, "Parties, Elites, and Political Developments in Western Europe," J. La Palombara and M. Wiener, eds., Political Parties and Political Development (Princeton: Princeton University Press, 1966), pp. 43-78, and V. Lorwin,

all-out conflict in the past moved participants to avoid such conflict in the future, by removing issues of survival from the political arena.

The visible expression and instrument of these decisions has been the formation of broad coalition governments. The attempt to bring all or most significant forces into government is often a response to internal fragmentation, and has characterized the recent experience of many smaller European nations. Since 1917 the Dutch have been governed by extensive coalition regimes. An even more striking example is Austria. After World War II, the Austrian political system was literally divided (in proportional terms) at all levels between Catholic and Socialist blocs. These arrangements were a response to a past history of civil war and represented an attempt to remove the causes of civil war by eliminating the issue of survival. Both sides were guaranteed a place in the political system. In Latin America, the case of Colombia is particularly relevant. In Colombia, a ten-year civil war between Liberals and Conservatives was ended in 1958 by a pact which established a National Front government jointly guaranteed by the two parties. The National Front agreements guaranteed the alternation of Liberals and Conservatives in power regardless of the electoral outcome. In this way, the threat of survival was removed from politics.[14]

In Venezuela, these accommodation arrangements have never been formalized to the same extent as in the Netherlands or Austria, and the element of free party competition has never been removed from the system as in Colombia. Nevertheless, the accommodation-through-coalition pattern

---

"Segmented Pluralism: Ideological Cleavages and Political Cohesion in the Smaller European Democracies," *Comparative Politics*, 3:2 (January 1971), 141-176.

[14] On Colombia, see R. Wienert, "Violence in Pre-Modern Societies: Rural Colombia," *American Political Science Review*, 60:2 (June 1966), 340-347, and J. Payne, *Patterns of Conflict in Colombia* (New Haven: Yale University Press, 1968).

is applicable to Venezuela in two respects. First, the participation of COPEI in the government from 1959 to 1963 was
central to the reconciliation of the entire Catholic sector—
it provided a political shield, an implicit guarantee of survival. Once these guarantees were ensured, it then became
possible to move to more limited approaches to politics:
bargaining, negotiation, and the like. Second, the general
orientation toward coalition enhanced the possibility of
inter-bloc accommodation by implicitly excluding consideration of explosive or sensitive issues, or at least putting them
off for as long as possible. As we have seen, since 1958,
methods of action and issues too hot to handle without
straining the delicate fabric of compromise have been shut
out.

The importance of these agreements may be illustrated
by a counter example. Consider the course of the Spanish
Republic from 1931 to 1936. Spain under the Republic is
strikingly reminiscent of Venezuela during the *trienio*: no
accommodations were made and issues were pushed, by all
sides, to the breaking point. Within a short period, antagonisms grew and polarization sharpened into a Civil War; the
outcome still stands as a warning to democratic politicians
and as a silent argument for prudence.[15]

THE PRICE OF DEFEAT

At first glance, the Venezuelan story seems to have a
happy ending. Institutions are legitimized and "everyone"
is united behind the new system and its rules. It is worth
emphasizing, however, that a process of incorporation,
whereby hostile elements are brought into new institutions
and patterns of action, presupposes (and indeed may be
contingent upon) a measure of exclusion. Parties which
challenge the bargain are either victors or vanquished: they

[15] I am indebted to Juan Linz for suggesting this parallel. For a
description of the politics of the Spanish Republic, see J. Linz, "The
Breakdown of Democracy in Spain" (unpublished paper).

223

overturn the system or are defeated by it. Remember that the basic thrust of the bargains and accommodations described so far is to mute partisan hostility in the name of stability. Parties to the bargain moderate their demands and tactics as a means of guaranteeing institutional strength and continuity. In policy terms, this kind of accommodation has clear social costs: those groups which reject the incorporation of traditional sectors, and their conservative impact on policy formation, are defeated. Traditional oppositions are incorporated as the dominant party moves to the center. The center is strengthened. Who used to be left out? The traditional Right. Who is excluded from the new revised spectrum of democratic politics? The Left.

In explaining the nature of opposition to a political system, and predicting the possibility (and cost) of incorporation of excluded groups, distinctions should be drawn between the situation of a "traditional" and a "modern" outgroup. "Traditional" and "modern" here distinguish groups whose claim to power and authority is based on custom and divine sanction and which lack mass organization (traditionals) from those whose mass organization provides the very basis of their claims to legitimate power (moderns). In some ways, traditional outgroups are more easily reconciled to a new system and incorporated into its processes than modern outgroups. For excluded traditional groups, the value of self-organization on a mass basis and of competition within the system is relatively easy to demonstrate. Extended experience within new structures and patterns of action (whatever the motive for their initiation) may work subtle changes in attitudes and values, as they guide action in concrete settings. As Fagen has pointed out, "participatory activity,—not in itself dependent on the internalization of new norms—may eventually lead to very basic changes in the value and belief systems of those who are swept into participation."[16] In Venezuela, this process is particularly

[16] Richard Fagen, *The Transformation of Political Culture in Cuba* (Stanford: Stanford University Press, 1969), p. 10.

clear for the Catholic sector. The reader will recall how Catholic elites decided to build mass organizations in order to compete within the system. The very process of building an organizational base, one might argue, brought the Church closer to the operative norms of the system. In this context, "cultural" and "structural" factors are not clearly distinguished: they have a mutual and reciprocal impact. I will return to this point in greater detail in Chapter 9.

If a group based on mass organization is shut out by a bargain of this kind, incentives to incorporation are few and far between. Such groups take the existing system as a starting point, as an object to be changed. The advantages of accepting limitations and seeking accommodation are less obvious to such groups since they already are organized along mass lines. To gain new advantage, they need to change the system, not freeze its rules and procedures. Yet the terms of the bargain exclude some crucial issues and methods, among them the option of total revolutionary change. The bargains struck in Venezuela after 1958 had the effect of freezing the rules of the game, freezing the political market. For mass revolutionary groups excluded by such a bargain, incorporation is contingent on total defeat.

The phenomenon we are trying to explain here is two-fold: the severity of the reaction of excluded groups, and their prospects of success or failure. So far, we have considered the impact of mass organization in shaping a group's probable reaction to exclusion. Clearly the impact of this factor depends on the context in which it operates—the kind of system in which the organization functions. The greater the strength and complexity of existing institutions, the more severe will be the reaction of excluded groups. Reaction will be most severe, then, when a mass "modern" group is excluded in a society where institutions are strong and complex.[17]

[17] As we have seen, the strength and complexity of institutions means that fewer persons are available for new forms of social commitment. Institutions are strong in the degree to which they incorporate the

A good example would be a challenge by mass groups in a society with complex and powerful institutions, where stable class and caste relations, backed up by religious sanctions, provide a reserve of support for the traditional order.[18] In this case, the most likely outcomes of the encounter of existing groups with challenging parties are two: revolutionary takeover and hegemonic rule by the challengers, or stalemate, stagnation, and endemic conflict where no new system is imposed. Why such bleak and limited alternatives? Basically because the greater initial strength and complexity of existing institutions lets them offer a longer, stronger battle. Power holders can limit the erosion of their base while repressing challengers successfully and checking them continuously.[19] Moreover, strong institutions imply an elite capable of uniting against threats, and hence fewer defections by elites to the new groups where they may provide key leadership.[20] In this situation, the only way challengers can get anywhere at all is through total revolutionary change. There is little room within the system for a gradual expansion of influence.

---

population into stable roles and authority relations. Economic, social, political, and religious sanctions all converge to support existing social arrangements.

[18] In a traditional society, for example, elites are better able to isolate the rural population from the organizational drive of new political parties. In this case, landowner, police chief, and priest work for a common goal—preventing the organization and mobilization of peasants. For a discussion of rural communities in Latin America, and the need for change to come from the outside, given the strength of the system in isolation, see R. Schaedel, "Land Reform Studies," *Latin American Research Review*, 1:1 (Fall 1965), 75-122.

[19] More is at stake here than a simple difference in power between *ins* and *outs*. After all, many traditional institutions, while concentrating power to a high degree, are nevertheless weak. Power may be centralized, but there is little of it, and regimes that often looked solid from the outside have proven fragile and brittle, falling easily to minimal pressure.

[20] See T. Di Tella, "Populism and Reform in Latin America," C. Veliz, ed., *Obstacles to Change in Latin America* (New York: Oxford University Press, 1965), pp. 47-74.

The link of organizational strength and complexity in the social structure to radical reactions to exclusion helps explain the depth of contemporary left-wing alienation in Venezuela. The Left seriously misjudged the nature of Venezuelan society, and underestimated the degree to which most social groups were already organized by and committed to existing democratic political parties. The fertile organizational material of 1936 was now occupied ground—rural support was never achieved, the students were isolated, and the urban slums could not be effectively mobilized.[21] Only after recognizing these facts were the Communists able to justify abandoning armed struggle and adapting themselves to the new rules of the game. The MIR has never recognized these facts, and as a result has been converted into a socially and politically irrelevant group— an isolated, armed micro-faction able to sting, but not bite.

The preceding argument on the relation of social structure to political outcomes is summarized in Figure 8.1, which offers a tentative model of the evolution of different systems of conflict. The central thrust of this model is that the nature of the social structure (its strength and complexity, in the senses already given) conditions the impact of new mass organization and thereby affects the kind of incentives the system offers for settling legitimacy conflicts and institutionalizing procedures for conciliation.

Let me elaborate on the model. An organizational vacuum is, of course, rare, but the term was chosen deliberately to emphasize the paucity of traditional social ties and loyalties. It does not, of course, imply that there are no organizations. Many institutions (armies, for example) may persist and offer effective opposition to new groups. But this is irrelevant to the basic issue considered here: the impact of differences in social structure on the nature of mass loyalties, and through them, on the penetration of mass organizations. In Venezuela the organizational vacuum of

---

[21] For an account of the strategic and tactical errors of the Left, see T. Ray, *op.cit.*, pp. 129-130; 154-155.

FIGURE 8.1

The Evolution of Conflict Systems

Independent Variable	Intervening Variable	Resulting System
Impact of new mass ⟶ organization	Nature of social structure	
	Organizational vacuum ⟶	Successful pluralism
	Organizational strength and complexity	Stalemate / Revolution

pre-1936 social structure laid the bases for a very deep penetration by the new political parties. This set up a conflict of traditional defense (made more extreme by the organizational weakness of traditional groups), culminating in a move to reconciliation. There was a stage of radical conflict (the *trienio*), but as we have seen, the very weakness of tradition stimulated a search for compromise.

Where social structure is complex and powerful, two kinds of outcomes are distinguished. In one case, stalemate prevails—when the clash of existing power groups with challengers reaches an impasse. The strength of existing institutions enables power holders to protect their base and retain a grasp on social loyalties. From a position of strength, elites can apply violence successfully in order to enforce a stalemate which protects their position. The scope of membership in the nation and of political participation remain powerful issues. Divergent resources, methods of action, and criteria of power coexist in the society since unresolved legitimacy conflicts dominate politics. Because no single group can marshal sufficient power to impose a new and definitive system, institutions and processes remain "tentative,"[22] and the society is locked into an endless cycle of civil strife and stagnation.[23]

In the second case, the clash of new forces with the institutions of a powerful and complex social structure leads to a one-party hegemonic regime—the end product of successful revolutionary war. Here one might argue that existing structures of power were so strong that only by liquidating them could reformist groups make any headway at all. Within existing institutions there is no place to go: most political ground is already occupied, and the cost of organization and change is high.[24] In this case, the strength of existing institutions is crucial in radicalizing the initial reformist drive of challenging groups. The extremely rapid radicalization of the Cuban Revolution, occurring in a highly complex and dependent social structure, is a case in point.[25]

[22] See C. W. Anderson, op.cit., Chapter 4, for a discussion of this concept.

[23] A useful example here is Argentina. For an analysis of the Argentine crisis along these lines, see K. H. Silvert, "Argentina: The Costs of Anti-Nationalism," K. H. Silvert, ed., Expectant Peoples, Nationalism and Development (New York: Random House, 1963), pp. 347-372.

[24] Many that at first glance seemed to represent cases of organizational vacuum leading to one-party rule, such as some West African nations, have on closer examination, turned out to involve considerable bureaucratization of the mass party stemming from concessions made to existing centers of power in an effort to gain their cooperation or acquiescence. Preexisting social structures were obviously not the vacuums they appeared to be from the outside. See I. Wallerstein, "The Decline of the Party in Single-Party African States," J. La Palombara and M. Wiener, op.cit., pp. 201-214.

[25] On the Cuban Revolution, especially with regard to the rapidity and thoroughness of change, see W. MacGaffey and C. R. Barnett, Twentieth Century Cuba: The Background of the Castro Revolution (Garden City: Anchor Books, 1965), especially Chapters 14-16. On the complex nature of the prerevolutionary Cuban system

This model is offered in a tentative vein. It is not a tightly integrated general theory, nor does it pretend to be. It helps explain some key differences in the evolution of different political systems, and highlights a number of important common variables and sequences of events, distinguishing the factors that helped produce the contemporary Venezuelan system from those that might have turned it in other directions. With these concepts and their structural-organizational bases well in hand, let us now consider the subjective dimension: the explicit and implicit norms which have guided political elites in the post-1958 period.

---

and the situation this created for revolutionary leadership, see J. O'Connor, *The Origins of Socialism in Cuba* (Ithaca: Cornell University Press, 1970), especially Chapters 1-4.

CHAPTER 9

Conflict and Consensus: Operative Norms

A MAJOR theme of this book is that elite norms have
changed profoundly since the introduction and consolidation of the party system in Venezuela, above all after 1958.
Part of this change lies, of course, in the altered composition of the political elite.[1] But more is at stake than this,
for perspectives on conflict and opposition, and the fundamental norms that guide party elites have also changed.
This chapter will describe and explain the system of shared
norms developed in Venezuela which has permitted social
and political conflict to be carried out on a regular basis
without institutional breakdown. These rules and norms
provide the framework for an ongoing system of social conflict. They grow out of and (in action) continuously reinforce agreements on the scope and content of conflict.

THE RULES OF THE GAME

The concepts of "culture" and "political culture" which
dominate recent studies by American social scientists con-
ceive culture largely in ideational terms, as a set of beliefs and orientations to public objects.[2] Thus, to Verba,
political culture is the "system of beliefs about patterns of
political interaction and political institutions,"[3] a mix of
descriptive and normative ideas about politics. This orien-

[1] Bonilla offers a detailed analysis of the composition of economic,
cultural, and political elites, see F. Bonilla, op.cit.
[2] A full discussion of this concept of culture is offered in D. Levine,
"Issues in the Study of Culture in Latin America" (forthcoming).
[3] S. Verba, "Comparative Political Culture," L. Pye and S. Verba,
eds., *Political Culture and Political Development* (Princeton: Princeton University Press, 1965), p. 516.

231

tation has weighted analysis (in much of anthropology and especially in political science) heavily toward psychological variables, primarily attitudes, with little emphasis on the direct observation and analysis of behavior.

Behavior patterns have, on the whole, been treated as dependent variables, determined by political values and attitudes, but analytically separate from them. In establishing patterns of values and culture, then, emphasis has been placed on the internal validity of the measuring instrument. Political culture thus becomes identified with a pattern of responses about attitudes to public objects. There is no validity check outside the questionnaire or interview schedule. Predictions are made concerning behavior, but no actual behavior is described or explained.

Political culture or political norms, however, cannot be so easily separated from political experience. There is a close, reciprocal relationship between norms and action. If this be the case, it stands to reason that new methods of organization and new forms of action will produce new configurations of culture. Culture then is not static, but changing, in response to changing patterns of behavior. In light of these considerations, an alternative approach to political culture might refocus attention to studies of behavior in concrete settings over time. Here, we need not inquire directly about a subject's attitudes to public objects or processes. Rather, analysis would infer operative norms, which may be held only implicitly, from examination of an ongoing system of behavior. In this case, the validity check lies in the ability of the pattern of norms extracted from this behavioral set to account for past and future behavior, not merely in their internal consistency. This is the method pursued in this book.[4]

This approach to the study of political norms has one further advantage. Reliance on expressed public attitudes makes it difficult to account for situations where people

4 See D. Levine, "Issues . . ."

compartmentalize their values. In certain roles, for example, the institutionally defined incentives and constraints on behavior may make general attitudes inoperative. Political actors may compromise deeply held values in order to conform to the demands of the role, or to maintain the institution of which it is a part. Since people can and do compartmentalize their lives to a great extent, the leap from attitudes and values in a generalized sense to norms which guide behavior in concrete situations is not always as clear and direct as a first glance might indicate. Some way is needed to provide for this institutionally defined variation in a political system. In this book, this has been done through case studies, working with observed behavior over time, in situations of conflict. Such data have many advantages, for they allow analysis to take account of the subjective and objective aspects of a situation, looking at a conflict as it is experienced by participants—given their own characteristic resources and methods of action, their perceptions of the opposition, their goals, hopes, and fears. This "sympathetic" approach to the analysis of conflict, rooted in the perspectives of Max Weber, is disciplined by a check on external observed behavior.[5]

One might argue that conflicts, once encapsulated in a set of common rules, may be self-regulating.[6] Norms of conflict are self-enforcing since they constrain groups to act within previously established patterns. Moreover, it is the very process of interaction which drives participants to impose self-defined limitations on the goals and methods of conflict. The whole field of industrial sociology, in which conflict tends, over time, to the establishment of common rules and expectations, speaks to this point.[7] As we have

[5] A useful discussion of the limitations of *verstehen* as a means of validating knowledge is offered by W. Connolly, *Political Science and Ideology* (New York: Atherton Press, 1967), pp. 7-8.
[6] See A. Etzioni, "On Self-Encapsulating Conflicts," *Journal of Conflict Resolution*, 8:3 (September 1964), 242-255.
[7] For a summary and discussion of relevant writings, see R. Dahrendorf, *op.cit.*

233

seen, in Venezuela the initial agreement to encapsulate conflict, building a set of rules to limit, contain, and regulate it, stemmed from fear—the fear of all parties that further uncontrolled conflict would harm them all. In the ensuing analysis, my goal is not to pass judgment on these norms or on their bearers, but rather to explain how the system operates, and further to delineate the consequences of this pattern of norms for the political system as a whole.

Changes in elite norms were central to the overall process of political reconciliation. The views of elites, defined here as organizational leaders, are particularly crucial because, as we have seen, leaders of an organization often influence followers by committing the organizations to paths of action which followers accept because of their general faith in the leaders.[8] The expression of new elite attitudes in organizational policy then changes mass behavior. Followers act as if their attitudes had changed along the same lines as the attitudes of leaders, but without the same prior attitudinal changes being necessary. Mass attitudes may not change, but effective patterns of behavior are altered in the desired direction.[9] Looked at in this way, the distinction between strictly cultural and strictly structural (or behavioral, for what we mean by structures is regular and repeated patterns of behavior) factors loses much of its presumed sharpness. Cultural and structural factors intertwine and support

[8] For a general analysis of the role of leaders in shaping the political world of followers, see M. Edelman, *The Symbolic Uses of Politics* (Urbana: University of Illinois Press, 1967).

[9] This process of "disorderly change," where attitudes are acquired ex post facto, as a result of new patterns of behavior, rather than vice versa, is discussed by R. Fagen, *op.cit.*, p. 150, in these terms:

> It should be pointed out that an interaction between behavioral change and attitudinal change might possibly be established right from the outset, thus rendering the "disorder" model (with its reverse linearity) quite inappropriate for understanding the way change takes place—or could take place. Dialectical or cybernetic models that begin with behavioral change certainly seem the most appropriate for representing the attitudinal-behavioral interaction in revolutionary Cuba, as well as in many other situations.

one another. Political actors behave as if they believed in certain "cultural" norms. But the "cultural norms" themselves emerge from the actual experience of certain patterns of behavior, however motivated.

Venezuela's dominant norms of political interaction may be described as a set of rules. These rules are more than window dressing: idealized cultural values displayed on ceremonial occasions only. They are, rather, both cause and consequence of new structural arrangements. They reflect understandings built into the key structures of contemporary Venezuelan politics. Taken together, these rules describe a self-perpetuating system for the management of political conflict.

Rule I: Freedom for Leaders

In Venezuela, the structure of organizations and the beliefs of political actors combine to reinforce the maneuverability and freedom of leaders to lead. The rank and file of political parties and organizations behave as if they believed that leaders should have a great deal of leeway. As we have seen, the ability of leaders to lead—to carry their organizations along on compromises often distasteful to the rank and file—has been crucial to the entire process of stabilization and reconciliation since 1958.

Party leadership per se has been able to establish effective independence from sectoral ties and demands. General political goals and needs have been successfully advanced as more urgent than any particular sectoral claim. AD and COPEI are good examples of this process. We have seen how AD restrained and moderated the actions and demands of the teachers. COPEI filled a similar role with respect to Catholic education. Indeed, the entire history of COPEI reveals a growing independence and self-definition as a political party, free of confining ties to the Church, right-wing interests, or regional identities.[10]

[10] See E. J. Williams, *Latin American Christian Democratic Parties*

In general, parties drawing on a wide variety of sectors can more easily resist pressure from any single component group. On the other hand, parties without broad strength are more tied to the resources of a strong intra-party group, and hence more open to pressure. Recall the role of left-wing students in promoting the insurrection within the PCV and the MIR. Single sector domination has gone very far in the MIR, a majority of whose leaders are now students or ex-student leaders. In the PCV, on the other hand, once the decision was made to return to normal political life, the relative weight of students (or of any single group) was consciously reduced.

Indeed, as the Communists abandoned armed struggle, the emphasis on leadership, internal party discipline, and the need to save the party organization grew apace. A Communist dissident, expelled from the party, complained in a letter to the Political Bureau that,

> . . . as revolution has stopped being discussed, growing emphasis has been placed on the role of the party. This is a deception, for if we put the party first, the revolution becomes secondary. But the party is an instrument, not an end in itself. The primary goal is the revolution, and the party is just a form of making it. To change these priorities reveals a mystifying attitude, basically reactionary, bureaucratic, elitist, and at the service of particular individuals, and not the working class.[11]

Rule II: The Fragility of Politics

Political leaders seem to be constantly looking over their shoulders in Venezuela since 1958. They behave as if politi-

---

(Knoxville: University of Tennessee Press, 1967), pp. 21-22, for a similar view.

[11] From a letter by Pedro Duno to the Political Bureau of the PCV, dated September 15, 1968. The letter is reprinted in P. Duno, *Sobre Aparatos, Desviaciones, y Dogmas* (Caracas: Editorial Nueva Izquierda, 1969), p. 33.

cal institutions might fall apart at any moment, and therefore require constant care and attention to stay afloat. The memory of past conflicts and the fear of renewed military dictatorship arising in response to uncontrollable conflict drove many leaders to handle politics with extreme care. During the *trienio*, elites were genuinely unaware of the consequences of all-out conflict. The tremendous extension of mass organizations and popular participation had greatly increased the potential scope of conflict. As we have seen, however, shared norms for the containment of conflict were not developed.

Acknowledging the fragility of political institutions led AD leadership to pursue a careful policy of coalition-building—muting expressions of partisan hostility. In policy terms, AD's leaders made their central goal less social revolution than the achievement of institutional stability and continuity. Because the potential consequences of all-out conflict were now recognized, great care was taken to avoid such conflict.[12] Many explosive issues were consciously set aside or delayed. When such questions were finally put on the table, efforts were made to ensure a broad base of support for common actions and to reduce, insofar as possible, the level of political passion involved.

Reporting on a recent survey of Venezuelan elites, Frank Bonilla has noted the pervasiveness of this sense of fragility among political leaders. His data fit Rule II very well:

Behind the overlay of conflict and aggressiveness there is more often great caution, timidity, accommodation, self-imposed limits on action, and fear of exceeding imagined restrictions. In short, what is most apparent is the operation of subjective constraints on action and acknowledged deference to power blocs with a marginally legitimate

[12] This is true with the constant exception of relations with the Communists. The exclusion of the Communists was in itself tactically useful since it further consolidated the center behind Betancourt's regime.

political role—the army, economic pressure groups, oil companies, the United States.[13]

Two key sectors with which the fragility argument was consciously and successfully employed are the Church and the military. For the Church, the treatment of educational reform described in Chapter 5 is a good example of the general process. With the military, it is clear that Betancourt consciously pushed the fragility argument, warning military officers that his government was the only thing that stood between them and a Cuban-style revolution, which, as they knew, had ended with total liquidation of the traditional military establishment. Participation in attempted coups, Betancourt argued, would only crystallize a general anti-military coalition—a coalition likely to be captured by the extreme Left.[14]

The impact of Rules I and II, working together, is also visible in the many party divisions which mark recent Venezuelan politics. AD, for example, has suffered three major divisions since 1960. In each case, more left-wing elements have split off, rejecting the top leadership's attempt to impose solutions justified in terms of fragility and thus the need for compromises often repugnant to party doctrine. Other parties have suffered similar divisions, for example URD and the Communists. In each case, the split has come over issues of general orientation: should the party accommodate itself to the dominant system, and its built-in limitations on politics and policies, or should a firmer, more ideologically principled line be followed? The latest such division came in December 1970 when the Communist Party leadership expelled a large proportion of its own Central Committee and top officials in a dispute over these issues.

[13] F. Bonilla, *op.cit.*, p. 318.
[14] For a discussion of Betancourt's relations with the military, and an outline of the arguments he used, see E. Lieuwin, *op.cit.*, pp. 86-91, and R. Alexander, *op.cit.*, pp. 105-117.

Rule III: The Agreement to Disagree

In Venezuela, many of the philosophical and ideological differences that sparked extended conflict during the *trienio* are now accepted as basic realities which cannot and should not be changed. In many cases, such differences have been taken for granted and set aside, in order to allow discussion and negotiations to proceed on commonly accepted grounds. The agreement to disagree in Venezuela is both generalized and specific. On a general level, conflict and dissent are accepted as normal social phenomena, and institutional provision is made to handle them.[15] The right of opponents to seek and assume power is acknowledged, within specified legitimate patterns of action.[16] There is broad agreement on how political power is to be generated and allocated— according to the distribution of votes in elections. On a specific level, broad areas of policy agreement have been staked out, leaving room for disagreement over details and implementation.[17]

Once a general agreement to disagree was reached, and areas of joint policy commitment outlined and reinforced

[15] For a discussion of the general impact of such an agreement, see R. Dahrendorf, *op.cit.*, especially Chapter 6. On pp. 225-226, Dahrendorf argues as follows:

First, for effective conflict regulation to be possible, both parties to a conflict have to recognize the necessity and reality of the conflict situation, and in this sense, the fundamental justice of the cause of the opponent. . . . A second prerequisite of effective conflict regulation is the organization of interest groups. So long as conflicting forces are diffuse, incoherent aggregates, regulation is virtually impossible. . . . Thirdly, in order for effective regulation to be possible, the opposing parties in social conflicts have to agree on certain formal rules of the game that provide the framework of their relations.

[16] F. Bonilla, *op.cit.*, p. 238, provides valuable data on attitudes toward opposition held by Venezuelan political leaders. His findings bring out the absence of paranoid and extreme views of opponents.

[17] The fascinating thing in Venezuela has been the explicit nature of this agreement. Remember that the Pact of Punto Fijo, signed on the eve of the 1958 elections, pledged AD, URD, and COPEI to support a common minimum program. Areas of joint policy commitment were consciously emphasized.

through governmental coalitions, then conflicts on a more specific level could be raised and resolved within the general framework of accommodation which had been agreed on. Once the idea of conflict came to be accepted as normal, then specific issues could more easily be isolated and conciliated without calling the structure of institutions into question.

Rule IV: Concentration

One of the most important rules of Venezuelan politics since 1958 has been the monopolization of political action by political parties. The rule might be stated this way: political actions should be restricted to a limited range of organizations and forms of action. The concentration of political action in party and official channels offers a clear alternative to a Praetorian system, where all groups and sectors intervene in politics because the identity and autonomy of political institutions are insufficiently developed.[18]

The concern of Venezuelan leaders with limiting the scope of conflict and building legitimate, powerful, and effective institutions dictated an alternative strategy of making politics a specialized, autonomous sphere of action. The primary goal of this strategy was to increase the leaders' control over the consequences of action, also increasing the uniformity of political structures and thus the predictability and regularity of political interaction. Concentration is a norm designed to permit the implementation of other norms. It increases the freedom of leaders to lead, and enhances their ability to put conflicts on ice or handle them, if necessary, in secrecy. The attempt to concentrate politics, to make it a monopoly of the political parties, was an issue of public debate in Venezuela, epitomized in the bitter polemics between President Betancourt and the left-wing students in the early 1960's. Bonilla again has provided valuable data

[18] See S. Huntington, *op.cit.*, especially Chapter 4 for a discussion of these points.

confirming this Rule since he shows the extent to which interactions and the use of influence by political leaders are weighted toward techniques of persuasion. In this way, leaders concentrate on generating support from other leaders, rather than fomenting direct mass involvement at every stage.[19]

SUPPORTING ELEMENTS

The rules of the game of Venezuelan politics constitute a method of political action. Elite attitudes on these counts are crucial, but while elite commitment is the method, the rules and the attitudes they reflect do not emerge out of thin air. It may be useful, in this regard, to specify some of the factors which support and facilitate them. The historical evolution of these factors has already been described. Now, let us bring them into sharper analytic focus.

In some cases, traditional values of deference to authority have been critical in freeing elites to maneuver and compromise.[20] In Venezuela, the structure of organizational ties and loyalties has provided a functional equivalent to social deference values. As we have seen, in Venezuela the penetration of party was exceptionally profound, and party affiliation became a key social tie, cutting across class and functional lines. Yet this organizational strength has not translated itself into a purely manipulative relation of the leaders to the masses, because the built-in factor of party competition has made organizational life at all levels (national and local) lively and vigorous.[21]

[19] F. Bonilla, *op.cit.*, pp. 233-234.
[20] As in the Netherlands. See A. Lijphart, *The Politics of Accommodation*.
[21] On local level organizational vitality, see J. D. Powell, *op.cit.*, and C. Erasmus, "Upper Limits of Peasantry and Agrarian Reform: Bolivia, Venezuela, and Mexico Compared," *Ethnology*, 6:4 (October 1967), 349-380. Erasmus' study is particularly relevant to this point as he shows that the life styles of Venezuelan peasants have changed more than those of Mexican or Bolivian peasants, and traces

Clearly, organizational loyalties cannot be pushed too far or too long, as the three divisions of AD and the numerous splits of other parties demonstrate. But it is important to recognize that the fear of instability long provided a powerful stimulus to unity.[22] Fear of uncontrolled conflict also reinforced elite commitments to organizational concentration and the moderation of partisan hostility. A contributing factor here is the degree to which politics is no longer viewed as a zero-sum game, a contest where A can win only to the extent that B loses. The emphasis in Venezuelan politics has shifted to one of broader incorporation and sharing. Behind the elimination of zero-sum visions of politics lies elite recognition of effective social pluralism. The decline of AD's overwhelming hegemony has made conflict and opposition less threatening to minority sectors, and has operated within AD to sensitize leadership to the dangers of riding roughshod over minorities. The decline of one-party domination meant concretely that others could win by playing according to the new rules. The game no longer works solely to AD's advantage. Only at this stage can the idea of compromise emerge and gain acceptance—why compromise with a system which regularly and routinely excludes one's interests? These new perspectives on the rules of the game were crucial in undermining antisystem attitudes within the Catholic sector.

Let me emphasize once again that the consensus described here is primarily an operational code of coexistence, not an agreement on substantive policies or issues. Hence

these differences to the more open, competitive nature of peasant politics. Open competitive politics at the local level prevented the reestablishment of traditional authority relations between politicians and peasants by forcing politicians to compete for support, and by giving peasants a real alternative.

[22] It is worth noting that the most serious of AD's splits, the division of Prieto and the MEP in late 1967, came only after a long period of intra-party tension, and broke out in competition for the party's presidential nomination, whose winner would presumably determine party and national policy for years to come.

the tremendous emphasis, by all sides, on procedural questions and mutual guarantees. Issue concerns come into the picture more by way of exclusion, by marking off certain areas as untouchable, than by direct agreement. This roundabout approach was central to the success of the whole enterprise, for only when the untouchable issues were safely buried could substantive agreement on more limited questions get under way.

The importance of coalitions in this strategy has already been noted. Coalitions, of course, are built on compromise and concession, and in Venezuela the powerful organizational loyalties already described have been central to the coalition process by providing elites with tremendous leverage at all levels. Elite decisions to reduce the level and intensity of open partisan conflict helped enforce the behavioral equivalent of these decisions at other levels. Through agreement on common forms of action, reformulation of the issues, and the like, people came to behave as if old hostilities had declined, when in fact change came primarily at the elite level. Elite decisions then spread throughout the system by virtue of leadership control over organizations.

OTHER EXPLANATIONS

The picture of a new political style, embodied in the rules of the game just outlined, differs in many respects from other recent views on Venezuelan society and politics. A major research effort, conducted jointly by the M.I.T. Center for International Studies and CENDES (the Center for Development Studies of the UCV) argues that the Venezuelan polity is marked by "cultural heterogeneity," that is, by the coexistence of distinct and often conflicting cultures within the same formal institutional framework.[23] The CENDES studies represent a massive collection and synthesis of elite and mass data on a national scale, and for that

[23] The titles published as a result of this research are listed above in Chapter 1, note 6.

243

reason alone, a complete review is both impossible and unnecessary here. It is important, however, to note the analytic thrust of the CENDES research, and to explore the empirical consequences of its guiding premises.

As used in the CENDES studies, cultural heterogeneity is manifest in two kinds of phenomena: (1) the coexistence of different cultures within the same political system, and (2) the coexistence within the same social stratum and institution of persons with radically divergent value orientations. According to Ahumada, "Venezuelan society is dual in both senses."[24] This intranational cultural diversity makes for profound differences in the meaning of institutions and events to different political actors, and implies related variations in the formulation of issues, evaluation of possible solutions, and the mobilization and use of resources in political conflict:

> The approach is in this sense structural, functional, and strongly normative, but centers on conflict and change rather than on system maintenance. While it considers the social location of interests and capacity to act, the focal political matrix, expressive of conflict and its resolution, is one in which evaluations of events change, rather than one in which interests are balanced.[25]

The political effects of cultural heterogeneity are primarily lack of consensus on basic issues, lack of consensus on proper methods of action, and as a general result, governmental inefficiency and inefficacy, social and political violence, and inability to engage in rational planning. Combined with the fragmentation of power resulting from rapid economic growth, cultural heterogeneity helps intensify conflict by inhibiting the creation and use of institutions for the conciliation of conflicts on a regular basis. The CENDES researchers assume that a decline in conflict

[24] F. Bonilla and J. Silva Michelena, eds., *op.cit.*, p. 27.
[25] *Ibid.*, p. 30.

means an increase in the possibility of rational policy-formation and decision-making:

> The diagnostic approach focuses in a very general sense on the national capacity to provide authoritative and practicable solutions to policy issues at minimal or at least tolerable social costs. . . . The emphasis is on locating and defining the nature of stress or conflict in the society that impedes the achievement of specific goals or blocks anticipated policy action.[26]

It should be noted that the CENDES studies do not reject conflict, nor do they always assign it a negative role. Rather, conflict and consensus, in general and for any particular instance, are placed in the context of given issues and policies:

> The assumption here is that if conflict, anticipated or actual, surpasses certain limits, both the political realism and feasibility of a policy fade away. However, we do not regard conflict by itself as necessarily either prejudicial or beneficial. Nor do we wish to imply that all conflicts hinder the policy-making and policy-implementing process. . . . All we are suggesting is that when conflict reaches certain levels—levels that may vary for different areas—it usually hinders the applicability of a given policy.[27]

One way to evaluate the validity and utility of this approach is to outline some specific areas of concern and assess the contributions of the CENDES studies to understanding the course of events. The first area of concern is a fundamental one, and arises with respect to the concept of consensus. One troubling aspect of the CENDES studies is the extremely broad scope given to (and required of) consensus. The problem becomes evident if we consider the rela-

[26] *Ibid.*, p. 25.
[27] J. Silva Michelena, *The Politics of Change in Venezuela: Volume III*, 253.

245

tion posited between consensus and violence. Clearly there is much violence in Venezuela, as in many societies. The incidence of violence by itself, however, tells us little about its social scope and political implications. Violence cannot be considered in isolation. It must be taken as part of a configuration of factors in a society. Only then can its social meaning be properly understood. If violence is generalized, and institutions are unable to contain it, then we could with justice speak of an anarchic situation or of anomie. But if violence is perpetrated by small, well-organized revolutionary cadres, and furthermore is effectively contained, then violence is a different kind of social phenomenon.[28]

Issue consensus is not absolute. That is clear. But what is the scope and content of the consensus that does exist? In terms of issues, it should be noted that by 1958, the major parties had agreed on a joint reform program, centering on agrarian reform, economic development, the expansion of health and educational services, promotion of urban and rural unionism, etc. There was disagreement between the parties, of course, but it was disagreement within a framework of commonly accepted goals. These general policy goals were cemented by the explicit determination of the major parties, and of nonparty elements such as the Church, to preserve open competitive politics. The general thrust of this study is that this determination has been made manifest in a procedural consensus, a set of limited agreements which allow institutions to function in the absence of universal agreement on issues. The problem with the CENDES approach is that it leaves little room for conflict and opposition as the normal, inevitable manifestations of social change and diversity. Cultural heterogeneity is seen as a

[28] F. Bonilla and J. Silva Michelena, eds., *op.cit.*, pp. 175-211 offer evidence: first, that there is general agreement among political, cultural, and economic elites on the nature of the problem of political violence and terrorism (pp. 185-187), and second, that broad agreement exists within the political elite on how to respond to it. There is no sense of unpreparedness or panic (pp. 207-209).

problem precisely because of the issue conflict it generates. As J. Silva Michelena puts it, "the political capacity of the country has been impaired by the cultural heterogeneity of key groups of the population."[29] The basic premise of the CENDES studies, then, is that for institutions to function effectively, value consensus must be reconstituted: cultural heterogeneity must be overcome.

Consider the following statement:

The most acute conflicts are probably those among groups within the most nationalist sector. Government officials, university professors, students and labor leaders display strong commitment to the nation but are unable to co-ordinate their activities because of political differences. Lack of agreement as to details of strategy, purpose, and leadership makes inoperative what should be a central, unifying value for development.

From this perspective, a crucial political need at all levels of the society is the linking of individual and group interests, present and emergent, to commitments and identifications transcending lower order loyalties. Mobilization in this sense seems indispensable in Venezuela.[30]

What is being argued here? The most nationally oriented groups are the most divided, and their division impedes national progress by inhibiting common action. What is needed, then, is some form of mobilization, to unify these now dispersed energies in the struggle for development. This implies that mobilization does not now take place, and moreover, that when it does occur, to be effective it must be monolithic, so as to ensure a more unified set of commitments. But if the struggle for development is really a struggle, why expect unanimity or even take it as a goal? If nothing else, development entails growing diversity, and the premise of unanimity is likely to serve as the pretext for re-

[29] J. Silva Michelena, *op.cit.*, p. 79.
[30] F. Bonilla and J. Silva Michelena, eds., *op.cit.*, p. 372.

pression (i.e., "we cannot afford the luxury"). Mobilization does indeed take place in Venezuela, but it is mobilization in a framework of competition, not uniformity.

The general premise of cultural heterogeneity focuses analytic attention on the search for "underlying" value splits and "fundamental" lines of conflict flowing from diversity, and away from more proximate explanations of political conflict and change.[31] This may explain why neither elite nor mass respondents were asked for party affiliation: the search is for deeper levels of conflict, and hence party membership received little systematic attention.[32] This creates some very grave problems for analysis. In explaining patterns of conflict and predicting future trends, CENDES researchers constructed a complex simulation of the political system (VENUTOPIA).[33] In the simulations, patterns of future alliances and coalitions are predicted for each group on the basis of attitudes and values tapped by survey questionnaires. Each sample group (e.g., parish priests, municipal councilmen, student leaders) was taken in isolation and a probable course of action calculated on the basis of the survey data.

Problems are apparent at once. The model ignores those linkages which cut across social and functional lines, setting up intra-group conflicts between members of different parties. By not asking for party affiliation, the CENDES model

[31] This distinction of levels of analysis is spelled out in J. Silva Michelena, "Desarrollo Cultural y Heterogeneidad Cultural en Venezuela," 67:2 (July 1967), *Revista Latinoamericana de Sociología*, especially 187.

[32] F. Bonilla, *op.cit.*, Chapter 7, does deal with party as a perceived context of action, but his discussion is of limited value for the question being raised here. For a study which compares the CENDES elite data with similar work in the U.S., France, Israel, and Germany (all of which did ask party affiliation), see D. Searing, "The Comparative Study of Elite Socialization," *Comparative Political Studies*, 1:4 (January 1969), 471-500.

[33] A variety of numbers and kinds of models were run through the computer. The most complete account of them is provided by J. Silva Michelena, *op.cit.*, Chapter 9.

fails to consider organizational ties which bind groups (or factions of groups) together and thus inhibit some of the polarizations and coalitions predicted by the model. Social and political groups in Venezuela do not exist in isolation. Their responses to issues can only be understood in terms of their relation to one another and to certain overarching structures such as political parties. If these factors are not built into the model, it loses empirical relevance.

Another problem with the CENDES research is that the concept of cultural heterogeneity is literally beaten to death. It is used and overused and used again and again to explain every fact of political life even where there is no problem that seems to demand explanation. For example, cultural heterogeneity is used by Silva Michelena to explain the formation and dissolution of coalition governments. As we have seen, coalitions have been central to Venezuelan politics since 1958. The composition of the coalition has shifted but nevertheless a policy of coalition was clearly pursued by both AD governments. The fact of coalition is surely more important than its shifting party base. To Silva Michelena, however, there is a basic problem here, traceable to normative disagreement. He argues that government by coalition

... has proved very unstable because of the heterogeneity of the normative patterns existing within and among the different parties. Even, for example, when the same party wins two consecutive elections, the coalition that existed in the first period will not necessarily be re-formed. This happened when the AD-COPEI coalition during Betancourt's regime was supplanted by the coalition of AD with URD.[34]

But why assume that identical coalitions will be formed in successive governmental periods? If the same coalition

[34] *Ibid.*, p. 70. Silva Michelena is in error here, for the coalition which replaced AD-COPEI was a three-party pact between AD, URD, and FND. FND later dropped out and for most of the governmental period, the effective coalition was AD-URD.

does not re-form, can this be attributed to normative heterogeneity? The most central norm at issue in this case was the relative assessment of COPEI's value to the coalition. The Christian Democrats wanted to build strength in opposition and develop a public image as a viable alternative government. Thus it made sense to leave the coalition. Moreover, the majority in AD favored experimentation with new coalition partners.[35] This explanation of coalition formation is quite proximate, and flows easily from an understanding of the way institutions operate in Venezuela. Cultural or normative heterogeneity have no great relevance here.

But assume, for the moment, that the nation is indeed riven by cultural heterogeneity. Why then do the postulated political effects of this condition not hold? What keeps the society from complete fragmentation and total inefficacy in the face of crisis? The basic reason lies in the independent role of political and leadership variables. As Arend Lijphart has pointed out, cultural and sociological determinism must be avoided, for there is more than one possible outcome to a situation of subcultural fragmentation: "The leaders of the rival subcultures may engage in competitive behaviors and thus further aggravate mutual tensions and political instability, but they may also make *deliberate efforts to counteract the immobilizing and unstabilizing effects of cultural fragmentation*."[36]

Clearly, the CENDES studies have brushed aside one obvious and important question: given the deep and cumulative conflicts that divide Venezuelans, how, in fact, have these been managed or regulated? The reason they brush this question aside is that from the CENDES perspective, conflict and consensus take on meaning only in terms of issue efficacy, the ability to provide "acceptable" solutions

[35] The formation of these coalitions is described by E. J. Williams, *op.cit.*, p. 209.

[36] A. Lijphart, "Consociational Democracy," *World Politics, op.cit.*, 211-212 (italics in original).

to problems. From this point of view, the costs built into the present system have been so high, especially in policy terms, that the efforts expended in its maintenance have not been worth it. Issue efficacy, "real progress" in other words, is sharply distinguished from institutional capacity for survival or continuity. Thus, for example, although Bonilla presents data on elite values which confirm the general propositions outlined here, he sees these data as evidence of the problem, not the solution.

Although his work demonstrates beyond a doubt that the elite, and particularly the political elite, represent a new leadership group, Bonilla constantly hammers home the theme that things are not as they seem, that although the system seems open, traditional paternalistic attitudes lie just below the surface. Thus he decries the shallowness and conventionality of the personal views and private lives of Venezuelan political leaders:

> Beneath the thin overlay of technicism, sophistication, and intellectuality that marks the professional activity of these men, lies a world of private relations in which more simple formulas and modes of action dominate. . . . These men are, by and large, the vanguard of a social group in ascent. Their private lives are still embedded in a class-marked milieu heavily preoccupied with status, conformity, and provincial canons of decorum. . . . *In short, these* [religion, family, friendship] *have not been in the past nor do they seem to be becoming areas of life in which informed, principled, and emotionally satisfying action patterns are taking root.*[37]

[37] F. Bonilla, *op.cit.*, p. 144 (italics in original). In general, Bonilla and Silva berate the middle classes for their unreliability, inconsistency, and the like. A source both cite for such views on the middle classes is Guillermo García Ponce, *Política y Clase Media* (Caracas: Editorial La Muralla, 1966). They fail to mention that García Ponce is a very high-ranking leader of the Communist Party, hardly the most objective source possible for views on middle-class political functions.

251

This is a very dubious proposition, for it says little more than that middle-class elites are middle class, not supermen, and perhaps lacking the intellectual polish, "principle," or dash of university professors. They are conventional, hardworking, career politicians of a type familiar in the evolution of many political systems.[38] I stress this point because the thrust of the CENDES studies as a whole, and of Bonilla's work on elites in particular, is to argue that this in itself poses the central problem. But elite conventionality, and the associated fact that not all social problems have been resolved to anyone's complete satisfaction, are not adequate substitutes for analysis and explanation of the way the system actually functions, the bases of its strength, and the reasons for its persistence.

Conclusions

At issue in my criticisms of the CENDES studies are fundamental differences in two central areas: first, concerning the proper role of political analysis; and second, regarding underlying theoretical premises about social reality (how and why societies hang together).[39] In the first case, it is important to distinguish explanation from prescription, and not to confuse an analysis of how institutions do run from a recommendation on how they should run. The tasks of explanation and prescription, of course, are not mutually exclusive, but some effort should be made to keep them

[38] A good discussion of the development of this kind of politician in U.S. history is R. Hofstadter, *The Idea of a Party System, op.cit.,* particularly Chapter 6.

[39] There is a methodological issue here as well, already presented in Chapter 1 and the early pages of this chapter. Basically, this concerns the most appropriate means for studying political values and culture: a survey-questionnaire approach, of the kind relied upon by CENDES, or an institutionally focused, in-depth study of actual behavior along the lines attempted here. For a fuller discussion of these issues and their bearing on the operational meaning of "culture," see D. Levine, "Issues in the Study of Culture in Latin America" (forthcoming).

analytically separate. The "diagnostic" approach employed by CENDES, with its clear commitment to certain kinds of policies and solutions blurs this distinction. Because elites have not been completely successful (who is?), they cannot therefore be dismissed as wholly ineffective, unable to work in more than trivial ways on social problems. The research reported in these pages has as its goal an understanding of the origins and operations of the present system: why it became the sort of system it is. This approach carries the danger of putting politics into a vacuum. To consider interelite agreements apart from their social and political consequences would clearly be a small contribution to understanding. Of course having elections and regular transfers of power is not the whole story. That point has not been argued here. But it is a key part of that story—the grease that makes the wheels turn. For without regular transfers of power, agreed-on procedures for the conciliation of conflict, and the norms and institutions on which they depend, little can be done.

In terms of basic social theory, a choice must be made between models and theories which view conflict as somehow dysfunctional and abnormal, something to be "overcome," and those which consider conflict as both normal and necessary, and then proceed to ask how societies contain and regulate it. The first perspective, associated in sociological theory with structural-functionalism,[40] assumes that societies are held together by some kind of value consensus. As we have seen, it then follows that cultural heterogeneity is a condition to be overcome, a state of affairs with unfor-

[40] I do not wish to enter, here, the debate over the merits of structural functionalism. I have outlined my views elsewhere ("Issues in the Study of Culture in Latin America"). I merely wish to note that despite disclaimers, the theoretical basis of the CENDES studies carries key structural-functional premises concerning social conflict and change. For a summary of the debate, and many valuable contributions to it, see N. J. Demerath and R. A. Peterson, eds., *System, Change, and Conflict: A Reader on Contemporary Sociological Theory and the Debate over Functionalism* (New York: Free Press, 1967).

253

tunate and unavoidable consequences. But the whole theory of cultural heterogeneity rings of determinism, as cultural fragmentation is supposed to make it impossible for a system to operate "effectively." Yet, as we have seen, there are many cases of "accommodation politics" (typical of the segmented pluralism of smaller European states and reproduced in many ways in Venezuela) where deeply fragmented societies have reached agreements to reduce tension and violence through the creation of minimal rules of accord. Perhaps analytic attention should turn to the mechanisms by which such systems emerge and survive. Surely more understanding will be gained this way than by mourning the heterogeneity underlying them.

Recognizing the possible range of accommodation systems, moreover, has immense significance for the theory of social and political change. For the existence of such systems belies simplistic, unilinear views of development which posit a neat and straightforward path from "tradition" to "modernity," from the disintegration of some previous consensus to the construction of a new one. Perhaps we need to provide theoretical room for systems which, rather than producing a new consensus, display instead the flowering of internal segmentation, and then try to work out some ways of living with it.

CHAPTER 10

Conclusions: The Future of Conflict

In drawing conclusions about Venezuela's political system, it is wise to consider the future not as a path determined once and forever after by forces beyond human control, but rather as a set of alternatives. Building alternative futures into analysis provides a healthy antidote to determinisms of any kind (racial, economic, or cultural) for it forces us to consider the role and capacity of leadership in moving systems on their way, simultaneously designing and implementing the future.

In studying the Venezuelan experience, a number of basic questions have been raised for the theory and strategy of political change. In theoretical terms, I have tried to distinguish the factors that helped Venezuela develop a pluralist and competitive political system from those which produce hegemonic revolutionary regimes or systems marked by stalemate between new forces and existing institutions and power groups. In strategic terms, it is important to specify the values served by a structure of competitive pluralism which are not fulfilled by other systems. What does a competitive system do that others fail to do?

In this regard, Venezuela offers strong evidence to support the view that the crucial vehicle for organizing and managing political change is the modern mass political party.[1] The Venezuelan party system combines effective popular mobilization with a new, widely shared sense of political authority and identity for the society. Moreover,

[1] For example, S. Huntington, op.cit., or I. L. Horowitz, *Three Worlds of Development: The Theory and Practice of International Stratification* (New York: Oxford University Press, 1966), Chapter 8.

in the long haul, the authority of party leadership has been used to moderate, channel, and control political conflict without eliminating it. Parties have provided organizational links between hitherto isolated sectors and groups, extending the effective social base of the nation by sponsoring the participation of previously marginal and excluded groups.

In this regard, there is one very visible problem clouding the future of the party system. Most major political parties have their most solid base in the countryside. For example, peasants have long provided a rock-hard base of support for AD and COPEI.[2] Given the fragmented and fickle nature of urban vote patterns (particularly in Caracas), this small but very consistent base has enabled AD and COPEI to dominate the political system. The urban vote has tended to be nonparty (and often, antiparty)[3] fluctuating wildly from election to election and leader to leader. In the long run, if the dominant parties cannot extend their organizations into Caracas, which now holds about one-fifth of the nation's population, then the future capacity of the system must be in doubt, as the strength of its institutions will continue to depend on control of a declining element in the population.

The Venezuelan experience is also relevant to one of the fundamental dilemmas of development strategy—the choice between systems of single-party mobilization and multi-party competition.[4] Many authors have described the advantages of open competitive systems, notably their lower level of coercion and correspondingly higher level of infor-

[2] J. D. Powell, *op.cit.*, shows that rural population (less than 1,000) correlates .65 with AD votes (1963) by state, and .76 with COPEI votes (p. 52).

[3] On Venezuelan vote patterns, see B. Bunimov-Parra, *op.cit.*, and J. Martz, *The Venezuelan Elections of December 1, 1963, Part III, Final Provisional Election Returns, Presidential and Legislative, Broken Down by Region and State* (Washington: Institute for the Comparative Study of Political Systems, 1964).

[4] See D. Apter, *The Politics of Modernization* (Chicago: University of Chicago Press, 1965), Chapters 6, 10, 11.

mation and potentially rational decision-making.[5] The Venezuelan experience highlights a slightly different facet of this question by revealing that in a society with a complex and varied structure of social and economic life, which naturally generates many situations of conflict and opposition, a political strategy of living with conflicts—one which tries to reconcile rather than repress them—is both feasible and effective.

The title of this chapter, "The Future of Conflict," is, in this respect, self-explanatory. For in Venezuela, the future of conflict is more conflict. The system itself is open-ended, and builds conflict and change into its operative mechanisms. Moreover, political parties in Venezuela manage to combine a mobilizing function—they are year-round, comprehensive parties of the integral kind,[6] with a commitment to methods of political action that center on elections. Thus, they do not fit the conventional models of "mobilization systems"[7] or "organizational weapons"[8] while in effect they perform the same functions. Moreover, it follows from our analysis of the development of organizations and norms, that the kind of conflict likely to dominate the future will be organization-focused, rather than issue-focused.

The general pattern of political change is best understood in terms of the interpenetration of structural and cultural factors. As we have seen, structural elements made certain patterns of conflict and confrontation probable, if not inevitable, while changes in political norms and culture shaped the pattern of conflict management that emerged.

[5] See Apter, *op.cit.*, Anderson, *op.cit.*, and C. Lindblom, *The Intelligence of Democracy* (New York: Free Press, 1965).

[6] On types of parties, see M. Duverger, *Political Parties* (London: Methuen and Co., Ltd., 1964).

[7] On mobilization systems, see D. Apter, *op.cit.*

[8] P. Selznick, *The Organizational Weapon* (New York: McGraw-Hill, 1952), provides a discussion of the typical view of Marxist-Leninist total parties.

The mutual determination of structural and cultural factors is inescapable. New patterns of action stimulated changes in political perspectives, just as new attitudes spurred elites to tentative efforts at accommodation. The interaction of structure and culture is also necessary for a full understanding of the dynamics of social change. Mapping changes in the generation and distribution of power is a necessary first step for any political analysis. But to understand the uses to which power is put, the form and content of political conflict, analysis of the distribution of power must be infused with culturally defined significance. Only then can we hope to understand the meaning of change as experienced by the actors, or appreciate the significance with which their actions are imbued.

A major premise of this book has been the central role of prudent leadership in making the system work. In closing, let me return to this theme. The Venezuelan system works. Its construction has entailed clear costs, in the abandonment or shelving of possibly more radical programs for change, but in the eyes of political elites, the achievement of institutional continuity, and thereby of the opportunity to work for more change in the future, was a price worth paying. The system seems well founded and solid, but like any artifact, it is fragile, and its continued survival requires constant care and attention.

As we have seen, in many conflict situations, once common rules are agreed upon, they are, in action, self-enforcing. This is so to a certain degree. But it should be remembered that conscious choice must be exercised at all levels, all the time, to stay within the rules. For a set of institutions is not an abstraction, but rather a system of behavior, continuously reconstituted and formed anew by the everyday, routine actions of its members. The agreement to disagree is fragile, and easily smashed. The care lavished on coalitions reflects vital awareness of this need. In any case, agreement and consensus alone are not enough. There must be sufficient power at the center to implement the agreements reached. Here, political parties are key. The imposition of the party system in Venezuela has had its most vital impact in the establishment of new legitimate methods of action and new criteria of power. The autonomy and independence of political institutions has grown immensely. Although the political spectrum is fragmented into many parties, and there is a constant problem of party division, so far most splinter groups have been wiped out at election time, and coalition strategies have provided a firm base of support for moderate politics and policies. For the system as a whole, noncoalition government is clearly not a viable strategy in the long term. COPEI, AD, or any of the major parties undoubtedly has the skills and personnel to rule alone, but the lessons of the past argue strongly for coalition, even at the possible loss of efficiency and governmental harmony.[9]

Venezuela seems to have solved some of the deepest riddles of political development: mobilization with legitimate authority, containing the military, and combining conflict and competition with institutional and procedural consensus. In reaching these solutions, Venezuelans have built a powerful and complex political infrastructure, a solid foundation for future development and change with institutional continuity. But authority and legitimacy are delicate creatures, and bargains can be broken. In Venezuela, the future lies with cautious men.

[9] Although COPEI came to power as a minority government and had formed no coalition by November 1971, it seems to have reached working agreements with AD for sufficient cooperation in the congress to allow essential legislation to be considered and passed.

AD   *Acción Democrática,* Democratic Action, a party founded in 1941

adeco   Member of AD

AD-OP   AD-Opposition, a party founded in 1961 as a result of a division in AD

AJV   *Asociación Juvenil de Venezuela,* AD's youth wing in the mid-1940's

allanamiento   A general term referring to a police search and seizure (In the text, this refers to police and army occupations of universities)

APRA   *Alianza Popular Revolucionaria Americana,* a party founded in Peru which served as an early model for AD

APRO-FEP   *Asociación Pro Fomento de la Educación Popular,* a group formed to sponsor Catholic candidates for the National Pedagogical Institute

AVEC   *Asociación Venezolana de Educación Católica,* a national organization of Catholic primary and secondary schools

Carúpano   A major naval base in Eastern Venezuela, scene of an attempted left-wing insurrection in May 1962

claustro   The electoral body of the autonomous universities: faculty are members of the *claustro,* and students and alumni elect delegates to it in differing proportions (The *claustro* elects the rector, vice-rector, and secretary of the University)

CEFEL   *Centro de Estudiantes Federados de Educación Libre,* an organization of students at Catholic schools

261

CJV   *Confederación de Jóvenes de Venezuela,* a youth organization sponsored by the Communist Party in the mid-1940's

COPEI   *Comité de Organización Política Electoral Independiente,* a Christian Democratic party, founded in 1946

copeyano   Member of COPEI

CPV   *Colegio de Profesores de Venezuela,* organization of secondary school teachers

CTV   *Confederación de Trabajadores de Venezuela,* the major national trade union organization

CUTV   *Confederación Unica de Trabajadores de Venezuela,* a group of left-wing trade unions formed after the expulsion of left-wing labor leaders from the CTV

cupo   A numerical limit or capacity (As used in the text, this refers to the policy of limiting admissions to university faculties and schools)

delito militar   Military crime, the classification under which left-wing deputies and senators arrested in 1963 were brought to trial

estado docente   A doctrine giving the primary role in the organization and supervision of education to public authorities

Fé y Alegría   Faith and Joy, a program of vocational and artisan training under Catholic sponsorship

FALN   *Fuerzas Armadas de Liberación Nacional,* the military arm of the guerrilla movement, set up to coordinate the actions of the various parties sponsoring guerrilla units.

FAPREC   *Federación de Asociaciones de Padres y Representantes de la Educación Católica,* national federation of parents' associations of Catholic schools

FCU   *Federación de Centros Universitarios,* the university wide student organization at each university (In formal terms, it is a federation of the student centers of the various faculties)

FEV	*Federación de Estudiantes de Venezuela*, the major national student organization active in 1928 and from 1936 to the mid-1940's
FEV-OP	*Federación de Estudiantes de Venezuela—Organización Política*, a group founded in 1936 as a front to allow the FEV to engage in political action
FLN	*Frente de Liberación Nacional*, the political expression of the guerrilla movement, set up to coordinate the activities of various revolutionary parties and groups
FND	*Frente Nacional Democrático*, a party founded in 1964, around the person of Arturo Uslar Pietri
FDP	*Fuerza Democrática Popular*, a party based on the candidacy and person of Admiral Wolfgang Larrazábal
FVM	*Federación Venezolana de Maestros*, national organization of primary school teachers
JRC	*Juventud Revolucionaria Copeyana*, the national youth organization of COPEI
LUZ	*La Universidad del Zulia*, the University of Zulia, located in Maracaibo
libertad de enseñanza	A doctrine giving the primary role in the organization and supervision of education to the family and the Church
liceo	Secondary school
MAS	*Movimiento al Socialismo*, a party formed by dissidents from the PCV, who were expelled by more orthodox leaders in late 1970
MEP	*Movimiento Electoral del Pueblo*, the People's Electoral Movement, a party formed in late 1967 as a result of a split in AD
MIR	*Movimiento de Izquierda Revolucionaria*, Movement of the Revolutionary Left, a party founded in 1960 as a result of a split in AD

ORVE	*Organización Venezolana,* left-wing front formed in 1936
Puerto Cabello	A major port and naval base in Western Venezuela, scene of a bloody left-wing insurrection in June 1962
PCV	*Partido Communista de Venezuela,* the Communist Party, first founded in 1931
PDV	*Partido Democrático Venezolano,* a party supporting the government of President Medina in the 1940's
PDN	*Partido Democrático Nacional,* a coalition of left-wing groups organized in 1936 (It was denied legal status by the government of López Contreras, and later became the seedbed of AD)
PRIN	*Partido Revolucionario de Integración Nacionalista,* a party formed out of a combination of the PRN, elements of the MIR, and other small left-wing groups; the PRIN dissolved after the 1968 elections.
PRN	*Partido Revolucionario Nacionalista,* a party based on the AD-OP, which split from AD in 1961
Pbro.	A contraction of *Presbítero,* the term for a parish priest (i.e., a priest not connected with an order, like the Jesuits or Dominicans)
RR	A common way of referring to the Regulations on Repeating Students, issued in the Central University in 1964
trienio	As used in the text, this refers to the three-year period of AD rule from 1945 to 1948
UCV	*Universidad Central de Venezuela,* the Central University, in Caracas
ULA	*Universidad de Los Andes,* the University of the Andes, in Mérida
UNE	*Unión Nacional de Estudiantes,* a Catholic group which split from the FEV in 1936 (Its principal leader was Rafael Caldera)

UPA   *Unión Para Avanzar*, the Union for Progress, a Communist front formed for the elections of 1968

URD   *Unión Republicana Democrática*, the Democratic Republican Union, a political party formed in 1946

VPN   *Vanguardia Popular Nacionalista*, a political party formed in the mid-1960's by leftist dissidents from URD

GENERAL

Books

Adams, R. N. *Crucifixion by Power: Essays in Guatemalan National Social Structure, 1944-1966.* Austin: University of Texas Press, 1970.

Anderson, C. W. *Politics and Economic Change in Latin America.* Princeton: D. Van Nostrand Company, Inc., 1967.

Apter, D. *The Politics of Modernization.* Chicago: University of Chicago Press, 1965.

Bosworth, W. *Catholicism and Crisis in Modern France.* Princeton: Princeton University Press, 1962.

Coleman, J. *Community Conflict.* New York: Free Press, 1957.

Connolly, W. *Political Science and Ideology.* New York: Atherton Press, 1967.

Crick, B. *In Defense of Politics.* London: Pelican Books, 1964, rev. edn.

Dahl, R. A., ed. *Political Oppositions in Western Democracies.* New Haven: Yale University Press, 1966.

————. *Polyarchy. Participation and Opposition.* New Haven: Yale University Press, 1971.

Dahrendorf, R. *Class and Class Conflict in Industrial Society.* London: Routledge and Kegan Paul, 1959.

Demerath, N. J., and Peterson, R. A., eds. *System, Change, and Conflict: A Reader on Contemporary Sociological Theory and the Debate over Functionalism.* New York: Free Press, 1967.

Dexter, L. A. *Elite and Specialized Interviewing.* Evanston: Northwestern University Press, 1970.

Diamant, A. *Austrian Catholics and the First Republic: Democracy, Capitalism, and the Social Order, 1918-1934.* Princeton: Princeton University Press, 1960.

Duverger, M. *Political Parties.* London: Methuen and Co., Ltd., 1964.

Edelman, M. *The Symbolic Uses of Politics.* Urbana: University of Illinois Press, 1967.

Emmerson, D., ed. *Students and Politics in Developing Nations.* New York: Frederick A. Praeger, 1968.

SELECTED BIBLIOGRAPHY

Fagen, R. *The Transformation of Political Culture in Cuba.* Stanford: Stanford University Press, 1969.

Gamson, W. *Power and Discontent.* Homewood: The Dorsey Press, 1968.

Horowitz, I. L. *Three Worlds of Development: The Theory and Practice of International Stratification.* New York: Oxford University Press, 1966.

Huntington, S. P. *Political Order in Changing Societies.* New Haven: Yale University Press, 1968.

Janowitz, M. *Political Conflict: Essays in Political Sociology.* Chicago: Quadrangle Books, 1970.

Landsberger, H., ed. *The Church and Social Change in Latin America.* South Bend: University of Notre Dame Press, 1969.

LaPalombara, J., and Weiner, M., eds. *Political Parties and Political Development.* Princeton: Princeton University Press, 1966.

Lieuwin, E. *Generals vs. Presidents: Neomilitarism in Latin America.* New York: Frederick A. Praeger, 1964.

Lijphart, A. *The Politics of Accommodation: Pluralism and Democracy in the Netherlands.* Berkeley: University of California Press, 1968.

Lindblom, C. *The Intelligence of Democracy.* New York: Free Press, 1965.

Lipset, S. M. and Rokkan, S., eds. *Party Systems and Voter Alignments.* New York: Free Press, 1968.

Lipset, S. M. and Solari, A., eds. *Elites in Latin America.* New York: Oxford University Press, 1967.

MacGaffey, W. and Barnett, C. R. *Twentieth Century Cuba: The Background of the Castro Revolution.* Garden City: Anchor Books, 1965.

McConnell, G. *Private Power and American Democracy.* New York: Alfred A. Knopf, 1966.

Moore, B. *Social Origins of Dictatorship and Democracy.* Boston: Beacon Press, 1967.

O'Connor, J. *The Origins of Socialism in Cuba.* Ithaca: Cornell University Press, 1970.

Payne, J. *Patterns of Conflict in Colombia.* New Haven: Yale University Press, 1968.

Schattschneider, E. E. *The Semi-Sovereign People: A Realist's View of Democracy in America.* New York: Holt, Rinehart, and Winston, 1960.

Selznick, P. *The Organizational Weapon.* New York: McGraw-Hill, 1952.

Silvert, K. H., ed. *Churches and States: The Religious Institution and Modernization.* New York: American Universities Field Staff, 1967.

Steward, J. *Theory of Culture Change.* Urbana: University of Illinois Press, 1963.

Vallier, I. *Catholicism, Social Control, and Modernization in Latin America.* Englewood Cliffs: Prentice-Hall, Inc., 1970.

Williams, E. J. *Latin American Christian Democratic Parties.* Knoxville: University of Tennessee Press, 1967.

Articles

Brown, B. E. "The Decision to Subsidize Private Schools," B. E. Brown and J. B. Cristoph, eds., *Cases in Comparative Politics.* Boston: Little, Brown and Company, 1965, pp. 113-147.

Di Tella, T. "Populism and Reform in Latin America," C. Veliz, ed., *Obstacles to Change in Latin America.* New York: Oxford University Press, 1965, pp. 47-74.

Etzioni, A. "On Self-Encapsulating Conflicts," *Journal of Conflict Resolution*, 8:3 (September 1964), 242-255.

Leeds, A. "Commentary," *Latin American Research Review*, 3:2 (Winter 1968), 79-87.

Linz, J. "The Breakdown of Democracy in Spain" (unpublished paper, n.d.).

Lijphart, A. "Typologies of Democratic Systems," *Comparative Political Studies*, 1:1 (April 1968), 3-44.

———. "Consociational Democracy," *World Politics*, 21:2 (January 1969), 207-223.

Lipset, S. M. "University Students and Politics in Underdeveloped Countries," *Comparative Education Review*, 10:2 (June 1966), 132-162.

Lorwin, V. "Segmented Pluralism: Ideological Cleavages and Political Cohesion in the Smaller European Democracies," *Comparative Politics*, 3:2 (January 1971), 141-176.

Merelman, R. "Learning and Legitimacy," *American Political Science Review*, 60:3 (September 1966), 548-561.

Schaedel, R. "Land Reform Studies," *Latin American Research Review*, 1:1 (Fall 1965), 75-122.

Scott, R. E. "Student Political Activism in Latin America," *Daedalus* (Winter 1968), 70-98.

Searing, D. "The Comparative Study of Elite Socialization," *Comparative Political Studies*, 1:4 (January 1969), 471-500.

SELECTED BIBLIOGRAPHY

Silvert, K. H. "Leadership Formation and Modernization in Latin America," *Journal of International Affairs*, 20:2 (1966), 318-331.
———. "The University Student," J. J. Johnson, ed., *Continuity and Change in Latin America*. Stanford: Stanford University Press, 1964, pp. 206-266.
———. "Some Psychocultural Factors in the Politics of Conflict and Conciliation: Setting Up the Problem." Prepared for delivery at the 1965 Annual Meeting of the American Political Science Association, Washington, D.C., September 8-11, 1965.
Verba, S. "Organizational Membership and Democratic Consensus," *The Journal of Politics*, 27:3 (August 1965), 467-497.
———. "Comparative Political Culture," S. Verba and L. Pye, eds. *Political Culture and Political Development*. Princeton: Princeton University Press, 1965, pp. 512-560.
Wienert, R. "Violence in Pre-Modern Societies: Rural Colombia," *American Political Science Review*, 60:2 (June 1966), 340-347.

VENEZUELA

Books

Acedo de Sucre, M., and Nones Mendoza, C. *La Generación Venezolana de 1928: Estudio de una élite política*. Caracas: Ediciones Ariel, 1967.
Acedo Mendoza, C. *Venezuela: Ruta y Destino*, 2 vols. Barcelona: Ediciones Ariel, 1966.
Agudo Freytes, R. *Vida de Un Adelantado (Intento Biográfico Sobre José Pío Tamayo)*. Caracas: Editorial Universitaria, 1948.
Alexander, R. *The Venezuelan Democratic Revolution*. New Brunswick: Rutgers University Press, 1964.
Alonso, I., Luzardo, M., Garrido, G., and Oriol, J. *La Iglesia en Venezuela y Ecuador*. Bogotá: FERES, 1962.
American University. *U.S. Army Handbook for Venezuela*. Washington, D.C.: U.S. Government Printing Office, 1964.
Arellano Moreno, A. *Mirador de la Historia Política de Venezuela*. Caracas: Ediciones Edime, 1967.
Betancourt, R. *Trayectoria Democrática de Una Revolución, Discursos y Conferencias*, Vols. I, II. Caracas: Imprenta Nacional, 1948.

270

SELECTED BIBLIOGRAPHY

———. *Tres Años de Gobierno Democrático*, Vols. I, II, III. Caracas: Imprenta Nacional, 1962.

———. *Venezuela: Política y Petróleo*, rev. edn. Caracas: Editorial Senderos, 1967.

Betancourt Sosa, F. *Pueblo en Rebeldía.* Caracas: Ediciones Garrido, 1959.

Bonilla, F. *The Politics of Change in Venezuela: Volume II, The Failure of Elites.* Cambridge: M.I.T. Press, 1970.

Bonilla, F., and Silva Michelena, J., eds. *The Politics of Change in Venezuela: Volume I, A Strategy for Research on Social Policy.* Cambridge: M.I.T. Press, 1967.

Bunimov-Parra, B. *Introducción a la Sociología Electoral Venezolana.* Caracas: Editorial Arte, 1968.

Cardenas, R. J. *El Combate Político: Sólo Para Líderes Nuevos.* Caracas: Editorial Doña Bárbara, 1966.

Centro de Estudios del Desarrollo (CENDES), Universidad Central de Venezuela. *Estudio de Conflictos y Consenso, Série de Resultados Parciales, No. 4, Muestra de Líderes Estudiantiles.* Caracas: Imprenta Universitaria, 1967.

Cockcroft, J. D. *Venezuela's Fidelista's—Two Generations.* Washington: National Student Association, 1963.

Cuenca, H. *Ejército, Universidad, y Revolución.* Buenos Aires: Ediciones Movimiento, 1962.

———. *La Universidad Revolucionaria.* Caracas: Editorial Cultura Contemporánea, 1964.

De Sola, R. *Balance Inconcluso de Una Actitud Universitaria.* Buenos Aires: Ediciones Casasola, 1962.

Doyle, J. "Venezuela 1958: The Transition from Dictatorship to Democracy." Ph.D. dissertation, Department of History, George Washington University, 1967.

Duno, P. *Sobre Aparatos, Desviaciones, y Dogmas.* Caracas: Editorial Nueva Izquierda, 1969.

Febres Cordero, F. *Autonomía Universitaria.* Caracas: Imprenta Universitaria, 1959.

Friedman, J. *Venezuela from Doctrine to Dialogue.* Syracuse: Syracuse University Press, 1965.

———. *Regional Development Policy: A Case Study of Venezuela.* Cambridge: M.I.T. Press, 1966.

Fuenmayor, J. *Veinte Años de Política, 1928-1948.* Caracas, 1968.

Gabaldón Marquez, J. *Memoria y Cuento de la Generación de 1928.* Caracas, 1958.

Gallegos Ortiz, R. *La Historia Política de Venezuela de Cipriano Castro a Pérez Jiménez.* Caracas: Imprenta Universitaria, 1960.

García Ponce, G. *Política, Táctica, y Estrategia.* Caracas: Ediciones Documentos Políticos, 1967.

——. *Teoría Política y Realidad Nacional.* Caracas: Editorial La Muralla, 1967.

Gilmore, R. L. *Caudillism and Militarism in Venezuela, 1810-1910.* Athens: Ohio University Press, 1964.

González Baquero, R. *Análisis del Proceso Histórico de la Educación Urbana (1870-1932) y de la Educación Rural (1932-1957) en Venezuela.* Caracas: Imprenta Universitaria, 1962.

Levy, F. *Economic Planning in Venezuela.* New York: Frederick A. Praeger, 1968.

Luzardo, R. *Notas Histórico-Económicas 1928-1963.* Caracas: Editorial Sucre, 1963.

Machado, G. *En el Camino del Honor Los Parlamentarios Acusan Desde el Cuartel San Carlos.* Caracas, 1966.

Márquez, P. *La Vigencia del PCV No Está en Discusion.* Caracas: Ediciones Documentos Políticos, 1967.

Márquez Rodríguez, A. *Doctrina y Proceso de la Educacion en Venezuela.* Caracas, 1964.

Martz, J. *The Venezuelan Elections of December 1, 1963, Part III, Final Provisional Election Returns, Presidential and Legislative, Broken Down by Region and State.* Washington: Institute for the Comparative Study of Political Systems, 1964.

——. *Acción Democrática: Evolution of a Modern Political Party in Venezuela.* Princeton: Princeton University Press, 1966.

Medina Angarita, I. *Cuatro Años de Democracia.* Caracas: Pensamiento Vivo, 1963.

Medina Silva, P. and Hurtado Barrios, N. *Por Qué Luchamos.* Caracas, 1963.

Mudarra, M. *Historia de la Legislación Escolar Contemporánea en Venezuela.* Caracas: Tipografía Vargas, 1962.

Otero Silva, M. *Fiebre.* Caracas, 1941.

Perales, P. *Manual de Geografía Económica de Venezuela.* Caracas: Ediciones Jaime Villegas, 1955.

Powell, J. D. *The Role of the Federación Campesina in the Venezuelan Agrarian Reform Process.* Madison: Land Tenure Center Research Paper No. 26, University of Wisconsin, December 1967.

Prieto, L. B. *Problemas de la Educación Venezolana.* Caracas: Imprenta Nacional, 1947.

————. *De Una Educación de Castas a Una Educación de Masas.* Havana: Editorial Lex, 1951.

Quintero, R. *Universidad y Política.* Caracas: Boletín Bibliográfico, Facultad de Economía, Edición Especial, UCV, 1961.

Rangel, D. A. *Los Andinos al Poder.* Caracas: Talleres Gráficos Universitarios, 1964.

————. *La Revolución de las Fantasías.* Caracas: Ediciones OFIDI, 1966.

Rangel, J. V. *Se Llamaba S.N.* Caracas: José Augustin Catalá, Editor, 1964.

Ray, T. *The Politics of the Barrios of Venezuela.* Berkeley: University of California Press, 1969.

Rodríguez Iturbe, J. *Iglesia y Estado en Venezuela (1824-1964).* Caracas: Imprenta Universitaria, 1968.

Rourke, T. [pseud.]. *Gómez Tyrant of the Andes.* New York: William Morrow and Co., 1936.

Sanoja Hernández, J. *La Universidad: Culpable o Víctima?* Caracas: Fondo Editorial Venezolano, 1967.

Silva Michelena, J. *The Politics of Change in Venezuela, Volume III: The Illusion of Democracy in Dependent Nations.* Cambridge: M.I.T. Press, 1971.

Sugon, A. *El Papel de los Militares.* Edinburgh: Centro de Estudios Latinoamericanos, 1963.

Taylor, P. *The Venezuelan Golpe de Estado of 1958: The Fall of Marcos Pérez Jiménez.* Washington, D.C.: Institute for the Comparative Study of Political Systems, 1968.

Uslar Pietri, A. *Sumario de Economía Venezolana.* Caracas: Fundación Eugenio Mendoza, 1960.

Articles

Agudo Freytes, R. "Ni Un Paso Atrás," *El Nacional,* June 8, 1946.

García Ponce, G. "La Línea Política y el IX Pleno del Comité Central del PCV," *Documentos Políticos,* No. 10, April 30, 1968.

López, C. [pseud.]. "El Partido Comunista de Venezuela y la Situación Actual en el País," *Principios,* segúnda época, No. 3 (March-April), 1965.

Martz, J. "Venezuela's 'Generation of '28': The Genesis of Political Democracy," *Journal of Inter American Studies,* 6, No. 1 (January 1964), 17-33.

SELECTED BIBLIOGRAPHY

Montes, E. [pseud.]. "La Historia Pública de la Federación de Estudiantes," *El Nacional*, February 17, 1966.

Muñoz, F. "FCU: Estudiar, Luchar: Una Lema Que Define Una Conducta," *Cultura Universitaria* (October 1963-March 1964), 153-160.

Ortega Díaz, P. "La Ideologia Pequeño-Burguesa en las Ideas de Regis Debray," *Documentos Políticos*, No. 9, March 31, 1968.

————. "Las Elecciones Universitarias," *Documentos Políticos*, No. 11, May 31, 1968.

Paz Galarraga, J. A. "Universidad Autónoma y Democrática," *La República*, February 3, 1966.

Plaza, C. G. "Pliego de Peticiones de la Federación Venezolana de Maestros," No. 93, *SIC* (March 1947).

Polanco, T. "Los Percances de Un Proyecto de Ley," *El Nacional*, July 16, 1966.

Quintero, J. H. "Alocución del Eminentísimo Cardenal Quintero," *AVEC Boletín*, segúnda epoca, No. 33 (September-October 1965).

Rangel, D. A. "El Destino de las Izquierdas," *El Universal*, December 5, 1968.

Rodríguez, G. "El Fracaso de la Insurección," *La República*, September 3-10, 1962.

Silva Michelena, J. "Desarrollo Cultural y Heterogeneidad Cultural en Venezuela," *Revista Latinoamericana de Sociología* 67:2 (July 1967), 164-195.

Documents

1. AD

Observaciones de Ultima Hora al Proyecto de Ley de Educación. March 19, 1965.

Informe de la Secretaría Nacional de Educación Ante el Secretariado Nacional Ampliado. July 24, 1965.

Resúmen del Informe del Secretario Nacional de Educación del CEN de Acción Democrática Ante la XV Convención Nacional del Partido. September 10, 1965.

Conclusiones y Tareas Derivadas del VII Pleno Nacional de Educadores. November 13, 1965.

Informe del Secretariado Nacional de Educación de Acción Democrática, para el VII Pleno Nacional de Educadores, sobre "FVM y Nueva Ley de Educación." Caracas, November 13, 1965.

Primer Seminario Universitario Nacional de Acción Democrática. Ponencia: "Bases Para Una Política Universitaria del Partido." Caracas: June 24, 25, and 26, 1966.

Paz Galarraga, J. A. *Carta Pública del CEN de AD (Pre-Convención Nacional)*, No. 7, July 5, 1966.

Conclusiones de la Comisíon del CEN Sobre Nueva Ley de Educación. February 9, 1967.

2. CATHOLIC EDUCATION

Carta Pastoral Colectiva Sobre Los Problemas Planteados a la Educación Católica en el País. Dirigida al Pueblo con Motivo de las Conferencias Extraordinarias, Celebradas en Caracas de 25 de agosto a 30 de septiembre de 1947. Caracas: Editorial Venezuela, 1947.

"Hablan los Padres de Familia: Memorandum Dirigido al Episcopado," No. 98, *SIC* (October 1947).

"Nosotros los Arzobispos y Obispos de Venezuela, a los Padres de Familia y Estudiantes Católicos de la República, Paz y Benedición," No. 98, *SIC* (October 1947).

Resúmen de la relación presentada por el R. P. Carlos Guillermo Plaza, S.J., Presidente Nacional de la AVEC ante la I Asamblea Nacional de Colegios Católicos, 1951. Mimeographed.

"Comunicado: La Educación Católica al Pueblo de Venezuela," *La Esfera*, July 8, 1966.

X Asamblea Nacional de AVEC, 19-23 de agosto de 1962. Caracas, 1962.

AVEC XI Asamblea Nacional, 26-30 agosto, 1964. Caracas, 1964.

XII Asamblea Nacional de AVEC, 17-23 de diciembre de 1966. Caracas, 1967.

AVEC: Planteles y Estadísticas Curso 1965-66. Caracas, 1967.

3. THE PCV AND THE MIR

Luchar Contra el RR, Sí. Pero Hacerlo en las Mejores Condiciones y Sabiendo Utilizar Oportunamente las Formas de Lucha Más Adecuadas. Propaganda flyer of the University Bureau of Communist Youth. Mimeographed, no date.

"Posiciones de Unidad Que Formulamos a Los Militantes Comunistas," No. 31, *Confidencial* (July 4, 1966).

SELECTED BIBLIOGRAPHY

"Remitido: Julio Escalona, Jorge Rodríguez, Carlos Muñoz, y José Enrique Mieres Opinan Ante los Estudiantes y el Pueblo de Venezuela," *El Nacional*, March 10, 1967.

"Remitido: Juvencio Pulgar, Alexis Adam, y Américo Díaz Nuñez," *El Nacional*, April 2, 1967.

4. OFFICIAL

Universidad Central de Venezuela, División de Planeamiento, Dirección de Economía y Planeamiento, Oficina de Estadística. *Boletín Estadístico No. 4, Años Lectivos 1964/65-1965/66*. Caracas, 1965-66.

Venezuela, Asamblea Nacional Constituyente. *Diario de Debates*, December 1946-September 1947. Caracas: Imprenta Nacional, 1947-48.

Venezuela, Congreso Nacional, Cámara de Diputados. *Diario de Debates*, August-September 1948. Caracas: Imprenta Nacional, 1948.

————. Cámara del Senado. *Diario de Debates*, September-October 1948. Caracas: Imprenta Nacional, 1948.

Gaceta Oficial de la República de Venezuela, No. 28.262, February 17, 1967.

Venezuela, Ministerio de Educación. *1966 Memoria y Cuenta que el Ministro de Educación Presenta al Congreso Nacional de la República de Venezuela en Sus Sesiones de 1967*, Vols. I, II. Caracas: Imprenta de la Dirección Técnica, 1967.

————. *1967 Memoria y Cuenta que el Ministro de Educación Presenta al Congreso Nacional de la República de Venezuela en Sus Sesiones de 1968*. Vols. I, II. Caracas: Imprenta de la Dirección Técnica, 1968.

————. Dirección Técnica. *Más y Mejor Educación, Análisis Estadístico*. Caracas: Imprenta de la Dirección Técnica, 1967.

Venezuela, Ministerio de Fomento, Dirección General de Estadística y Censos Nacionales. *Anuario Estadístico de Venezuela, 1965*. Caracas: Taller Gráfico, 1967.

————. Dirección General de Estadística y Censos Nacionales. *Compendio Estadístico de Venezuela*. Caracas: Taller Gráfico, 1968.

————. Dirección General de Estadística y Censos Nacionales, Oficina Central del Censo. *Noveno Censo General de Población (26 de febrero de 1961), Resúmen General de la*

República, Partes A, B, C. Caracas: Taller Gráfico, 1966, 1967.
Ley de Presupuesto General de Ingresos y Gastos Públicos Para el Año Fiscal, 1951-52 to 1967-68. Caracas, 1952-68.

Newspapers and Periodicals

El Nacional, 1945-69.
La República, 1962-69.
El Universal, 1958-69.
Izquierda, 1960.
Joven Patriota. Organo Nacional de la Juventud del MIR. IV Epoca. No. 1. June-July, 1968.
Tribuna Popular. Organo del Comité Central del PCV. VI Epoca. Advance No. 7. February 28, 1967.
Nueva Voz Popular, 1968-69.

INDEX

Acción Electoral, 31
Acción Nacional, 31
accommodation politics, 254
AD, anticlericalism, 38; attitude
to opposition in trienio, 40;
conditions of growth, 214;
conflict over Decree 321,
88-89; divisions, 59-60n, 139;
educational reform, 66f;
formation, 25, 28; internal
conflict, 42-43; internal
conflict over education,
123-24; Plenum of Educators,
112; power of students,
186-87; program, 65-66;
relation to Church, 38-40,
42-46; relation to FVM,
136-37; relation to military,
41, 46
Adam, A., 181
adeco, definition, 38
agrarian reform, 37
Aguilar, J. L., 103, 135
Aguirre, Padre J., 102, 117
Ahumada, J., 204
AJV, 30
allanamiento, 196-203; debate
in Left, 199-203; reaction of
political parties, 198-99
anticlericalism, 66n; in AD, 38
Anzola Carillo, A., 78n
April Bloc, 24
APRO-FEP, 102
Argentina, 229n
Arías Blanco, Msgr., 148
autonomy, of universities, 197-98
AVEC, 73, 77, 78, 79, 85, 90,
99, 102, 106, 117, 118, 119,
121, 126, 128; revival after
1958, 101

Barrios, G., 35

Betancourt, R., 24, 28, 35, 43,
51, 74, 99, 105, 151, 155n;
relations with Church, 45, 109;
relations with military, 46
Bianco, J. M., 198n
Bloque Nacional Democrático, 24
Bonilla, F., 231n, 240-41, 251
Bravo, D., 53, 199
brigades of order, 150-51
buffers, organizational, 91
Burelli Rivas, M. A., 56n

Caldera, R., 30
Cardozo, H., 181n
Carúpano, 52
case studies, method, 6, 233;
summary, 7-8
Castro, Cipriano, 46
Catholic Church, 213, 238;
challenges to, 63; opposition
to Pérez Jiménez, 45;
organizational growth, 106;
organizational weakness, 31-33,
63-64; organizational weakness
and conflict, 77; rebuilding,
32; relation to COPEI, 33, 39;
relation to FVM, 45; relation
to political change, 31-33;
relation to political parties
after 1958, 43-44; subsidies,
44; traditional strategies,
63-64
Catholic education, growth, 32;
internal debates, 118;
relation to lay educators,
99-100; reorientation, 103
Catholic leadership, perceptions,
41-43, 89-90, 111
Catholic sector, post-1958
summary, 107
caudillo, 19
CEFEL, 102, 128

279

diagnostic approach, 245, 253.
See also CENDES studies
Duno, P., 236n

ecclesiastical patronage, 45
education, growth, 69, 70, 95-98;
issue, 66n, 219-20. *See also*
school issue
Education Law, reform, 112ff
educational reform, 112;
Catholic goals, 123; elite
restraint, 123-25, 135; internal
conflict in AD, 123-24;
negotiations, 118-22, 124-25;
source in parties, 113-15;
submission to Congress, 128
elite norms, changes, 234;
impact in masses, 234
Episcopal Conference, 83, 126
Erasmus, C., 241-42n
Escalona, J., 180n
estado docente, 65, 79; Decree
321, 73
exclusion, and legitimacy
conflicts, 224; modern
response, 224-27; traditional
response, 224-26

Fagen, R., 224, 234n
FALN, 190n, 210n
FAPREC, 101, 102, 118, 128
FCU, 52
FEV, 20, 21, 23, 151; decline,
30-31
FEV-OP, 24
Fernández, E., 35
Fe y Alegría, 103, 118, 128
FND, 121, 126
formulation of issues, 216-17
fragility political, 237
Frente Universitario, 149, 150
Fuenmayor, J. B., 24
functional spheres, 9n
FVM, 32, 79, 99, 112, 116, 117,
119, 121, 136, 144; relation
to AD, 136-37

Gallegos, R., 27
García Mackle, M., 147n

García Ponce, G., 251n
General Association of Students,
20
general strike (1936), 25
generational solidarity, 181
Gilmore, R., 19n
Gómez, J. V., 14, 19, 21, 23, 159,
211, 213; opposition to, 19;
summary of period, 22
González, A., 113, 134
González Cabrera, J., 82n
government, growth, 15-16
Guatemala, 214n
guerrilla movement, 53; and
elections, 53
Guzmán Blanco, A., 31

Hamilton, W., 186
Henríquez, R., 180n
Herrera Campins, L., 147n
Huntington, S., 8, 220-21

incorporation, and legitimacy
conflicts, 223-24
industrial sociology, 233
institutionalization, 132-35. *See
also* conflict, institutionalization
insurrection, role of students,
161-63; strategy, 51
inter-party relations, impact
military rule, 42; post-1958, 99
interviews, subjects, 6
interviewing, 7
isolation of conflict, 10. *See also*
conflict, isolation
Izquierda, 156-57

Janowitz, M., 9n
jefes civiles, 37
Joven Patriota, 189
JRC, 31, 181n, 182

labor organizations, 18n, 37
Lairet, G., 149n
Lara Law, 25
La Riva Araujo, E., 197
Larrazábal, W., 155n
Law of Universities, 200

PDV, 29
Pérez Jiménez, M., 43, 46, 58,
61, 99, 146, 150, 152, 159,
210, 211
Pérez Marcano, H., 149n, 180n
petroleum, impact on social
structure, 16-17, 213
Pío Tamayo, J., 20-21n
Pizani, R., 158, 159n
planning, 3
pluralism, 11
Polanco, T., 131
polarization of conflict, 10-11
political change, dimensions of
analysis, 212; post-Gómez, 26;
post-1958, 55-61
political culture, and behavior,
232; study of, 231
political elites, changed
composition, 231
political fragility, 237
political leadership, 258
political legitimacy, 5, 10-11. *See
also* legitimacy conflicts
political norms, 231ff; agreement
to disagree, 239-40;
competition, 241-42;
concentration, 240-41;
fragility, 237-38; leadership,
235-36; mutual guarantees,
242-43; of Catholic elites,
141-43; organizational
loyalties, 241ff; pluralism, 242;
procedural consensus, 242-43;
supporting elements, 241ff
political parties, 18, 255-56,
258-59; atomization, 56n;
autonomous role, 9;
leadership, 235; relation to
sectors, 9; relation to social
structure, 18-19; rural base,
256; single-class, 18; types,
256
political roles, emergence of
new, 29; for student leaders,
167-68
political systems, accommodation,
254; alternatives for
Venezuela, 209ff;

competitive, 256;
mobilization, 256-57
praetorianism, 9, 240-41
Prieto, L. B., 35, 67, 78, 126,
134, 139, 242n
procedural consensus, 243
proportional representation,
student elections, 46, 153;
trade unions, 46
Provisional Statute of
Education, 95
PRP (Partido Republicano
Progresista), 24, 29; ("Black
Communists"), 37n
Puerto Cabello, 21, 53
Pulgar, J., 181

Quintero, Cardinal, 116, 117,
120

radical conflict system, 219
Ramírez Labrador, D., 166n
Rangel, D. A., 207
Rangel, J. V., 147n
regionalism, 15
religious conflict, 77-78
revolution, conditions, 228-29
revolutionary idealogy, 59
Rodríguez, G., 52
Rodríguez Bauza, H., 147n, 149n
Rojas, Pbro., 83
RR, 193-95
rules, political, 5, 231-41

Sánchez, D., 181n
Sánchez Espejo, Pbro., 82
save-the-yearism, 202
school issue, 66n; France, 221;
Netherlands, 221; Venezuela,
220
scope of conflict, objective and
subjective, 9-10, 217-18
secondary students, 51
Silva Michelena, J. A., 18, 48n,
247, 249
Silvert, K. H., 8n, 220n
Siso Martínez, J. M., 81

INDEX

social structure, changes, 17-18;
consequences of weakness,
212; relation to political
parties, 214
Sociedades Cívicas Bolivarianas,
31
Spanish Republic, 223
stalemate, 228-29; Argentina,
229n
strikes, general, 25; petroleum,
25-26, 147; students, 148, 167
strong conciliation system,
218-19
structural-functionalism, 252-53
students, new political
orientations, 22; decline of
autonomy, 29;
and political parties: 22,
177ff; activity in liceos,
178-79; age of enrollment,
177-78; conditions of power,
186; coordination processes,
182-84; orientation to
universities, 179-80; role in
AD, 186-87; role in COPEI,
160-61; role in MIR, 152f,
189; role in PCV, 55, 188-89,
203-04
students and politics, 7-8;
attempts to neutralize, 158-59;
conditions of autonomy,
145, 207; conditions of
isolation of conflict, 146, 159,
188; conditions of power,
145, 159, 207; impact on Left,
151; prestige of students in
1958, 150-51; relation to
legitimacy conflicts, 146,
159-60, 168-69, 187; role in
insurrection, 161-63; role of
party organization, 147;
thesis of irresponsibility, 175
student elections, proportional
representation, 152; role of
parties, 152
student leaders, career patterns,
180-81; salience of political
roles, 167-68
student opposition, 51; to

Betancourt, 50; to Gómez,
20-21; to Pérez Jiménez,
146-50
student organizations,
structure, 184
Student Week, 20-21
subsidies, to Church, 44
systems of conflict, 217-19

Táchira, 213
Tribuna Popular, 199
trienio, 35ff; absence of
organizational buffers, 91;
Catholic political perceptions,
89-90; expansion of
participation, 36; failure of
guarantees, 41; growth of
education, 69-70; growth of
unions, 37; norms of conflict,
90-91; relation of AD to
other groups, 38-41; relation
of Church and COPEI, 39;
religious conflict, 77-78; scale
of conflict, 76
Trujillo (state), 213
Trujillo, R. L., 155n

UCAB, 95, 97
UCV, 19; closure, 157; Reform
Council, 148; resignation of
authorities, 163. See also
allanamiento
ULA, 19, 195
UNE, 30; and Catholic social
doctrine, 30; relation to
COPEI, 31
unemployment, 51
Unión Nacional Republicana, 24
Unión Popular, 29
Universidad Santa María, 97
university autonomy, 197-98
university, official image, 164-65;
left-student image, 164-66
university elections, 169-75,
203-05; campaign styles, 204;
candidate selection, 185;
procedures, 191
university students, opposition to
Betancourt, 50; opposition to
Gómez, 19-20; opposition to

284

university students (*cont.*)
Pérez Jiménez, 146-50; role in
Left, 50-51. *See also* students
and political parties, students
and politics, student
opposition
UPA, 54, 181
urbanization, 17-18
URD, formation, 36

Vallier, I., 33n, 63
Vargas, M., 35
Venezuelan Peasant Federation,
37
Verba, S., 231
Villalba, J., 24, 36, 134n
Vivás Terán, A., 181n

Weber, M., 233